Chag sameach from Oorah to you
We hope you'll enjoy this gift, through and through.

Immerse yourself in it, enjoy, take a look
Get inspired, as you read from this book.

Enjoy the Chag throughout every stage
With the lessons you'll learn and gain from each page

And while you read, you'll know Oorah's near
Wherever you are, we're always here!

from
Rabbi Chaim Mintz

This book was donated in loving memory of
Dovid Winiarz z"l דוד אברהם בן חייא קהת ז"ל
by the Winiarz family

732-730-1000

Torah sp⚙t

www.oorah.org

Little Star

from Buffalo Burgers *to* Monetary Mysteries

Fascinating Expositions on Contemporary Halachic Issues

RABBI YIRMIYOHU KAGANOFF

Published by:
Torah Temimah Publications
40/15 HaMemGimmel St.
Jerusalem 94470
Israel
tel: +972-2-650-8779
ttp.information@gmail.com

Distributed by:
The Judaica Press, Inc.
123 Ditmas Avenue
Brooklyn, NY 11218
tel:800-972-6201
      718-972-6200
info@judaicapress.com
www.judaicapress.com

Printed in the USA

בס"ד

Rabbi Zev Leff

Rabbi of Moshav Matityahu
Rosh HaYeshiva—Yeshiva Gedola Matityahu

הרב זאב לף

מרא דאתרא מושב מתתיהו
ראש הישיבה—ישיבה גדולה מתתיהו

D.N. Modiin 71917   Tel: 08–976–1138 'טל   Fax: 08–976–5326 'פקס   71917 ד.נ. מודיעין

Dear Friends,

I have read the manuscript of *From Buffalo Burgers to Monetary Mysteries* by HaRav Yirmiyohu Kaganoff *shlita*. Rav Kaganoff presents a variety of halachic topics on virtually every aspect of Torah living. He presents real life situations that require halachic guidance and presents that guidance in a thorough, comprehensive, and well organized fashion. Hashem Yisborach has blessed Rav Kaganoff with the perception one needs to discern the pertinent issues and apply the proper halachic information to reach a genuine *psak halacha*. Rav Kaganoff's vast Torah knowledge, his ability to research the pertinent facts of the issue at hand that impact on the *halacha*, and to systematically apply the *halacha* to the facts is truly impressive.

I found Rav Kaganoff's presentations halachically sound, lucid, interesting, and peppered with enhancing humor and candor.

I strongly recommend this work. Aside from the wealth of Torah knowledge this work contains, it will also give the English speaking community a glimpse of how decisions are arrived at by competent *poskim* such as Rav Kaganoff.

I commend Rav Kaganoff for a job well done and pray that Hashem Yisborach grant him and his family life and health to continue to merit the community in their many and varied ways.

Sincerely,
with Torah blessings

Rabbi Zev Leff

Contents

Introduction 7

1 Meet the Adams Family 11

2 Tribal Rivalry 21

3 When the Jews Observed Two
Different Pesachs 33

4 Is It a Lemon? 47

5 Revealing the Skeletons in Your Closet. 59

6 The Spurned *Shadchan* 65

7 Marriage and Yom Kippur 75

8 Is Your *Kesubah* Kosher? 87

9 The Torah and Derech Eretz. 97

10 What Will the Neighbors Think?. 107

11 The Big Critic. 119

12 Snitching on Your Coworker 129

13 Double Jeopardy 139

14 To Buy or Not to Buy? 149

15 When There Is a Will,
the Relatives Will Complain 161

16 Monetary Mystery – A Drama in Real Life 171

17 The Dry Cleaner and the Gown 183

18 How Do I Know that I'll Get It Back? 191

19 How Not to Do a *Chesed* 201

20 Anyone for a Buffalo Burger? 211

21 Beeing Kosher 221

22 The Chocolate Riddle 231

23 Kindler on the Roof 241

24 The *Chol HaMoed* Outing Saga 251

25 Grave Issues about Graven Images 261

26 Do the Clothes Make the Kohein? 271

27 Should a Kohein Be Afraid of
Confederate Ghosts? 283

28 Sifting the *Makom HaMikdash* 291

29 Here Comes the King 301

Introduction

O ver the past thirty years, I have had the distinct pleasure of serving as a *rav* in three diverse communities. I first served as *rav* of the Young Israel of Greater Buffalo, New York, followed by my tenure in the same capacity at Congregation Darchei Tzedek in Baltimore, Maryland, and for the last fifteen years I have been serving unofficially as a *rav* in the *chareidi* neighborhood of Neve Yaakov, Yerushalayim.

Since my relocation to Yerushalayim, I have been privileged to teach at *kollelim* whose graduates serve their communities in various capacities. Consequently, I now have many *talmidim* who are involved in the rabbinate, teaching, and outreach in dozens of communities throughout the world. This generates all types of interesting questions on the entire spectrum of Jewish experience – from archaeology to Jewish identity, life insurance to loan collection, and buffalo burgers to monetary mysteries.

It was this collective experience as a *rav*, teacher, and writer that inspired me to collect the appropriate articles, edit them, and then edit them some more until this wonderful mission reached fruition.

It is not the purpose of this book to provide a basic overview of Jewish observance since there already exist many excellent works in Hebrew, as well as English, that accomplish this goal superbly. As most *rabbonim* lament, more than 90 percent of the questions we are asked would be unnecessary if our questioners were familiar with the simple, classic *Kitzur Shulchan Aruch*. For those who would like to broaden their halachic knowledge relatively easily, halachic classics such as the *Chayei Adam, Shemiras Shabbos Kehilchasah*, and other *seforim* of similar stature can assist them immensely.

In addition, this book does not aim to answer the most common twenty-first-century halachic queries. That role has always been, and should remain, the role of an individual's *rav* or *posek*. For better or for worse, the current market has also been inundated with an ever-increasing range of halachic literature that endeavors to provide quick answers to specific inquiries.

My goal, both in this book and in my general teaching, is quite different. I strongly believe in introducing people to the halachic process and the concepts on which a *halachah* is based. Therefore, I emphasize studying the *halachah* from its most basic sources, usually emphasizing the differences of opinion that we find among our earlier halachic masters. In fact, occasionally my essays present a range of halachic opinions without taking sides.

My aim is to be informational, explanatory, and challenging so that readers can enjoy rolling up their sleeves and sweating through a halachic topic – while at the same time appreciating the practical issues. Indeed, studying *halachah* can be quite entertaining, and it is certainly the ultimate fulfillment of the *mitzvah* of learning Torah.

I must mention one very important item: Although all of the cases I discuss in this book are based on actual *she'eilos* that I received over the years, some of the tangential and complex details may have been omitted for the sake of simplifying the *halachah*, extraneous facts may have been inserted in order to allow us to investigate additional angles, and **all of the names have been changed in order to preserve anonymity.**

Prior to assuming my first position in Buffalo, I had studied for almost ten years in Yeshivas Ner Yisrael in Baltimore. I am profoundly indebted – beyond what words can express – to my *rosh yeshivah*, Rav Yaakov Ruderman, *ztz"l*, for being an outstanding role model and teacher. Above all, however, I am indebted to him for inspiring an American yeshivah high school graduate (who had typical American ambitions) to aspire to grow in the depth and breadth of knowledge of our Holy Torah. Were it not for the *Rosh Yeshivah*'s influence, I would no doubt be a *frum* professional – a knowledgeable graduate of the yeshivah system, but one with fairly limited ambitions regarding Torah accomplishments. Although there is yet a long road to travel, I *daven* to merit appreciating and understanding the thoroughfares of Torah as extensively and thoroughly as I can.

I also owe a huge debt of gratitude to the indefatigable Rabbi Naftali Neuberger, *z"l*, who was always available when I needed him, a rather impressive achievement when one realizes that virtually all of Klal Yisrael depended on him – and he always found time for each individual.

Most of the material in this book was first published in the form of articles in a regular *halachah* column that I have been writing for *Yated Ne'eman* during the last ten years. I thank Rabbi Pinchos Lipschutz and his staff for their assistance throughout the years, and for permission to publish this material in book form.

Converting this work from articles written for periodicals to book form required an enormous amount of labor, most of which was provided by an exceptional editor, Mrs. Sonya Matsui. She has become more like a partner in this endeavor than simply an editor, and she will rightfully derive as much joy as I do in seeing this work published as a book.

I have had the utmost pleasure interacting with my publisher, Rabbi Eliyahu Miller. His copy editor for this work, Mrs. Talya

Rosenstein, did an extremely thorough job, and Mr. Refoel Pride did an excellent job proofreading and polishing up the manuscript. I wish Torah Temimah Publications much *hatzlachah* in spreading the words of Torah through their future publications.

This book is dedicated to the memory of my parents, both of whom graduated to the *Yeshivah shel Maalah* many years ago, as well as to the memory of my parents-in-law, who were called there more recently. Each of these four admirable people was raised and educated in an American environment that preached allegiance to a melting pot culture that required sacrificing one's time-honored traditions, exchanging the timeless values of Torah for the in-vogue goal of Americanization. Notwithstanding this atmosphere, each of them remained completely committed to Torah and *shemiras hamitzvos*, a mission they successfully transmitted to their progeny and that is now maintained by their many dozens of descendants living Torah-true lives.

Certainly, *acharon, acharon chaviv*: Without my life's helpmate, this book, as well as my learning and teaching, would not have been possible. Rather than thanking her in a public format, I will simply express the wish that we should share many more decades together in good health, teaching Hashem's children His ways, and enjoying *nachas* from our children, grandchildren, and their future progeny.

1

Meet the Adams Family

John Adams and the Adamites

I am about to introduce you to someone who is extremely concerned and knowledgeable about *halachah*, yet he doesn't even keep a kosher home. Nor has he ever observed Shabbos. On the other hand, he is meticulous about observing every detail of *Choshen Mishpat*.

Who is this individual?

Allow me to introduce John Adams, who is a practicing Noahide – or, as he prefers to call himself, an Adamite.

Adams asserts that he descends from the two famous presidents, a claim that I have never verified, but have no reason to question. Raised in New England and a graduate of Harvard Law School, John rejected the tenets of the major Western religions, but retained a very strong sense of G-d's presence and the difference between right and wrong. Study and introspection led him to believe that G-d had probably detailed instructions for mankind. Sincere questioning caused him to discover that, of the Western religions, only Judaism does not claim a monopoly on Heaven. A non-Jew who observes the seven laws taught to Noah, and believes that G-d commanded them at Har Sinai, has an excellent place reserved for him in *Olam Haba*.

John began practicing the Noahide laws. He is quick to point out that, with only one exception, these laws were all commanded originally to Adam. Since John is proud of his family name and lineage, he enjoys calling himself an Adamite.

What Are the Basics of Noahide Practice?

We all know that a gentile is required to observe seven *mitzvos*, six of which are prohibitions: idolatry, incest, murder, blasphemy, theft, and *eiver min hachai* (which we will soon discuss). The particulars of the seventh, the *mitzvah* of having *dinim*, are controversial.

The *Sefer HaChinuch* and others note that these seven *mitzvos* are actually categories, and a non-Jew is in fact required to observe several dozen *mitzvos*.[1]

Kosher, Noah-Style

I asked John whether eating meat presents any religious problems for him.

"Well, you know that Noah was prohibited from eating meat or an organ that was severed from an animal before it died, a prohibition you call *eiver min hachai*," said John, obviously proud that he could pronounce the expression correctly. "So, sometimes I come across meat that I may not eat. Muslim slaughter, called *halal*, involves killing the animal in such a manner that many of its internal organs are technically severed from the animal before it is dead. Because of this, we are very careful about where we purchase our organ meats."

May a Noahide Eat Out?

"This issue had further ramifications," John continued. "Could we eat in a restaurant where forbidden meats may have contaminated equipment?"

I admit that I had never thought of this question before. Must a gentile be concerned that a restaurant's equipment absorbed the flavor of *eiver min hachai*? Does a Noahide need to "*kasher*" a *treif* restaurant's utensils before he can eat there? *Oy, s'iz shver tzu zein a goy!* (Oy, the difficulty of being a *goy!*)

"How did you resolve this dilemma?" I timidly asked.

"Well, for a short time our family stopped eating out," he replied. "You could say that we ate *treif* only at home. My wife found the situation intolerable – no McDonald's or Wendy's? I know that observant Jews do not understand why this is such a serious predicament, but please bear in mind that we made a conscious decision *not* to become Jewish. One of our reasons was that we enjoy eating out wherever we want.

"So I decided to ask some rabbis I know, but even then, the end of the road was not clearly in sight."

"Why was that?"

"I had difficulty finding a rabbi who could answer the question. From what I understand, a rabbi's ordination teaches him the basics necessary to answer questions that apply to kosher kitchens. But I don't have a kosher home – we observe the Adamite laws. As one rabbi told me, 'I don't know if Noahides need to be concerned about what was previously cooked in their pots.'"

How *Treif* Is *Treif*?

"How did you resolve the predicament?"

"Eventually, we found a rabbi who contended that we need not be concerned about how pots and grills were previously used. He explained that we could assume that they had not been used for *eiver min hachai* in the past twenty-four hours, which certainly sounds like a viable assumption. Therefore, using them would only involve the possibility of a rabbinic prohibition, and we gentiles are not required to observe rabbinic restrictions. The last contention makes a lot of sense, since there is nothing in the Seven Laws about listening to the rabbis, although I agree that they are smart and sincere people. [Note: I am not certain who it was that John asked. According to the *Chasam Sofer*,[2] there would be no *heter* to use pots that had once absorbed the flavor of *eiver min hachai*. There are *poskim* who disagree with the *Chasam Sofer*, but many of them hold that there is no prohibition whatsoever with a gentile using pots that absorbed flavor from *eiver min hachai*.[3]]

"The result is that we now go out to eat frequently, which makes my wife very happy. It was a good decision for the sake of our marital bliss, what you call *shalom bayis*. Although I understand that this is another idea we are not required to observe, it is good common sense."

Milah in the Adams Family

The birth of John's son raised an interesting *she'eilah*. To quote him: "Circumcision as a religious practice originates from G-d's covenant with Abraham, the first Jew. But my covenant with G-d predates Abraham and does not include circumcision. However, even though there was no religious reason for my son to be circumcised, my wife and I thought it was a good idea for health reasons."

John is a very gregarious type, and loves to provide detailed explanations. "We actually had two concerns about whether we could circumcise John Jr. The second issue was that many authorities contend that the seventh *mitzvah* of instating 'laws,' which you call 'dinim,' includes a prohibition against injuring another person.[4] According to this opinion, a person who hits someone else during a street fight may lose his World to Come for violating one of our seven tenets. I have come too far to risk losing my share in the World to Come, so I try very hard not to violate any of the laws. I called a rabbi I know to ask whether there was any problem with circumcising my son for health reasons. The rabbi I asked felt that since we are performing this procedure for medical reasons, it is comparable to donating blood or undergoing surgery. The upshot was that we did what no self-respecting Jew should ever do: we had a pediatrician circumcise John Jr. on the third day after his birth, to emphasize that we were not performing any *mitzvah*."

No *Bris*

Proud to show off his Hebrew, John finished by saying: "So we had a *milah*, but no *bris*. We also decided to skip the bagels and lox.

Instead, my wife and I decided it was more appropriate to celebrate with shrimp cocktails, even though primordial Adam didn't eat shrimp. All types of meat were only permitted to Noah after the Deluge, which you call the Mabul. I believe that some authorities rule that Adam was permitted roadkill and was only prohibited from slaughtering, while others understand he had to be strictly vegetarian. My wife and I discussed whether to go vegetarian to keep up the Adams tradition, but decided that if meat was 'kosher' enough for Noah, it is 'kosher' enough for us. We decided that we would not keep any stringent practices, even if they become stylish."

Earning a Living

"Have you experienced any other serious dilemmas due to your being an 'Adamite'?"

"Oh, yes. I almost had to change my career."

I found this very curious. As John Adams seemed like an honest individual, it seemed unlikely that he had made his living by stealing or any similar dishonest activity.

Non-Jews are forbidden to perform abortions, which might affect how a Noahide gynecologist earns a living, but John is a lawyer, not a doctor. Even if John used to worship idols or had the bad habit of blaspheming, how would that affect his career?

May a Gentile Practice Law?

John's research into Noahide law led him to the very interesting conclusion that his job as an assistant district attorney was halachically problematic. John discovered that one of the *mitzvos* (or probably more accurately, categories of *mitzvos*) that a Noahide must observe is that of *dinim* – literally, *laws*. The authorities dispute the exact definition and nature of this *mitzvah*. The commandment definitely includes a requirement that gentile societies establish courts and prosecute those who violate the Noahide laws.[5] Some authorities contend that the *mitzvah* of *dinim* prohibits injuring or abusing others or damaging their property.[6]

However, this dispute leads to another issue that was more

germane to John's case. A major dispute exists among halachic authorities as to whether Noahides are governed by the Torah's rules of property laws, which are referred to as *Choshen Mishpat*,[7] or whether the Torah allows non-Jews to formulate their own property and other civil laws.[8] If the former is true, a non-Jew may not sue in a civil court that is governed by any system of law other than the Torah. Instead, he must litigate in a *beis din* or in a court of non-Jewish judges who follow halachic guidelines. Following this approach, if a gentile accepts money based on civil litigation, he is considered to be stealing, in the same way as a Jew. This approach is accepted by many early *poskim*. Some authorities extend this *mitzvah* further, contending that the *mitzvos* governing proper functioning of courts and civil laws apply to Noahides.[9] Following this approach, enforcing a criminal code that does not follow the Torah rules violates the *mitzvah* of *dinim*.

As John discovered, some authorities extend this idea quite significantly. For example, one of the *mitzvos* of the Torah prohibits a *beis din* from convicting or punishing a person based on circumstantial evidence.[10] If the same tenet applies to the laws of *dinim*, a gentile court has no right to use circumstantial evidence.[11] Thus, John was faced with an interesting predicament. According to the aforementioned opinions, a gentile who prosecutes because of circumstantial evidence might violate the Seven Noahide Laws, even if the accused party appears to be guilty. It is understood that according to these opinions, one may not prosecute for the violation of a crime that the Torah does not consider to be criminal, or sue for damages founded on a claim that has no halachic basis.

The Napoleonic Code and *Halachah*

On the other hand, other authorities contend that non-Jews are not obligated to observe the laws of *Choshen Mishpat*. Rather, the Torah requires them to create their own legal rules and procedures.[12] These authorities rule that gentiles perform a *mitzvah* when they create a legal system for themselves, such as the Napoleonic Code, English common law, or any other commercial code. Following this approach, a non-Jew may use secular courts to resolve his litigation and even fulfills a *mitzvah* by doing so.

It is interesting to note that following the second approach in this case creates an interesting halachic ramification. According to those who rule that a gentile is not required to observe the laws of *Choshen Mishpat*, a gentile may not study these laws, since the Torah prohibits a gentile from studying Torah.[13] (Note, however, that others rule that a gentile who decides to observe a certain *mitzvah* may study the laws of that *mitzvah* in order to fulfill it correctly.)[14] However, according to those who contend that the *mitzvos* of *dinim* follow the laws of *Choshen Mishpat*, a gentile is *required* to study these laws in order to observe his *mitzvos* properly.[15]

John's Dilemma

The rabbis with whom John consulted maintained that a gentile could work as a district attorney. However, John had difficulty with this approach. He found it inconceivable that G-d would allow man to decide such consequential matters, and felt it more likely that mankind was expected to observe the Torah's code. He therefore gravitated toward the opinion of those who maintained that gentiles are required to observe the laws of *Choshen Mishpat*. As a result, he felt that he should no longer work in the DA's office, since his job entailed prosecuting based on laws and a criminal justice system that the Torah does not accept.

"What did you do?" I asked him.

"I decided to 'switch sides' and become a defense attorney, a choice that also affords a practical advantage, in that I make a lot more money."

"How do you handle a case in which you know that your client is guilty?"

"First, I ask myself – is he guilty according to *halachah*? Did he perform a crime? Is the evidence halachically acceptable? If no halachically acceptable evidence is available, he is not required to plead guilty. Furthermore, since none of my clients are practicing Noahides or observant Jews, they can't make it to heaven anyway, so let them enjoy themselves here. Even if my client is guilty, the punishment determined by the court is not halachically acceptable. It is very unclear whether jail terms are halachically acceptable punishment for gentiles. Philosophically, I was always opposed to jail time. I think that there are better ways to teach someone to right their ways than by incarceration, which is a big expense for society."

Interesting Noahide Laws

"Have you come across any other curious issues?"

"Here is a really unusual question that I once raised," John responded. "Am I permitted to vote in elections for a local judge? According to some authorities, the Torah's prohibition against appointing a judge who is halachically incompetent applies equally to gentiles.[16] Thus, one may not appoint a judge to the bench who does not know the appropriate Torah laws, which precludes all the candidates. When I vote for one of those candidates, I am actively choosing a candidate who is halachically unqualified to judge. I therefore decided that although some authorities rule that this is permitted, and that therefore it is permissible to vote, I wanted to be consistent in my position. As a result, I vote religiously, but not for judgeships."

Becoming Jewish

"John, did you ever consider becoming Jewish?"

"First of all, I know that the rabbis will discourage me from becoming Jewish, particularly since I don't really want to. I know exactly what I am required to keep, and I observe those commandments properly. I have no interest in being restricted in where and what I eat, and I have no interest in observing Shabbos, which, at present, I may not observe anyway, and that is fine with me.[17] I am very willing to be a 'Shabbos *goy*' – and I understand well what the Jews need – but it is rare that I find myself in this role. Remember, I do not live anywhere near a Jewish community. Although I have never learned how to read Hebrew – why bother? I am not supposed to study Torah anyway – I ask enough questions from enough rabbis to find out all that I need to know."

Conclusion

Although it seems strange for a non-Jew to ask a *rav* a *she'eilah*, this phenomenon should actually be commonplace. Indeed, many non-Jews are concerned about their future place in *Olam Haba* and, had the nations not been deceived by spurious religions, many thousands more would observe the *mitzvos* that they are commanded. When we meet sincere non-Jews, we should direct them correctly in their quest for truth. Gentiles who observe these *mitzvos* because Hashem commanded them through Moshe Rabbeinu are called "*chassidei umos ha'olam*" and merit a place in *Olam Haba*.

NOTES

1. #416.
2. *Shu't Chasam Sofer, Yoreh Deah* #19 (at end).
3. See *Darchei Teshuvah* 62:5.
4. *Ramban, Bereishis* 34:13.
5. *Tosefta, Avodah Zarah* 9:4; Rambam, *Hilchos Melachim* 9:14.
6. *Ramban, Bereishis* 34:13.
7. *Shu't HaRema* #10.
8. For example, *Tumim* 110:3.
9. *Minchas Chinuch* #414; 415.
10. Rambam, *Sefer HaMitzvos, Lo Saaseh* #290; *Sefer HaChinuch* #82.
11. *Minchas Chinuch* #82, #409.
12. *HaEmek She'eilah* #2:3; *Chazon Ish, Bava Kama* 10:1.
13. See *Tosafos, Bava Kama* 38a s.v. *Karu*.
14. *Meiri, Sanhedrin* 59a.
15. *Shu't HaRema* #10.
16. *Minchas Chinuch* #414.
17. *Sanhedrin* 58b.

2

Tribal Rivalry

Did the Brothers Have a Right to Sell Yosef?

The Torah relates in *Parshas Vayeishev* that Yosef would report the "bad deeds" of his brothers to his father, Yaakov Avinu. Although his intentions were solely for the purpose of bettering his brothers' spirituality, nevertheless the brothers despised him for his actions. Additionally, Yosef related his dreams to his brothers, dreams that implied that Yosef would rule over his brothers, as well as his own parents. Initially, the brothers resolved to murder Yosef. Ultimately, they decided to sell him into slavery instead of killing him.

Righteous Brothers

Had this story occurred in the most dysfunctional family imaginable, we would still be shocked by the unfolding of its events. After all, even if brothers feel that their indulged, nasty kid brother is challenging their father's love for them, would they consider committing fratricide?

This question would apply even to members of a poorly functioning family. All the more so when we are discussing great *talmidei chachamim*, who constantly evaluate the halachic ramifications of every action that they perform! How can we possibly understand what transpired?

We must remember that all twelve of Yaakov's sons were *tzaddikim gemurim*.[1] In other words, the ten brothers were far greater *tzaddikim* than the Chafetz Chayim or Rav Aryeh Levin, *ztz"l*, and far greater *talmidei chachamim* than even the Chazon Ish or Rav Moshe Feinstein, *ztz"l*. (This comparison does not diminish the stature of any of these *tzaddikim*; on the contrary, mentioning them in this context shows how much we venerate them.) We cannot imagine any of these people hurting someone's feelings intentionally, much less causing anyone even the slightest amount of bodily harm. It is difficult to imagine any of these *tzaddikim* even swatting a fly!

Thus, how can we imagine Yosef's brothers, who were far greater *tzaddikim*, hurting their brother, much less doing anything that might cause any long-term damage?

Certainly, we cannot interpret this as an extreme case of sibling rivalry. Ultimately, we are left completely baffled by the actions of Yosef's ten saintly and scholarly brothers. How could these ten great *tzaddikim* consider killing their brother? And then, decide that selling him into slavery was more appropriate? As we see clearly, for the next twenty-two years, they assumed that their decision had been justified, although they did eventually acknowledge that they should possibly have given Yosef a "second chance."

Act One

Yosef is in the habit of reporting to his father *"dibasam raah"*[2] (usually interpreted as *slander*) – actions that he notices in his older brothers that he interprets as infractions. Rashi[3] quotes a *midrash* in which Yosef informs his father of whatever bad actions he observes in Leah's six sons. Specifically, Yosef reports:

1. They were consuming meat without killing the animal properly, a sin forbidden to all descendants of Noach.

2. They were belittling their brothers Dan, Naftali, Gad, and Asher, by calling them slaves.

3. He suspected them of violating the heinous sin of *gilui arayos*.

Others explain that Yosef accused his brothers of not caring properly for their father's flock.[4] Although Rashi makes no mention of this accusation, it is clear from his comments that, in his opinion, had Yosef suspected them of this, he would certainly have noted it to his father as well.

Is *Dibasam Raah* Equivalent to Slander?

We must be careful not to define *dibasam raah* as *slander*, which usually intimates malice and falsehood, and would imply that Yosef's intentions were to harm his brothers. Without a doubt, the righteous Yosef had no such intent. It is more accurate to translate *dibasam raah* as an *evil report*. Yosef certainly shared his interpretations of his brothers' actions with his father, but they were not fabrications, and he was not attempting to defame them.

Why Is Yosef Tattling?

Without question, Yosef's goal in reporting his brothers' misbehavior was the betterment of his brothers. He acted completely *lishmah*, with no evil intent; just as later, in *Parshas Vayigash*,[5] he holds no grudge against his brothers, despite the indescribable suffering they caused him.

Indeed, Yosef's motivation was his sincere concern for his brothers. He knew very well the *halachah* that if one sees someone sin, one must bring it to the offender's attention, explaining to him that he will acquire a big share in *Olam Haba* by doing *teshuvah*.[6] A person giving *tochachah* must always have the interests of the sinner completely at heart, and consider how to educate the malefactor in a way that his words will be accepted.

Yosef knew also that whoever has the ability to protest sinful activity and fails to do so is liable for his lack of action.[7]

At this point, we can already answer the following question: if one sees someone do something wrong, what should one do about it?

Answer: I am obligated to bring to the person's attention that it is in his or her best interest to do *teshuvah* and correct whatever he or she has done wrong. The admonition should be done in a gentle way, expressing concern, so that it can be received positively and thereby accomplish its purpose.

Roundabout Rebuke

Without a doubt, Yosef's goal in sharing his concerns with his father was that his brothers should correct their actions. If so, why didn't Yosef admonish them directly?

Yosef wanted his father to take appropriate action to correct the brothers' deeds, and thereby bring them to do *teshuvah*. Yosef believed that his father would be more successful than he in giving *tochachah* to the brothers.

Did Yosef Speak *Lashon Hora*?

The halachic authorities disagree regarding whether Yosef was guilty of speaking *lashon hora* by using this approach *in this instance*. The Chafetz Chayim contends that Yosef was guilty of speaking *lashon hora*, because he should have shared his concerns directly with his brothers, rather than first discussing them with his father.[8]

The Chafetz Chayim also sees Yosef as having neglected the *mitzvah* of being *dan lekaf zechus*, judging people favorably. Since the brothers were great *tzaddikim*, Yosef should have realized that they had a halachic consideration to permit their actions. Had he judged them favorably, he would have considered one of three possibilities:

1. Yosef's brothers had done nothing wrong, and he had misinterpreted what he had seen them do.

2. Alternatively, Yosef's brothers might have justified their actions, explaining them in a way that he might have accepted what they did as correct or, at least, permitted.

3. Although his brothers were not right, they had acted based on some mistaken rationale. If their rationale was mistaken, Yosef should have entertained the possibility that he might have successfully convinced them that their approach was flawed. He should have discussed the matter with them directly, and either convinced them of their folly, or gained an understanding of why they considered their actions as justified.

In any case, Yosef should not have assumed that the brothers sinned intentionally.

The Malbim's Approach

The Malbim disagrees with the Chafetz Chayim's approach, contending that Yosef felt that his rebuking his brothers would be unheeded under any circumstances, possibly even counterproductive, and only his father's reprimand would be successful. If one is certain that the sinner will not listen to one's *tochachah*, but may listen to someone else, one may share the information with the person one feels will be more successful at giving rebuke. Yosef felt that although his brothers would not listen to him, their father could successfully convince them of their errors; therefore, he reported the matters to his father.

Practical Applications

In the same vein, a student who sees his classmates acting inappropriately and feels that they will not listen to his rebuke may share the information with someone who he feels will be more effective at influencing their behavior.

Another related question is: may I inform a parent that I saw his child do something wrong, or is this considered *lashon hora*?

If a parent is able to do something to improve a child's behavior, one may notify the parent of the child's conduct. Not only is it not *lashon hora*¸ but it is the correct approach to use. However, if the circumstances are such that the parent will be unable to do anything to improve the child's behavior, or if one can bring about change in the child's behavior by contacting him directly, one may not inform the parents of the child's misbehavior.

Yaakov's Reaction

Yaakov reacts passively to Yosef's talebearing. He does not rebuke the brothers for their misbehavior as Yosef wanted him to, but he also does not reprimand Yosef for speaking *lashon hora*, or for neglecting to be *dan lekaf zechus*. Indeed, he demonstrates his greater love for Yosef than for the others by producing with his own hands a special garment for Yosef called a *kesones pasim*. Yaakov, an affluent sheep raiser who preferred to spend his time studying Torah, took time from his own learning to hand-weave Yosef a beautiful coat. Indeed, Yaakov felt a special kinship with Yosef for several reasons, including Yosef's astute Torah learning.

All of this makes us wonder: why does Yaakov not rebuke Yosef for reporting his brothers?

Was Yosef Wrong?

Yaakov agreed with Yosef's assessment that his reporting was not *lashon hora*, although this does not necessarily mean that he felt that the brothers were guilty. I will shortly rally evidence that implies that Yaakov was convinced that the brothers were innocent. Nonetheless, Yaakov concurred that Yosef behaved correctly in bringing the matters to his attention, rather than dealing with the brothers himself.

Yaakov agreed that the brothers would not accept Yosef's admonition, because they did not understand Yosef's greatness. At the same time, Yaakov realized that Yosef had leadership and scholarship skills superior to those of his brothers. He therefore gave Yosef the *kesones pasim*, to demonstrate his appointment as leader of the household.[9]

Yaakov's Perception of the Brothers

This of course leads to a new question. If Yaakov did not rebuke Yosef because he felt that his approach was correct, why do we not find anywhere that he rebuked the brothers for their behavior?

It appears that Yaakov realized that the brothers had not sinned, and that there was no reason to rebuke them. *Shemiras Halashon* rallies proof of this assertion, because the Torah teaches that Yaakov had a special love for Yosef, only because of Yosef's scholarship, and not because of any concerns about the brothers' behavior.[10] Yaakov understood that the brothers had not sinned, and that, indeed, Yosef had misinterpreted their actions.

In fact, because of his mistaken accusation of the brothers, Yosef himself was later severely punished: he was sold into slavery; and for wrongly suspecting his brothers of violating *arayos*, he himself was suspected by all Egypt of a similar transgression, as a result of Mrs. Potifar's fraudulent allegation.[11] Apparently, Yosef was indeed guilty of not having judged them favorably.[12] (The problem of an innocent man being tried and convicted in the media is not a modern phenomenon – Yosef was found guilty of a crime of which he was innocent.)

Was Yaakov Correct?

Was the *kesones pasim* an appropriate gift for Yaakov to give to Yosef?

Even asking this question places us in an uncomfortable position: it implies that we might condemn the educational practices of one of our *Avos*. Notwithstanding our awesome appreciation of the greatness of Yaakov Avinu, the Gemara indeed criticizes Yaakov's deed: "A person should never treat one son differently from the others, for because of two *sela'im* worth of fancy wool that Yaakov gave Yosef, favoring him over his brothers, the brothers were jealous of him, and the end result was that our forefathers descended to Egypt."[13]

Yaakov did not act without calculation. Presumably, seeing Yosef's high standard of learning, his refined personal attributes, and his concern for others' behavior, Yaakov felt it important to demonstrate that Yosef was the most exceptional of a very impressive group of sons. Yet Chazal tell us that this is an error. One should never demonstrate favoritism among one's sons, even when there appears to be appropriate reason for doing so.

Were the Brothers Justified?

At this point, we have presented Yaakov's and Yosef's positions on what happened, but we still do not know why the brothers wanted to kill Yosef, the most hideous crime imaginable.

Remember that the brothers were both righteous and talented *talmidei chachamim*. Clearly, they must have held that Yosef was a *rodef*, someone pursuing and attempting to bring bodily harm to another. No other halachic justification would permit their subsequent actions.

Indeed, Sforno and others note that the brothers interpreted Yosef's actions as a plot against them, to deny them a share of Yaakov's spiritual inheritance. Rav Hirsch demonstrates that the *pasuk* "*Vayisnaklu oso lehamiso*" means "They imagined him as one plotting against them – so that he was deserving of death." The brothers assumed that Yosef's goal was to vilify them in their father's eyes, so that Yaakov would reject them, just as Avraham had rejected Yishmael and the sons of Keturah, and Yitzchak had rejected Eisav.[14] After all, Yosef was falsely accusing them of highly serious infractions. The brothers interpreted Yaakov's gift of the *kesones pasim* to Yosef as proof that Yaakov had accepted Yosef's *lashon hora* against them.[15] The brothers needed to act quickly before he ruined them; they were concerned that Yaakov would accept Yosef's plot to discredit them and to rule over them. Therefore, they seized and imprisoned Yosef, and then sat down to eat a meal, while they were deciding what to do with him.

Not a Free Lunch

The brothers are strongly criticized for sitting down to eat this meal. Assuming that they were justified in killing Yosef, they should have spent an entire night debating their judgment. After all, when a *beis din* decides on capital matters, they postpone their decision until the next day, and spend the entire night debating the *halachah* in small groups, eating only a little while deliberating the serious matter.[16] Certainly, the brothers' sitting down to eat immediately after incarcerating Yosef was wrong, and for this sin they were subsequently punished.[17]

The brothers then realized that selling Yosef as a slave would accomplish what they needed, without bloodshed.

Later, in Egypt, they recognized that they should not have been so hard-hearted as to sell him; perhaps his experience in the pit had taught him a sufficient lesson, and he was no longer a danger. Not until Yosef presented himself to them in Mitzrayim did they realize that Yosef was correct all along: he did indeed rule over them, and he never intended to harm them.

Halachic Conclusions

When one sees someone doing something that appears wrong, one should figure out a positive way to tell the person what he can accomplish by doing *teshuvah* properly.

If one is convinced that he is unable to influence the evildoer, while believing that someone else may be more successful, one may share the information with the other person, so that he can deliver discreet and gentle admonishment.

The information should be shared with no one else, unless, otherwise, someone could get hurt.

One should always figure out how to judge the person favorably. The entire sale of Yosef occurred because neither side judged the other favorably. Also, bear in mind that we are often highly biased in our evaluation, making it difficult for us to judge.

One should never demonstrate favoritism among children, even when there appear to be excellent reasons for doing so.

Facing the Truth

To quote the Midrash: Prior to Yosef's revealing himself in Mitzrayim, he asked them, "The brother whom you claim is dead is very much alive; I will call him." Yosef then called out, "Yosef ben Yaakov, come here. Yosef ben Yaakov, come here." The brothers searched under the furniture and checked all the corners of the room to see where Yosef was hiding.[18]

By this time, Yosef had already revealed that he knew the intimate details of their household. They knew that Yosef had been taken to Mitzrayim. They now have someone telling them that he knows that Yosef is in the same room, and there is no one in the room save themselves and Yosef. Nonetheless, they cannot accept that the man that they are facing is Yosef!

Contemplate how these giants of spirit were blinded by their own interests! Is it not sobering how convinced a person can be, despite facts to the contrary, that he is entirely right? We can stare truth in the face, and still not realize that it is Yosef standing before us.

NOTES

1. Ramban, *Iggeres HaKodesh*, chapter 5.
2. *Bereishis* 37:2.
3. Ibid.
4. *Sforno*, ibid.
5. *Bereishis* 45:5–8.
6. Rambam, *Hilchos Dei'os* 6:7.
7. *Shabbos* 54b.
8. *Shemiras Halashon*, vol. 2, chapter 11 [*Parshas Vayeishev*].
9. *Sforno* ad loc.
10. See *Sifsei Chachamim* and other commentaries on Rashi who explain why the brothers had done nothing wrong, and what Yosef misinterpreted.
11. *Shemiras Halashon* ad loc.
12. Rav Samson Raphael Hirsch.
13. *Shabbos* 10b.
14. Malbim.

15. *Shemiras Halashon* ad loc.

16. Rambam, *Hilchos Sanhedrin* 12:3.

17. *Shemiras Halashon* ad loc.

18. *Bereishis Rabbah; Yalkut Shimoni.*

3

When the Jews Observed Two Different Pesachs

The Controversy over the Jewish Calendar in the Geonic Period

I magine the scene: You call your sister with the exciting news that you plan on visiting her family for Pesach, hoping to arrive on Monday, Erev Yom Tov, so that you do not disturb her plans for having the house ready for Pesach. But the ensuing conversation takes you by surprise:

> Of course, we would love to have you for Pesach, but our *rav* has ruled that we will be keeping Pesach two days earlier, beginning on Sunday. Of course, this means that Erev Pesach is on Shabbos, with all the ramifications of that particular observance. Remember the last time that happened a few years ago? Decide if you want to follow our rabbi, but that is what our entire community is doing this Yom Tov.

Surprised, you ask if they are also ending Yom Tov two days

earlier than everyone else you know, to which your sister answers:

> Yes. That is what our rabbi said we should do, and
> even the Jewish bakeries are going to be baking –
> even though it will be Pesach elsewhere. Our rabbi
> is arranging *mechiras chametz*, assuming that this is
> the schedule we will be following.

A bit incredulous, you hang up the phone, scratch your head, and wonder: What is going on here? How could their community be keeping Pesach two days earlier than we are? You double check the wall calendar sent by the local yeshivah before Rosh Hashanah, and it confirms the dates that you thought. Could your sister's community have a different calendar? Indeed, according to the calendar, your sister, her family and their entire community will be eating *chametz* on Pesach!

As shocking as the above scenario appears, this is exactly what happened once in Jewish history. And indeed, were it not for the scholarship and leadership of Rav Saadiah Gaon, to this day we might find different *frum* communities observing the Yamim Tovim on different days!

The Basic Story

In the year 4681 (920 CE), the greatest halachic authority in Eretz Yisrael, Rav Aharon ben Meir, proclaimed that the months of Marcheshvan and Kislev of the coming year (4682) would both have only twenty-nine days. As a result, the following Pesach (4682) would begin on a Sunday, and end after Shabbos in Eretz Yisrael and after Sunday in *chutz laaretz*. Prior to Ben Meir's proclamation, all had assumed that Marcheshvan and Kislev would both be thirty days long that year, which would result in Pesach beginning two days later – on Tuesday, and ending on Monday in Eretz Yisrael and on Tuesday in *chutz laaretz*. Thus, Ben Meir was pushing Pesach forward two days earlier than anticipated. Those communities that followed Ben Meir would be eating *chametz* when it was still Pesach, according to the original calculation![1]

Just as shocking, Rosh Hashanah and Yom Kippur of the following year were also two days earlier, according to Ben Meir's calculation; meaning, that Rosh Hashanah began on Tuesday and Yom Kippur was observed on Thursday, whereas according to the original calculation, Rosh Hashanah was to fall on Thursday, and Yom Kippur on Shabbos.

As a result of the dispute that ensued, most of the Jewish communities in Eretz Yisrael and Egypt observed Pesach, Yom Kippur, and Rosh Hashanah that year according to Ben Meir's calendar, whereas the communities of Syria, Bavel (today's Iraq), and presumably Europe and the rest of North Africa observed all these Yamim Tovim two days later! Thus, on the Shabbos before Sukkos of 4683, while Ben Meir's followers were festively enjoying their Shabbos repasts, the other communities were fasting because of Yom Kippur!

Why did Ben Meir observe the calendar differently? And why was his opinion rejected?

Background

The Jewish calendar that we use currently was instituted in the fourth century by Hillel HaNasi (not to be confused with his ancestor, Hillel HaZakein. The historians called Hillel HaNasi either Hillel the Second or Hillel the Third, but I will refer to him the way the Rishonim do.) Prior to this time, the *nasi* of the Sanhedrin appointed a special *beis din* that was in charge of determining the Jewish calendar, which included two areas of responsibility:

1. Determining whether each month is twenty-nine or thirty days.

2. Deciding whether or not the year should be made into a leap year, by adding the month of Adar Sheini.

On the "thirtieth" day of each month, a *beis din* of three judges representing the Sanhedrin, the *beis din* with the greatest authority in Klal Yisrael, would meet to determine whether that day was Rosh Chodesh and the previous month was only twenty-nine days, or whether to postpone Rosh Chodesh to the morrow, making that day the last day of a thirty-day month. The determination of which day was Rosh Chodesh was based heavily, but not exclusively, on whether witnesses appeared in the special *beis din* on the thirtieth day to testify that they had witnessed the new moon. We will soon see that Rosh Chodesh being dependent on the testimony of witnesses affects our permanent calendar, as well.

In addition, the head of the Sanhedrin appointed a panel of judges who met during the winter months to deliberate and decide if the year should have an extra month added and become a leap year. Many factors went into their considerations, including the weather, the economy, the *shemittah* cycle, and of course, whether the Jewish calendar year was early or late, relative to the annual solar cycle. It is a *mitzvah* of the Torah to ensure that Pesach falls out during the spring, which is a feature of the solar calendar.

History of the Jewish Calendar

The Gemara[2] states unequivocally that as long as there is a *beis din* in Eretz Yisrael that is qualified to establish the calendar, no *beis din* elsewhere is authorized to do this.

This system worked well for thousands of years – from the time of Moshe Rabbeinu until about three hundred years after the destruction of the Beis HaMikdash, which occurred during the time that the Gemara was being written. However, by this time, severe Roman persecutions had taken a tremendous toll on the Jewish community in Eretz Yisrael, and its yeshivos suffered terribly. It was at this time that the head of the last Sanhedrin then functioning in Eretz Yisrael, Hillel HaNasi (usually assumed to have been a great-grandson of Rabi Yehudah HaNasi, final author and editor of the Mishnah), established the Jewish calendar that we currently employ. In establishing this calendar, Hillel HaNasi instituted a cycle of nineteen years that included a set schedule of seven leap years. He also ordained that the months of Tishrei, Shevat, Adar Sheini (when there is one), Nissan, Sivan, and Av are always thirty days, whereas Teves, Adar (or Adar Rishon), Iyar, Tammuz, and Elul are all always only twenty-nine days.

Only the two months of Marcheshvan and Kislev would vary in length each year. A year in which both of these months is twenty-nine days is called *chaseirah* (deficient); one in which Marcheshvan is twenty-nine days and Kislev is thirty days is called *kesidrah* (regular), and a year in which both months are thirty days is called *sheleimah* (full).

Hillel HaNasi's established calendar made it possible for a Jew anywhere in the world to make the calculations necessary to determine the current Jewish calendar, or for that matter, any future calendar. All one needs to know is the pattern of the nineteen-year cycle, and the information necessary to determine how long the months of Marcheshvan and Kislev are in a given year.

One noteworthy point is that in the original calendar, the length of each month was determined primarily by the witnessing of the new moon, whereas in the calendar created by Hillel HaNasi, the lengths of all months are completely predetermined, regardless of when the new moon occurs. Only Rosh Hashanah is determined by the new moon, although, as we will soon see, even then, there are other contributing considerations.

History has demonstrated the unbelievable clairvoyance of Hillel HaNasi's calendar. So that we can gain an inkling of what he accomplished, bear in mind that at the time of the events of our story, almost six hundred years had passed since Hillel's passing and Jewish communities had already scattered across the entire known world. There were already, at that time, Jewish communities strewn throughout Europe and North Africa – those which eventually developed into the Ashkenazim and the Sefardim. Yet wherever Jewish communities lived, they kept the same Jewish calendar – whether under the rule of Christians, Muslims, or Zoroastrians.

One of the fascinating marvels of history is that although there was no absolute central authority to determine Jewish observance, Jewish communities everywhere followed and continued to follow the identical calendar, without any error or dispute, with the sole exception of the one incident we are discussing!

Creating a Calendar

Creating a calendar is fairly simple once one understands the nineteen-year cycle of leap and common years. Perhaps the most difficult aspect is determining the length of the months Marcheshvan and Kislev. What factors govern whether there will be twenty-nine or thirty days in any given year?

There are five factors that determine this decision, three of which are germane to understanding the dispute that we will soon discuss. However, before explaining them, we need to understand one astronomical concept, the *molad*.

The *Molad*

While the moon orbits the earth, we on the earth observe it as passing through its various phases, from the very smallest crescent until it reaches full moon, then subsequently shrinking until it disappears completely. This monthly cycle occurs because the moon has no light of its own, and only reflects sunlight back to the earth. As the moon travels around the earth, the angle at which it reflects light changes. This manifests itself in the moon's changing phases. When the moon is on the side of the earth away from the sun, we see the full moon, because it is now at an angle that reflects the greatest possible amount of light back to us. However, when the moon is on the side of earth nearest the sun, we see no reflection of its light at all, and that is the point during every month when the moon disappears from earthly view. The *molad* is the point at which the moon crosses the plane between the earth and the sun, which means that it is the beginning of a new cycle, called in English the *new moon* and in technical jargon, the *point of conjunction*.

Sod Ha'ibur

The length of time that it takes for the moon to orbit the earth varies, depending on the variant gravitational forces of the sun, the earth and the planets that pull on the moon. Hillel HaNasi's calendar bases itself on an estimate, an average time that it takes the moon to orbit the earth: each new moon appears twenty-nine days, twelve hours, and 793 *chalakim* (singular: *chelek*), or 793/1080 of an hour following the previous new moon. (The term *chelek*, also used when announcing the time of the current *molad* on Shabbos Mevorchim, equals 1/1080 of an hour, or 3 and 1/3 seconds.) This amount of time is called the *sod ha'ibur* ("the secret of intercalation," that is, of calculating the appearance of the new moon at its earliest visibility in the sky), because prior to Hillel HaNasi's creation of the new calendar, this information was not made public.

Once one knows when the new moon occurred on the previous Rosh Hashanah, one can add either twelve or thirteen times the *sod ha'ibur* figure (depending on whether it is a common or a leap year) and determine the *sod ha'ibur* time of the *molad* for Tishrei in the coming year, which is the most important factor in determining which day is the next Rosh Hashanah. Since Rosh Hashanah can never fall before the *molad* day, if there were no other factors in our calendar, one could rely on the *sod ha'ibur* calculation, determine which day Rosh Hashanah should fall the next year, decide how many calendar days one needs for Rosh Hashanah to fall on that day, and then decide whether Marcheshvan should be thirty days, rather than twenty-nine, because we need an extra day, or whether Kislev should be twenty-nine days rather than thirty because we have a day too many.

However, there are other factors that influence which day we want Rosh Hashanah to occur, and because of these other factors, Rosh Hashanah is often a day or two later than the day of the *molad*. Of course, this will in turn affect how many days there are in the months of Marcheshvan and Kislev.

The Four *Dechiyos*

In creating the "permanent" calendar, Hillel HaNasi incorporated four other features that influence when Rosh Hashanah should fall out. These factors are called *dechiyos* – literally, postponements – because they postpone when Rosh Hashanah falls out, relative to the *molad* of the month of Tishrei. Two of these *dechiyos* occur only rarely, and did not enter into the calendar dispute. However, the other two *dechiyah* factors did influence why different communities observed Pesach and Yom Kippur on different days.

Lo Adu Rosh

When Hillel established the calendar that we currently use, he also factored into his calculations the requirement that Yom Kippur never fall either the day before or the day after Shabbos, because of the difficulties entailed with observing two consecutive "Shabbos" days. He also included calculations to guarantee that Hoshana Rabbah should never fall on Shabbos, which would have necessitated the cancellation of the observance of the *hoshanos* with the *lulav* and *aravah* of that day.

In order to accommodate these innovations, Rosh Hashanah could only fall on Monday, Tuesday, Thursday, or Shabbos, since if it falls on Sunday, Hoshana Rabbah falls on Shabbos; if Rosh Hashanah falls on Wednesday, Yom Kippur falls on Friday; and if Rosh Hashanah falls on Friday, then Yom Kippur falls on Sunday. This calendar concept of guaranteeing that Rosh Hashanah not fall on Sunday, Wednesday, or Friday is called לא אד"ו ראש, *lo adu rosh*, meaning that *rosh*, Rosh Hashanah, does not fall on Sunday (א), Wednesday (ד), or Friday (ו).

The implication of this is that when Rosh Hashanah in the coming year would naturally fall on Sunday, Wednesday, or Friday, an extra day is added to the calendar to make sure that Rosh Hashanah falls on Monday, Thursday, or Shabbos instead.[3]

Molad Zakein

To understand the dispute between Ben Meir and the other leaders, we need to explain another calendar rule called *molad zakein*. According to the usual understanding of this rule, whenever the *molad* of the month of Tishrei takes place after the exact midday on a particular day, Rosh Hashanah is pushed off to the next day. Why Hillel HaNasi established this rule brings us back to the way the calendar existed prior to Hillel.

When the calendar was determined monthly by *beis din*, the date of Rosh Chodesh was not established according to the time the new moon occurred, but by when the new moon could be *witnessed* – thus, Hillel HaNasi ruled that Rosh Hashanah should never fall out before the new moon would be visible in Eretz Yisrael – which we assume is at least six hours after the *molad*. The phenomenon of delaying Rosh Hashanah because its *molad* could not be observed that day is called *molad zakein*, an "old", or late, *molad*.

A Highly Esoteric Dispute

Ben Meir disputed how much time we allow for *molad zakein*. According to the approach accepted both prior to his time and afterwards, the cutoff time to create a *molad zakein* is exactly midday. If the *molad* falls after midday, that day cannot be Rosh Hashanah, and an extra day (or days) must be added to the calendar to postpone the holiday. Ben Meir asserted that the cutoff time to create a *molad zakein* is 642 *chalakim* (which equals 35 2/3 minutes) after midday. In the year 4684 (923 CE), the *molad* occurred 237 *chalakim* after midday, which according to the usual calculation made it a *molad zakein*, whereas according to Ben Meir it was not.

But Why Two Days?

This explains why Ben Meir's Rosh Hashanah calculation was one day earlier than that of the other scholars; but why were all of his holidays *two* days earlier? The answer is that since Rosh Hashanah cannot fall on a Wednesday, once we postpone Rosh Hashanah because of *molad zakein*, we must postpone it to Thursday. Thus, the year in question could either be *chaseirah*, that is, with both Marcheshvan and Kislev twenty-nine days so that Rosh Hashanah could fall on Tuesday, or *sheleimah*, with both Marcheshvan and Kislev thirty days, so that Rosh Hashanah would fall on Thursday. The original calculation assumed that Rosh Hashanah could not fall on Tuesday in that year because of *molad zakein*, and could not be on Wednesday because of *lo adu rosh*, and therefore Rosh Hashanah had to be postponed two days to Thursday. Ben Meir ruled that Rosh Hashanah should fall on Tuesday, and, to accommodate this, he needed to make both Marcheshvan and Kislev twenty-nine days, which then made Pesach two days earlier than had been expected, and moved it back from Tuesday to Sunday.

Ben Meir vs. Rav Saadiah Gaon

Why Ben Meir felt the need to add 642 *chalakim* to the calculation is unclear. I have read several theories to explain why, none of which are very halachically satisfying, particularly when we realize that Ben Meir was without question a *gadol beYisrael* who, in any other generation, probably would have been the *gadol hador*. However, he was not a greater *talmid chacham* than Rav Saadiah Gaon.

One thing is certain: Ben Meir held that once his calculation was correct, all of the Jewish People were bound to follow it, since his *beis din* was the most qualified in Eretz Yisrael – and perhaps in the entire world – to decide on Klal Yisrael's calendar. Without question, he contended that the final decision on determining the calendar still rested with the highest halachic authorities in Eretz Yisrael, and that Hillel HaNasi's calendar had not changed this.

Historical Context

Some historical background information is useful. At the time of Hillel HaNasi, the Jewish community in Bavel had already surpassed that of Eretz Yisrael, not only in numbers, but also in scholarship, producing the greater *talmidei chachamim*. This is why the period of the Amoraim essentially ended earlier in Eretz Yisrael than in Bavel, and why the *Talmud Bavli* is more authoritative than the *Talmud Yerushalmi*. The main bastion of Torah in Klal Yisrael remained in Bavel for several hundred years. Throughout most of this era, the Geonim headed the two main yeshivos of Klal Yisrael, Sura and Pumbedisa, both located in Bavel.

However, at the time of this controversy, both of the yeshivos of Sura and Pumbedisa were in decline, and Rav Aaron Ben Meir, who headed his own yeshivah in Eretz Yisrael, surpassed in learning the heads of both Babylonian yeshivos.

Rav Saadiah Gaon

At the time of the dispute, Rav Saadiah, later to become Rav Saadiah Gaon, was only twenty-nine years old. Virtually nothing is known about Rav Saadiah's *rebbeim*. All we know is that he was born in Egypt, which was the second largest Jewish community at the time (after Bavel). At the age of about twenty-three, he traveled eastward, visiting the various Jewish communities of Eretz Yisrael, Syria, and eventually Bavel. He became very familiar with the many scholars residing in these communities. Although a very young man, we see from later correspondence that prior to leaving Egypt he already had established many disciples there, with whom he maintained correspondence after he journeyed and settled further east.

The *Machlokes*

About a year before his change was to affect the calendar, Ben Meir let people know that he was planning to implement this change in the calendar.

In response to Ben Meir's startling declaration, the authorities of Bavel addressed a letter to him, written with tremendous respect and friendship, but sharply disputing his halachic conclusions.

Rav Saadiah was in Aleppo, Syria, when he heard of Ben Meir's intentions to change the calendar. He immediately addressed a succession of letters to Ben Meir, explaining to him that the established calendar was correct and that one should not tamper with it.

Apparently, Ben Meir was not troubled by the letters from either Rav Saadiah or from Bavel. It appears that he then formalized his calendar change with a pronouncement made on Hoshana Rabbah from Har Hazeisim. Because of its proximity to the Beis HaMikdash grounds, the Torah leaders of Eretz Yisrael held an annual gathering on Har Hazeisim to perform *hoshanos* as close as they could to the former site of the Beis HaMikdash. At the same time, they used the occasion to discuss the issues facing their communities, and decided on plans and policies. It appears that Ben Meir used this opportunity to announce the decision of his *beis din* to change the planned calendar in the coming year.

Indeed, the communities of Eretz Yisrael, and several (if not all) of those in Egypt followed Ben Meir's ruling and kept twenty-nine-day months for both Marcheshvan and Kislev.

The *Machlokes* Heats Up

By Teves, after the two questionable *roshei chodashim* had passed, we find letters addressed back and forth between Bavel and Eretz Yisrael, but by now the letters are more strident. By this point, Rav Saadiah had arrived in Bavel, and the next correspondence includes letters from the established leaders of Bavel to Ben Meir, strongly rebuking his decision. At the same time, the leadership of Bavel, as well as Rav Saadiah, addressed circulars to the various Jewish communities, advising them to observe the established calendar and not to follow that of Ben Meir.

About the same time, Rav Saadiah wrote to his disciples in Egypt, advising them that all the leaders of Bavel had concurred to follow the old calendar and to proclaim Marcheshvan and Kislev as full months, and to observe Pesach, Rosh Hashanah, Yom Kippur, and Sukkos accordingly. "Close this breach and do not rebel against the command of Hashem. None of the people would intentionally work on Yom Tov, eat *chametz* on Pesach, or eat, drink, or work on Yom Kippur. May it be the Will of Hashem that no stumbling block be placed either in your place or in any other place in Israel."

What is amazing is that Rav Saadiah was barely thirty years old when these events transpired, and already he was held in such high esteem that the established leadership of Bavel requested that he join them in their correspondence on the issue, and that, of his own volition, he mailed letters instructing various communities concerning what to do.

Ben Meir Won't Retract

In reaction to the letters from the Geonim and from Rav Saadiah, Ben Meir sent his son to Yerushalayim to announce, once again, his planned calendar change. At the same time, he wrote in an aggressive and disrespectful tone that final authority in all matters of the calendar lie with the Torah leadership of Eretz Yisrael.

In the meantime, Pesach was fast approaching, and communities were bewildered as to what they should do. Rav Saadiah wrote a second letter to his disciples in Egypt.

It should be noted that, notwithstanding the personal attack leveled against him by Ben Meir, Rav Saadiah dealt specifically with the issues at hand and refrained from any remark belittling its author. Such is the way of Torah.

Why did Rav Saadiah not accept Ben Meir's assertion that the Torah leadership of Eretz Yisrael had the right to the final say in these matters?

Rav Saadiah wrote that Ben Meir's calculations were all in error. The traditional calculations used were based on an old *mesorah* from Sinai, as can be demonstrated from the Gemara.[4] Thus, Ben Meir's disagreement was not a matter of debate, but a grievous error. Rav Saadiah rallied support for his point from the fact that, since the days of Hillel HaNasi, no one had questioned the accuracy of the accepted calendar.

Two Different Pesachs

Indeed, that Pesach, many communities followed Ben Meir and others followed Rav Saadiah and the Geonim of Bavel. The dispute continued on for the next year, through the disputed Rosh Hashanah, Yom Kippur, and Sukkos.

History did not bequeath to us the final steps of this dispute, yet we know that by the following year, the strong, brilliant logic of Rav Saadiah's responsa swayed the tide against Ben Meir's contentions, Rav Saadiah became accepted as the *gadol hador*, and had the final say in *halachah*. Ben Meir himself blamed Rav Saadiah for torpedoing his initiative. History knows nothing more of Ben Meir after this episode, nor does it know of any community that subsequently followed his approach.

Six years later, Rav Saadiah was asked to assume the position of Gaon of Sura, the only time in history that the position was offered to someone who had not grown up and studied in Bavel. Indeed, we have Rav Saadiah to thank for the Jewish People's unanimity in always observing Yamim Tovim on the same day.

NOTES

1. Primary source for the historical information in this article is Dr. Henry Malter's *Saadia Gaon: His Life and Works* (Jewish Publication Society of America, 1921).

2. *Berachos* 63a.

3. Rambam, *Hilchos Kiddush Hachodesh* 7:1.

4. *Rosh Hashanah* 20b.

4
Is It a Lemon?

The History and *Halachah* of the Grafted *Esrog*

Micha Moka, who is fairly new to observant Judaism, presents the following question:

> This is the first time that I am purchasing my own *esrog*. I have been told that many *esrogim* may not be kosher because they, or their antecedents, were grafted onto other citrus trees. But I don't understand what the problem is. When you graft a branch of one species onto another tree, the fruit that grows should be identical to any other fruit of the branch species.

Pri Eitz Hadar

In *Parshas Emor*, the Torah teaches, "And on the first day you shall take for yourselves the fruit of a beautiful tree…and you shall rejoice with it before Hashem your G-d seven days."[1] The Hebrew term used to describe the fruit is *pri eitz hadar*. The word *hadar* is used many times in Tanach to refer to the glory of Hashem Himself.[2] The Ramban[3] explains the word *esrog* to be the Aramaic translation of the Hebrew word *hadar*; both words mean *desired* or *beautiful*. (The Modern Hebrew use of the word *hadar* to mean *citrus* has no basis in traditional Hebrew, but was borrowed from the *pasuk*. Unfortunately, as a result of this modern convention, Israelis often misunderstand the *pasuk*.)

The *Esrog*

The Written Torah does not provide any more details with which to identify this fruit, but the Oral Torah's *mesorah* from Sinai is that the Torah means the species that we call an *esrog*,[4] which is called *Citrus medica* in scientific jargon, based on its extensive medicinal value. Certainly, the oral *mesorah* itself provides sufficient basis for us to know which species is *pri eitz hadar*, but in addition, Chazal infer hermeneutically from the *pasuk* three features that are unique to the *esrog*.[5]

Feature 1: Its Bark Is as Good as Its Bite

The bark tastes like the fruit. This means that the natural oils, flavonoids, and other chemical components that impart the unique fragrance and flavor of an *esrog* exist in sufficient quantity in the bark such that it bears the smell and "taste" of the fruit.

Some early authorities note that this factor seems common to all citrus and is not unique to the *esrog*.[6] Other citrus fruits also bear their unique components in their leaves, peels, and bark such that one can identify the leaf or bark of a lemon or orange tree by its aroma.

However, the *Kappos Temarim*[7] explains that an *esrog* is unique in that the taste of "*its* fruit and bark are equal." In other words, the *esrog* is unique in that it has little or no pulp, unlike other edible citrus fruits. Therefore, the main part of the *esrog* is its "rind," which bears a much closer flavor to its bark than does the pulp of any other fruit.[8]

Feature 2: The Fruit Remains on the Tree

As a general rule, non-citrus trees drop their fruit at the end of the season. Most other citrus trees also drop their fruit when overripe, although some individual fruits still remain on the tree. *Esrogim* do indeed remain longer on the tree than any other citrus. Some fruit do fall off, but an impressive percentage remains on the tree, sometimes for as long as two years.[9]

Feature 3: Water, Water Everywhere

An *esrog* requires year-round irrigation to produce sizable fruit. As of the time of this writing, I have been unable to discover any unique feature of *esrogim* differentiating them from other types of citrus, all of which require year-round irrigation to produce large fruit.

Notwithstanding this description, a fruit still may have all these three features and still not be considered an *esrog* according to most authorities. We will soon see why.

Grafting

A common practice in the production of citrus is to graft the branches of the desired variety of fruit onto rootstocks that allow a greater yield, are more resistant to disease, and provide other commercial value. It is prohibited for a Jew to graft one species onto another stock, and there is a dispute among halachic authorities about whether or not a gentile may do so. Most authorities understand that different varieties of citrus are halachically considered different species concerning the prohibition of grafting fruits (however, see *Chazon Ish*[10] who conjectures whether the similar characteristics of citrus might allow them to be considered one species, in regard to the prohibition of grafting.)

May One Use a Grafted *Esrog*?

When one grafts the fruit of one species onto the rootstock of another, the fruit will grow according to the species of the scion branch, an observable phenomenon noted already by Rashi.[11] Our question: is the fruit of an *esrog* branch grafted onto a lemon stock halachically an *esrog*? Are there any other halachic concerns because it grew on a non-*esrog* stock?

Graft in Sixteenth-Century Poland

The earliest responsum on the subject that I discovered is authored by the Rema, who probably never saw an *esrog* tree in his life. Citrus trees are not generally frost hardy, and therefore grow in warmer areas than Poland, where the Rema lived his entire life. When reading his responsum on the matter, we should bear in mind the difficulty of obtaining *esrogim* for Sukkos in his place and era.

Rema writes very tersely that the fruit of a graft is not called an *esrog*, nor is it called the *fruit of a hadar tree*.

Rema notes that although there were earlier scholars who recited a *berachah* on grafted *esrogim* when they had no others available, we should not rely on this when we have access to nongrafted *esrogim*.[12] (For the balance of this chapter, when I refer to "grafted *esrogim*," I mean *esrogim* grafted onto a rootstock of a non-*esrog* species. All authorities allow use of a fruit grown on an *esrog* branch grafted onto another *esrog* tree.[13])

A Ransomed *Esrog*

A contemporary and second cousin of Rema, Rav Shmuel Yehuda Katzenellenbogen, the *rav* of Venice from 5326 to 5357 (1566 to 1597), was asked whether one may use an *esrog* grafted onto a lemon tree, and he responded that every child knows that these *esrogim* may not be used. Rav Katzenellenbogen writes that he heard from his father, Rav Meir Katzenellenbogen, the famed Maharam Padua (named for the city where he served as *rav* for many decades), a fascinating anecdote:

One year, the entire community of Padua was able to acquire only one non-grafted *esrog* for Sukkos, which had to service all the different congregations of the city. This is even though grafted *esrog* trees were apparently very popular decorative trees there and were readily available in the houses of the gentry. When the *esrog* was sent from one congregation to another, it was stolen by rowdy gentile students, who held the *esrog* for ransom. The community needed to redeem the kidnapped *esrog* for a considerable amount of money, which they did in order to fulfill the *mitzvah*, notwithstanding the fact that they had ready access to a large supply of very inexpensive, locally grown, grafted *esrogim*. Thus, the community purchased a non-grafted *esrog twice* in order to fulfill the *mitzvah*!

(Two interesting side points about Rav Shmuel Yehuda Katzenellenbogen: The first is that we do not have an extant edition of his responsa. This particular, undated responsum is published in the *Shu't Rema*.[14] The second is that he is often called the Mahari Padua, meaning *Rav Yehudah, who had been born in Padua*, to distinguish him from his father.)

Graft in the Holy Land!

A third responsum from the same era deals with the identical issue in Eretz Yisrael. Prior to Sukkos of 5346 (1585), the Alshich in Tzefas was asked about using a grafted *esrog*. He relates that one local *rav* wanted to permit the use of this *esrog*, notwithstanding the fact that all the other authorities prohibited the use of grafted *esrogim* for Sukkos. This *rav* contended that the nourishment drawn from the lemon stock was already nullified in the *esrog* branch, and the fruit was therefore considered to be completely *esrog*.

In his discussion on the subject, the Alshich demonstrates, from the laws of *orlah*, that we consider the branch to be nullified to the stock and not the other way around. This is due to the fact that a young branch grafted onto a stock more than three years old is not subject to the laws of *orlah*, whereas an older branch grafted onto a young stock is.

Furthermore, the Alshich contends that even if the *esrog* was not nullified to the lemon as the laws of *orlah* imply, the resultant fruit should be considered a blend of both species and not purely *esrog*. Therefore, even if the fruit is considered an *esrog*, it is an incomplete *esrog*, and therefore invalid, because it has some lemon content.[15]

A Different Graft Problem

A disciple of Rema, Rav Mordechai Yaffe, often called the "Levush" because of the titles of his published works, contended that a grafted *esrog* may not be used for Sukkos for a different reason: Since the Torah disapproves of grafting, one may not fulfill *mitzvos* with grafted products, just as a crossbred animal may not be used for a *korban*.[16] (By the way, both a fruit grafted from two kosher species, and an animal crossbred from two kosher species are considered kosher – for eating purposes.)

Not all authorities agreed with the Levush regarding this *p'sak*. The *Taz* questions whether this principle of the Levush is accurate, rallying sources that the fact that something sinful had previously been performed with an item does not automatically invalidate it for *mitzvah* use.

The *Taz* still concludes that one should not use a grafted *esrog* because of a different reason, one of those that the Alshich had mentioned: that a grafted *esrog* should be considered incomplete because of the admixture of other species. However, the *Taz* notes that a halachic difference results between his reason and that of the Levush, since the *halachah* is that a damaged or incomplete *esrog* (called an *esrog chaseir*) may be used to fulfill the *mitzvah* after the first day of Sukkos. Since, in his opinion, the shortcoming of a grafted *esrog* is its incompleteness as an *esrog*, one could use it after the first day of Sukkos.

The *Taz* then notes that perhaps an *esrog* from a grafted branch or tree is worse than an incomplete *esrog*, in that it is considered qualitatively to be only partially an *esrog*. If that is the case, one should avoid using it under any circumstances, so that people not err and think that it is a kosher *esrog*.

Identifying a Grafted *Esrog*

The vast majority of halachic authorities concluded that one does not fulfill the *mitzvah* with a grafted *esrog*.[17] A later debate focused on whether the fruit of a tree planted from the seed of a grafted *esrog* is also invalid, with the *Beis Efraim*[18] contending that these *esrogim* are kosher, and other authorities disputing its *kashrus*.

This led to a new debate. If the tree grown from a grafted *esrog* is no longer considered an *esrog* tree (for the purposes of fulfilling the *mitzvah*), how can one ever know that the *esrog* he wants to use is kosher?

This led to a dispute in the early nineteenth century. The *Beis Efraim* ruled that one may use an *esrog* if it has the physical characteristics, the *simanim*, of a non-grafted *esrog*. His contemporary, the *Chasam Sofer*,[19] disputed this, and ruled that just as we no longer rely on *simanim* to decide which birds we treat as kosher, but rely exclusively on a *mesorah* to determine the *kashrus* of a bird, so too, we can use *esrogim* only from places where we have a *mesorah* that they are kosher.

The *Simanim*

What are the characteristics that distinguish a grafted *esrog* from a non-grafted *esrog*?

In the above quoted responsum of the Mahari Padua, he writes that one can identify whether an *esrog* was grown on a branch grafted onto another tree by three characteristics:

1. **Smooth-skinned.** The skin of a grafted *esrog* is smooth, more like a lemon, whereas a pure *esrog* has a bumpy surface.

2. **Outward-stemmed.** The stem (the *ukatz*) of a grafted *esrog* looks like a lemon's stem, which sticks up from the bottom of the lemon, instead of being imbedded inward like that of an *esrog*.

3. **Fruity and thin-skinned.** A grafted *esrog* has a lot of edible fruit and juice in it and a thin peel, whereas a pure *esrog* has a thick peel and little juicy flesh.

4. **Vertical seeds.** Some later authorities noted another distinction between a regular *esrog* and a grafted one. In a

regular *esrog*, the seeds grow in the same direction as the length of the fruit, whereas grafted *esrogim* often have their seeds growing like a lemon's, in the same direction as the width of the fruit. Other authorities disputed whether this demonstrates that the *esrog* has been grafted.[20]

Variety of *Esrogim*

Let us note that today there are several different types of *esrogim* with a *mesorah* that they are not grafted. Aside from the conventional European or Israeli *esrog* that most of us are used to, there are also the Moroccan *esrog* and the Yemenite *esrog*, notwithstanding the fact that both the inside and outside of these *esrogim* are definitely distinguishable from the European or Israeli *esrogim* that Ashkenazim are accustomed to.

Genetic Testing

Research teams from the University of Catania, Italy, and Hebrew University jointly studied twelve varieties of *esrog*, including the standard Moroccan, Yemenite, Italian, and Chazon Ish, to investigate whether the DNA indicated that they were indeed consistently one species, or whether they were of different species and origins.

The study concluded that all twelve varieties are in fact *esrogim*, and indeed are genetically separable from other citrus fruits, including the lemon, which appears most similar to the *esrog*.

To quote the study:

> The results obtained are very clear and might be regarded as somewhat surprising. Notwithstanding diverse geographical origin and the considerable morphological variation, especially in fruit size and shape, presence of pulp and persistence of style, all the citron types examined revealed a high degree of similarity. There was no sign of introgression of lemon or other citrus genomes into any of the citrons examined.[21]

We should note that even though genetically, all the varieties tested are indeed *esrogim*, we cannot rely on genetic testing to prove the authenticity of a particular *esrog*, since, if it was grafted onto non-*esrog* stock, it would be invalid for use on Sukkos, according to most authorities. In addition, the decision as to whether one may plant his fruit or stock and use future generations of this *esrog* is dependent on the above-quoted dispute between those who follow *mesorah* and those who follow *simanim*.

Contemporary *Esrogim*

Two generations ago, many, if not most, *esrog* trees in Eretz Yisrael were grafted onto the stock of a variety of orange tree called the *chushchash*, which bears a fruit that is not edible raw. The farmers of the era claim that they were told that since the *chushchash* is not edible, using it as a stock for the *esrog* is permitted and would not invalidate the fruit, a position that is difficult to sustain and has been rejected by subsequent authorities.

A result of this is that the Chazon Ish and many other authorities had difficulty finding *esrogim* in Eretz Yisrael. Therefore, when the Chazon Ish chose an *esrog*, he was very careful that it did not come from an *esrog* tree that had been grafted onto *chushchash* or any other species. After Sukkos one year he entrusted a seed from the *esrog* that he had used to Rav Michel Yehudah Lefkowitz, *ztz"l*, to plant. Rav Michel Yehudah protested that he had no experience in horticulture, and *esrogim* require considerable knowledge to grow properly. The Chazon Ish told him, "Just plant this seed and make sure to water it regularly, and you will have plenty of *esrogim* to sell." Rav Michel Yehudah did as he was told, surprised at the instructions, notwithstanding his lack of experience.

His tree grew, and for over seventy years produced gorgeous *esrogim* without any efforts on his part. This in itself can be considered a miracle, for two different reasons:

1. *Esrogim* do not usually grow nicely on the tree without considerable work.

2. *Esrog* trees do not live this long.

Many of the "Chazon Ish" *pardesim*, which are very popular nowadays, originated from trimmings of branches taken from Rav Michel Yehudah's tree.

As of Nissan 5771 (2011), this *esrog* tree was still covered with beautiful blossoms, indicative of another beautiful crop. The tree was in excellent shape, notwithstanding that the Chazon Ish is gone almost sixty years and the tree is over seventy years old. Its regular customers were looking forward to selecting *esrogim* from this ancient tree.

Rav Michel Yehudah passed away in Tammuz 5771 (2011), at the age of ninety-seven. Although the same people watered the tree that year, the tree began to wither, completely stopped producing fruit in midseason, and suddenly showed signs of severe aging.

Certainly a miraculous sign, but the phenomenon can be readily explained. When Rav Michel Yehudah protested that he knew nothing of *esrog* horticulture, the Chazon Ish promised him that he need only water the tree and it would produce fruit. As long as Rav Michel Yehudah was alive, the *berachah* of the Chazon Ish was fulfilled. We have a rule: *Tzaddik gozeir, HaKadosh Baruch Hu mekayeim* – If a righteous person decrees something, Hashem fulfills it.[22] As long as Rav Michel Yehudah was alive, the *berachah* of the Chazon Ish had to be fulfilled, despite the long odds against it. Once Rav Michel Yehudah passed on, the decree of the Chazon Ish no longer had to be fulfilled, and the tree no longer lived.[23]

NOTES

1. *Vayikra* 23:40.
2. See, for example, *Tehillim* 96:6; 104:1.
3. *Vayikra* 23:40.
4. Rambam, introduction to *Peirush Hamishnayos*.
5. *Sukkah* 35a.

6. *Shu't HaRema* #117.

7. *Sukkah* 35a.

8. Quoted by *Shu't Chasam Sofer, Orach Chayim* #207.

9. Note that the *Kappos Temarim, Sukkah* 35a, explains the difference between *esrog* and other citrus slightly differently.

10. *Kelayim* 2:15; 3:7.

11. *Sotah* 43b.

12. *Shu't HaRema* #117.

13. *Shu't HaBach* #135; *Mishnah Berurah* 648:65.

14. #126:2.

15. *Shu't Maharam Alshich* #110.

16. *Orach Chayim* 649:4.

17. One authority that permitted its use is the *Shu't Panim Meiros*, vol. 2, no. 173.

18. *Orach Chayim* #56.

19. *Shu't Chasam Sofer, Orach Chayim* #183.

20. *Bikkurei Yaakov* 648:53.

21. *Proceedings of the International Society of Citriculture*, December 2000.

22. See *Moed Katan* 16b.

23. The author acknowledges the assistance of Dr. Joshua Klein, senior scientist at the Volcani Center, Israel Ministry of Agriculture, for technical information in this essay.

5

Revealing the Skeletons in Your Closet

Guidelines for What and When to Disclose in *Shidduchim*

Mrs. Weiss called to discuss the following sensitive matter:

> I was once treated successfully for a serious disease. My grandmother had the same illness, yet lived in good health to a ripe old age. The doctors feel that my daughter should be checked regularly from a fairly young age for this same disease. She is now entering the *shidduchim parshah.* Must I reveal this family information to *shadchanim* (matchmakers) and/or to the families of potential *chassanim,* and, if so, at what point must I disclose this information? I am truly concerned that this could seriously complicate her *shidduch* prospects.

Although this situation may be atypical, we all have medical, personal, and/or genealogical issues that we wish to keep private.

What information must we reveal while arranging *shidduchim* for our children (or for ourselves)? And at what point must we disclose the issues? And to whom must we reveal this sensitive information?

The prohibitions of *geneivas daas*, misleading someone, and *onaah*, fraud, apply equally to *shidduchim*. However, there are many complicating factors specifically involved in *shidduchim*, and therefore we need to explain the issues carefully.

Onaah – Fraud

Misrepresenting a product or service in order to make a sale is a form of cheating, just as painting an item to hide a defect is also a form of cheating. In *shidduchim*, the same rule is true: subject to some exceptions, which I will explain shortly, one must notify the other party of information that might concern them. Hoping that no one takes this personally, I will refer to this type of negative information as an "imperfection." For example, Mrs. Weiss is inquiring whether the family medical history constitutes an imperfection that must be revealed.

Mekach Ta'us – Invalidating the Marriage

The most serious ramification of withholding required information about *shidduchim* – or worse, of being deceptive – is that this can even result (in certain extreme cases) in a halachically invalid marriage. (This indeed applies to any contracted arrangement – an unrevealed, serious imperfection brings about a *mekach ta'us*, because the two parties never agreed to the arrangement as it presently exists.)

Here are a few interesting examples.

Vows

If someone specifies that his new wife should have no vows (*nedarim*) and finds that she is bound by *neder* to abstain from meat, wine, or nice clothes, the *kiddushin* is annulled![1] A husband wants to enjoy life together with his wife, and refraining from these activities may disturb the happiness of their marriage.

To quote the words of the *Sefer Chassidim*:

> When arranging matches for your children or other family members, do not hide medical issues from the other party to which they would object enough to decline the *shidduch*, lest they afterward choose to annul the marriage. You should also tell them about deficiencies in halachic observances that are significant enough that the other party would have rejected the marriage (had they known about them).[2]

Can't Smell

Another example of unrevealed information that invalidates a marriage is a woman's failure to notify her future husband that she has no sense of smell, since this flaw hampers her ability to prepare tasty meals. Similarly, working at a profession that causes a man's body to have a foul odor is sufficient reason to invalidate the marriage.[3]

Infertility

Withholding information concerning an inability to have children is certainly a *mekach ta'us*. In this last situation, a physician who is aware that his patient cannot have children is required to reveal this information to the other side, even though this violates patient confidentiality.[4] In a specific situation discussed by the *Tzitz Eliezer*, the physician was aware that the young woman had no uterus, and therefore it was physically impossible for her to conceive a child. He was also aware that they were hiding this information from the prospective groom. The same would be true should the male be unable to have children, since the assumption is that people of childbearing age marry, intending to bear offspring from the marriage.

What May One Hide?

What type of information may one withhold?

There are two categories of negative information, i.e.,

imperfections, that one does not need to reveal. These include information that the other party could find out on their own, and information that is not significant.

Known Information

A seller is not required to disclose an imperfection in his product that the buyer could discover on his own. Furthermore, as long as the buyer could have noticed something that may arouse attention, there is no *geneivas daas* and no *onaah* in making the sale.[5]

For example, if someone is selling a house with a drop ceiling, he is not required to notify the buyer that there was damage above the ceiling, since a drop ceiling in a residence should arouse attention. Similarly, if the entire neighborhood is susceptible to flooding basements, the seller does not need to mention that his basement has a severe water problem. If the buyer asks directly, the seller must answer honestly.

Similarly, in regard to stock trading: the seller is not required to mention that in the last recorded quarter, the company reported a sharp decline in profits, since this information is readily available to the buyer.

A similar concept is true concerning *shidduchim*. For example, if the scandalous activities of a family member are well known in one's hometown, one need not tell the other party, since this information could be discovered by asking around.[6] Halachically, when the other party asks neighbors for information about this potential *shidduch*, the neighbors should share the requested details.

Insignificant Information

A second category of information that need not be revealed includes factors that are insignificant to the buyer. One is not required to provide an in-depth list of every shortcoming the merchandise has. Similarly, *shidduchim* do not require revealing every possible medical or *yichus* issue. The Chafetz Chayim distinguishes between a medical issue one must reveal and a "weakness," which one does not.[7] Thus, someone need not reveal minor ailments that would not disturb the average person.

Of course, it is sometimes difficult to define what constitutes a "minor ailment" and what constitutes a serious one, and specific rabbinic guidance is usually warranted when one is in doubt. However, I will present one or two examples of each.

Although I know *rabbonim* who disagree with this position, I feel that juvenile diabetes is a malady that must be mentioned, whereas hay fever and similar allergies that are not life threatening may be ignored. On the other hand, an allergy that is so serious that it affects one's lifestyle and activities in a major way must be mentioned. My usual litmus test is: if the issue is significant enough that one might want to hide it, it is usually something that one should tell.

When to Tell?

At what point must one reveal a significant "imperfection"?

The *Sefer Chassidim*, quoted above, does not mention at what point one must notify the other party of the shortcoming. Contemporary *poskim* usually contend that one should reveal this information after the couple has met a few times; about the time the relationship is beginning to get serious, but after the two parties have become acquainted and see their overall qualities as individuals. This is the approach I personally advise in all such situations. There is no requirement for the parties to tell a *shadchan*, and in some situations, it is prohibited to do so.

My daughter has a close friend who unfortunately has celiac disease. She had been told by her *rav* that she should reveal this information on the third date. (Note that this precise detail will vary tremendously depending on the dating approach used in the couple's circles.) She was so nervous and concerned about how the young man would react that she was unable to bring herself to mention it then. Finally, on the fourth date, she was able to get the words out, to which he reacted nonchalantly, "Oh, so does my brother." This story has a very happy ending, since anyway her mother-in-law prepares food that is appropriate.

Rejection

However, if one knows that the other party will reject the *shidduch* because of this imperfection, I would recommend forgoing this *shidduch* from the outset. For example, if one knows that a particular family prides itself on a pure pedigree, one should not pursue a *shidduch* with them if one knows that they will ultimately reject it – when they discover that the other party's great-uncle was not observant.

At this point, we can discuss Mrs. Weiss's *she'eilah* about revealing information concerning the serious disease both she and her mother endured, and which the doctors recommend her daughter be checked for regularly.

Most *poskim* with whom I discussed this *she'eilah* contended that one should reveal this information to the other side after the couple has gotten to know one another and are interested in pursuing the relationship. One *rav* disagreed, contending that since the problem can be caught early and treated successfully, one need not divulge this information at all. All opinions agree that one has absolutely no obligation to mention this information to a *shadchan* or to anyone who has no personal need for this information.

Obviously, I cannot possibly discuss the various permutations of these *she'eilos* in a short essay, but can simply present the issues.

Wishing all much happiness in their marriages and their children's marriages!

NOTES

1. *Kesubos* 72b.
2. *Sefer Chassidim* #507.
3. *Kesubos* 76a.
4. *Shu't Tzitz Eliezer* 16:4.
5. *Shu't Igros Moshe, Yoreh Deah* 1:31.
6. *Shu't Panim Me'iros* 1:35.
7. *Be'er Mayim Chayim* #8 at end of *Hilchos Rechilus*.

6

The Spurned *Shadchan*

Practical *Halachos* of Paying *Shadchanus Gelt*

The phone rings. Mrs. Goldberg, a *shadchan* who often calls to ask *she'eilos,* is on the line.

"I suggested that a local girl meet a *bachur* who is currently learning in Eretz Yisrael," Mrs. Goldberg began. "Both families did their research and agreed that it sounded worth pursuing, but they decided to wait until the summer when the *bachur* would be visiting his family here in America."

"When the summer arrived," Mrs. Goldberg continued, "I called the families back to arrange for the young people to meet. However, they told me that someone else suggested the *shidduch,* and that they are following up through the other *shadchan.* Are they permitted to cut me out of the arrangements? After all, it was my idea first!"

Does Mrs. Goldberg have a claim? If she does, for how much money and against whom?

Shadchanus Gelt

Before we discuss these issues, we need to establish whether paying a *shadchan* is indeed a halachic requirement.

I often find that people feel that one is not required to pay a *shadchan*. However, this is a misconception, since the *poskim* require paying a *shadchan* a fee, usually called by its Yiddish name, *shadchanus gelt*.[1] Just as one expects to pay one's real estate broker, so too, one should assume one will pay the *shadchan*. Furthermore, there is nothing wrong with a *shadchan* requesting payment for services rendered, just as an attorney or accountant has every right to demand payment for services.

Brokerage Fees

Although it sometimes sounds strange, *shadchanus* fees are halachically categorized as brokerage fees. Just as one pays a real estate agent for arranging a transaction, so too, one pays a *shadchan* for making the necessary arrangements in order for the engagement and marriage to transpire. Therefore, we must first explain the halachic sources for brokerage fees.

The Gemara[2] mentions the responsibility to pay a broker's fee to the person who arranges the sale of property or merchandise.[3] This is a standard business practice, similar to paying a commission to a stockbroker, real estate agent, or personnel recruiter (sometimes called a "headhunter").

Unsolicited Service

People easily understand that if one approaches a broker or agent, one thereby obligates oneself to pay him for his services. However, some people assume that if one did not solicit the service, one is not obligated to pay. Does this distinction have any basis?

According to *halachah*, one is required to pay for any unsolicited benefit that one would usually pay for. Providing unsolicited benefit is called *yored lesoch sdei chaveiro shelo birshus* (entering someone else's field without authorization), and the provider of the benefit is referred to simply as the *yored*.[4]

The case in which the Gemara demonstrates this *halachah* is very instructive: Someone owns a field that he usually plants, but he has not yet planted it this year. Someone else planted the field *without asking the owner's permission* and now asks the owner to pay him! Is the planter entitled to compensation for his efforts? The Gemara rules that he is entitled to compensation, since the owner benefits from his work.

Amount Owed

The owner is required to pay the *yored* as much as he has benefited. If he performed work for the owner that would normally require one to hire someone, one must pay him the market rate for hiring someone for this work.[5] One must pay the *shadchan* the accepted fee in his community for this service.[6]

Obligation to Pay

When a single person or the parent of a single person asks someone if they know of any marriageable prospects, they are asking them to perform a valuable service on their behalf. This service has a market value, comparable to any other brokerage or recruiting fee.[7]

Unsolicited Service

Although there are halachic differences between whether one approaches the *shadchan* or the *shadchan* offers his services, in either case, one is required to pay the *shadchan*. The basis for this requirement is as follows:

In the latter instance, the *shadchan* is a *yored*, since one received benefit from him for an unsolicited service that one would normally pay for.[8] As explained above, one must pay him whatever one would have otherwise paid for that service.[9]

A Family Member or Friend

Am I required to pay *shadchanus* to a family member or a close friend? This *she'eilah* was discussed hundreds of years ago. A professional *shadchan* contacted Mr. Reuven suggesting a gentleman he thought appropriate for Mr. Reuven's widowed sister-in-law. Mr. Reuven was involved in researching the *shidduch* and in arranging the couple's meeting. When the couple announced their engagement, Mr. Reuven informed the professional *shadchan* that he was expecting half the *shadchanus gelt*, claiming that he was the *shadchan* who convinced the woman to consider this *shidduch*. The professional *shadchan* contended that he was the only *shadchan*, and that Mr. Reuven was an interested party and not a *shadchan*. Mr. Reuven countered that the professional had never made direct contact with his sister-in-law, but relied exclusively on him to encourage the *shidduch*. The matter was referred to Rav Yair Chaim Bachrach, author of the *sefer Chavos Yair*. The *rav* ruled that Mr. Reuven was indeed a *shadchan* since he influenced his sister-in-law to pursue the *shidduch*. He was therefore entitled to half the *shadchanus* fee, even though he was related to one of the principals.[10]

Who Is Obligated to Pay?

Who must pay the *shadchanus* fee, the parents or the couple? Usually the parents of an engaged party pay the *shadchanus gelt*. Are they required to pay this fee, or is it really the responsibility of the young couple that the parents assume? As we will see, there are halachic ramifications to this question.

The *poskim* debate this question, making razor-thin distinctions that have major ramifications. Some contend that the responsibility falls upon the young couple, since they are the ones who benefit, even though the prevalent custom is that the parents pay.[11] Others contend that since the parents usually pay, the *shadchan* expects payment only from them, and therefore he has no claim against the young couple.[12]

There is a major dispute between the advocates of these approaches. The first opinion holds that if the *shadchan* is unable to collect from the parents, he may collect from the couple. According to the second opinion, his only claim is against the parents, and if he cannot collect from the parents, he cannot claim his fee from the young couple.

Approaching the *Shadchan*

Since we have learned that one must pay the *shadchan* whether or not one solicited him initially, does it make any halachic difference whether I asked the *shadchan* or the *shadchan* approached me first?

There are several differences in *halachah* that pertain to whether one solicited the *shadchan* initially or vice versa, including when one is required to pay the *shadchan*, and whether one could potentially violate the *mitzvah* of *bal talin* for not paying the *shadchan* on time.

If one approached or telephoned the *shadchan* initially, then one has hired him or her to perform a job – in this case, to find an appropriate *shidduch*. If he succeeds in his mission, then one is required to pay when the job is completed, and therefore, according to most *poskim*, one must pay the *shadchan* as soon as the couple becomes engaged.[13] Others contend that one need not pay the *shadchan* until the wedding, unless the custom is otherwise.[14] Furthermore, if one does not pay him or her on time and the *shadchan* demands payment, one will violate a Torah prohibition called *bal talin*, not paying a worker on time, a *mitzvah* we will explain shortly.

However, if one did not hire the *shadchan*, then one does not violate *bal talin* if one do not pay him or her on time, since the *shadchan* is not one's employee. If the *shadchan* solicited you, then the time one is required to pay the *shadchan* depends on *minhag* – accepted local custom.[15] If the local custom is that people do not pay the *shadchan* until the wedding, then the *shadchanus gelt* is considered a marriage expense to be paid then, and not an engagement expense. However, as mentioned above, if one solicited the *shadchan* then one is required to pay the *shadchan* when his job is completed, which is when the couple becomes engaged.[16]

What Is Considered "On Time"?

As explained above, if one hired the *shadchan*, one must pay him on time because of the *mitzvah* of *bal talin*. What is considered "on time"?

There are two deadlines, sunset and daybreak, and one is obligated to pay one's worker before the first deadline after the job is completed. Therefore, if the worker finished his job before the end of the day, I must pay him by sunset. If he completed the work at night, I must pay him before daybreak.[17] (As mentioned above, one violates this prohibition only if the worker demanded payment and the owner refused to pay, and there was no understanding or prearrangement of late payment.) According to this approach, if one went to a *shadchan* who, *baruch Hashem*, arranged a successful *shidduch*, one should make sure to pay him or her immediately after the couple becomes engaged (or married, if following the minority opinion), before the next deadline arrives.[18]

Still other *poskim* contend that since the responsibility of paying the *shadchan* really lies with the bride and groom, there is no violation of *bal talin* if the *shadchan* is assuming that the parents are paying his fee, since they are technically not required to pay *shadchanus gelt*.

Dividing the Fee

What happens if two different *shadchanim* were involved at different stages of encouraging the *shidduch*? Are they both entitled to be paid? How does one divide the fee? As we can imagine, this is not a recent *she'eilah*.

An early *posek*, the *Shev Yaakov*,[19] discusses the following case: Levi recommended that Reuven's son meet Shimon's daughter. After the engagement of the young couple, Gad claimed that he had originally suggested the *shidduch* to the parties, and thus, he is entitled to part of the *shadchanus*.

The *Shev Yaakov* researched the claims. As it turned out, Gad had, indeed, originally suggested the *shidduch* to both parties, but Shimon and his family had no interest in pursuing it. Levi, however, was a more persistent *shadchan* and convinced Shimon to consider Reuven's son for his daughter.

The *Shev Yaakov* rules that Gad was not entitled to any part of the *shadchanus* fee. He contends that a *shadchan* is only entitled to a fee when he was involved in the part of the discussion that reached fruition. However, in this case, Gad's proposal did not accomplish anything, and therefore, he is not considered a *shadchan*.

By similar reasoning, when two real estate agents show a prospective client the same house, if the first was unable to interest the client in it, but the second succeeded in convincing him to make the purchase, according to *halachah*, the second agent is entitled to the entire commission. (In these instances, if accepted business practice is different, it might affect the *halachah*; this is a separate topic in itself.)

Thus, it seems in our situation that Mrs. Goldberg is not entitled to any *shadchanus* fee, since she was not part of the actual introduction that took place.

Notwithstanding the *Shev Yaakov's* ruling that Gad was not entitled to a share of the fee, there are cases in which the *shidduch* involves several parties, and each *is* entitled to a part of the fee. If Sarah suggested a *shidduch*, but then felt that Rivkah would be a better go-between, and eventually it was necessary to get Leah involved, and *she* (Leah) was instrumental in the couple subsequently becoming engaged, all three ladies are considered partial *shadchanim* according to many *poskim*. The accepted practice in this case is to divide the accepted *shadchanus* fee and to award one-third to each of the ladies. Other *poskim* contend that only the person who suggested the *shidduch* and the one who finalized it are considered *shadchanim*, and they split the fee – but that a go-between who neither suggested a *shidduch* nor finalized it is not viewed as a *shadchan*.[20]

Higher Fee

If a shadchan asks for a fee higher than the standard, am I required to pay it? If the *shadchan* did not provide any unusual *shadchanus* service, and the fee for a *shadchan* in one's area is fairly standard, then the *shadchan* is not entitled to the extra fee. However, if there is no standard *shadchanus* fee in one's area, or the *shadchan* performed a special service, then one must pay the *shadchan's* higher fee.[21]

Shadchanus is like any other profession, where one may not charge significantly above the going rate. However, when there is no fixed, accepted amount, then the *shadchan* is not overcharging, since there is no market amount. Similarly, if the *shadchan* extends himself more than is expected, he may command a higher fee, since one is paying for the extra service.[22]

An Interesting *Shadchanus* Story

A *shadchan* unsuccessfully attempted to arrange a *shidduch* between a daughter of the wealthy Weiss family and the son of the wealthy Schwartz family. Although the two families did meet and enjoyed one another, the *shidduch* did not materialize, and the Weiss girl subsequently married someone else. Later, other *shadchanim* suggested a match between a younger Weiss daughter and the widowed Mr. Schwartz, and the couple became engaged. The original *shadchan* then claimed that he is entitled to a percentage of the *shadchanus gelt*, claiming that his involvement in the previous unsuccessful *shidduch* was instrumental in forging the close relationship between the two families that caused the latter *shidduch* to happen. Does the original *shadchan* have a claim?

The parties referred this *she'eilah* to the *Avnei Nezer*.[23] In a very complicated ruling, he contends that the original *shadchan* might be entitled to a very small percentage of the *shadchanus gelt* for his role. He suggests a compromise on this basis, but rules that one could not be certain that he is entitled to any part of the fee.

The First *Shadchan*

According to the Midrash, Moshe Rabbeinu was the *shadchan* between Klal Yisrael and Hashem at the giving of the Torah. Furthermore, Hashem Himself is indeed the ultimate *shadchan* of every marriage. Thus, we should respect the wonderful role of the *shadchanim* in our midst, who are involved in a *mitzvah* that emulates both Hashem and Moshe Rabbeinu.

NOTES

1. *Rema, Choshen Mishpat* 264:7.
2. *Bava Metzia* 63b.
3. *Shulchan Aruch, Choshen Mishpat* 185:1; *Rema* 87:39.
4. *Bava Metzia* 101a.
5. *Bava Metzia* 76a; *Sma, Choshen Mishpat* 375:1.
6. *Pischei Teshuvah, Even HaEzer* 50:16.
7. *Rema, Choshen Mishpat* 264:7.
8. *Biur HaGra, Choshen Mishpat* 87:117.
9. *Bava Metzia* 76a, 101a.
10. *Shu't Chut HaShani* #3, quoted in *Pischei Teshuvah, Even HaEzer* 50:16.
11. *Shu't Avnei Nezer, Choshen Mishpat* #36.
12. *Shu't Halichos Yisrael* #3, quoting *Eirech Shai, Choshen Mishpat* #185.
13. *Shu't Halichos Yisrael* #1–2.
14. Introduction of Rav S. Y. Elyashiv to *Shu't Halichos Yisrael*.
15. *Rema, Choshen Mishpat* 185:10.
16. *Shu't Halichos Yisrael* #4.
17. *Bava Metzia* 111a.
18. *Shu't Halichos Yisrael* #11.
19. *Choshen Mishpat* #13.
20. *Shu't Avnei Nezer, Choshen Mishpat* #36.
21. See *Rema, Choshen Mishpat* 335:1 and 264:7; *Shach* 264:15.
22. See *Rema, Choshen Mishpat* 335:1.
23. *Choshen Mishpat* #36.

7

Marriage and Yom Kippur

Rules and Reasons for Fasting on the Wedding Day

The custom of the *chassan* and the *kallah* to fast on their wedding day has been observed by the vast majority of Torah-observant Jews in North America and Europe. It is a widely observed custom that seems simple and straightforward on first examination, but in reality is rich in levels of complexity. This intricacy can be illustrated by three very reasonable questions posed by ordinary Jews:

1. **Simcha wonders:** Our wedding is going to be after nightfall. Do we fast until the wedding, or may we break the fast when it gets dark?

2. **Yocheved asks:** I usually do not fast well, and I am concerned about how I will feel at my wedding if I fast that day. What do I do?

3. **Sheryl's dilemma:** What will I explain to my nonobservant parents when they exclaim at my pre-*chuppah* reception – "What! You can't eat anything at your own wedding?"

Sheryl comes from a very assimilated background. She explains:

> In my extended family, my parents were considered the religious ones, since they were the only ones who married Jewish. Furthermore, my Dad was the only one who fasted on Yom Kippur, albeit with a little cheating on the side. So, when my family members heard that I had become Orthodox, they were shocked at many of my new practices, despite my efforts to keep things as low-key as possible. None of them had a clue what it means to really keep kosher or Shabbos. Now that I'm getting married, many of them are curious to attend my wedding, and I would like to make the experience a *kiddush Hashem* for them. Therefore, I intend to explain our *mitzvos* and customs to them in the best possible light.

Sheryl's goals are indeed noble. How will she explain the reason for the custom that the bride and groom fast on their wedding day to someone who knows little about *Yiddishkeit*? The prospect seems almost ominous.

Why Do We Fast?

Although early authorities cite at least six different reasons for this custom, most halachic authorities[1] discuss only two of them:

To Avoid Inebriation

Some explain that the practice is to ensure that the *chassan* and *kallah* are fully sober when they participate in the wedding ceremony. If they are not eating and drinking, they will certainly not drink anything intoxicating prior to the ceremony. Some commentaries provide an interesting twist to this explanation. They explain that the concern is that if one of the marrying parties drinks anything intoxicating on the wedding day, he may subsequently claim that they were inebriated and that therefore the marriage is invalid![2]

To Achieve Atonement

Since a bridegroom is forgiven for all his sins, he should fast as atonement.[3] One allusion to this atonement is found in the Torah. In the very last verse of *Parshas Toldos*, the Torah records that one of the additional wives Eisav married was Machalas, the daughter of Yishmael. The *Yerushalmi* points out that although her name was actually Basmas and not Machalas, the Torah calls her Machalas to indicate that even someone as sinful as Eisav was forgiven on his wedding day.[4]

Who Fasts?

I am sure you are already asking why I said that the *chassan* fasts on his wedding day, and omitted the *kallah*. Are there any halachic differences between the two reasons given for the fast? Indeed, there are several. One issue that *might* be affected is whether only the *chassan* fasts, or also the *kallah*. The authorities dispute whether the wedding day atones for both parties, or only for the *chassan*. Indeed, Talmudic sources mention only the *chassan* in this connection, and some later authorities contend that the wedding is indeed an atonement day only for the *chassan* and not for the *kallah*. Following this approach, some authorities conclude that only the bridegroom fasts and not the bride.[5] Others contend that despite the fact that the Gemara mentions only atonement of the *chassan's* sins, since the *kallah* is a direct cause of his atonement, she also receives forgiveness on this day.[6]

However, if the reason for the fast is to guarantee the sobriety of the parties, the *kallah*, too, should fast, even if the day is not a day of atonement. Of course, it won't be easy for Sheryl to explain all this to her family at the reception prior to her wedding. I will soon mention other reasons she can provide for them.

On the other hand, many authorities rule that the wedding day atones for both *kallah* and *chassan*, the same as Yom Kippur.[7] Following this approach, the *kallah* should also fast, even if we are not concerned about her becoming inebriated at her wedding.[8] This, too, is why both *chassan* and *kallah* say *vidui* after Minchah on the day of their wedding.[9] In addition, the couple should pray for a happy marriage that is blessed with children who bring great credit to themselves and to Hashem.[10]

Sheryl can certainly tell her family this reason for the sanctity of the day and say that this is why she will be fasting. This will also provide her with the occasion to explain that a Torah marriage involves holiness, sanctity, and opportunity for spiritual growth, all ideas that will impress her family.

Fast Duration

There are other halachic differences that result from the two reasons quoted above. If the *chassan* and *kallah* fast to ensure that they remain sober, then they should not break their fast until after the wedding ceremony, even if it does not take place until after dark. Accordingly, if the ceremony takes place on a winter night, they should logically continue their fast, even if this means that it extends into a second halachic day.[11] On the other hand, if the fast is an atonement, then once they have completed the day they can break the fast. A third opinion holds that when the ceremony is at night, their fast does not *begin* until sunset that day – since prior to sunset is still the day *before* their wedding.[12] To the best of my knowledge, this last approach is not followed.

The *Chochmas Adam*[13] concludes that since the fast is only a custom, one need not be stricter than the requirements of *halachah* for established fast days, and therefore one may end the fast at dark. However, one should be careful not to drink anything intoxicating until sipping the wine at the *chuppah*.[14] The *Aruch Hashulchan* disagrees, but the accepted practice follows the *Chochmas Adam*.[15]

What about the opposite situation – when the ceremony takes place before nightfall? According to the rationale that the fast is an atonement, some contend that one should fast the entire day, even if the ceremony transpired in the afternoon.[16] This means that even after the wedding ceremony is complete, the *chassan* and *kallah* continue to fast until nightfall, even through the *chuppah* and the *yichud* room! However, accepted practice is for the couple to end their fast at the ceremony, even when it takes place before nightfall.

Ashkenazim and Sefardim

Most sources citing the custom of fasting on one's wedding day are Ashkenazic. Whether or not Sefardim fast on this day is subject to local custom. The popular Hebrew halachic anthology, *Hanesu'in Kehilchasam*,[17] mentions many Sefardic communities that followed the custom of fasting on the wedding day – at least for the *chassan* – including the communities of Algeria, Baghdad, the Crimea, Salonika, and parts of Turkey. On the other hand, the prevalent custom in Constantinople, Egypt, and Eretz Yisrael was not to fast on the day of the wedding.[18]

Some explain that in Egypt the custom was not to fast because the weddings were always conducted in the morning. They explain that when the wedding is held late in the day, we are concerned that the *chassan* and *kallah* may drink something intoxicating, but when the wedding is in the morning, there is no such concern.[19] One could therefore argue that when Egyptian Jews marry in the evening, they should follow Ashkenazic practice and fast.

Nevertheless, the common practice among Sefardim in Eretz Yisrael today is not to fast.[20]

Comparable to Receiving the Torah

What are the other reasons mentioned for the fast?

One early source states that the reason for the fast is that the wedding ceremony commemorates the giving of the Torah at Har Sinai.[21] Indeed, many of our wedding customs, such as the carrying of candles or torches by those accompanying the *chassan* and *kallah*, commemorate our receiving the Torah. Continuing this analogy, one early source mentions that just as the Jews fasted prior to receiving the Torah, so too a *chassan* fasts the day of his wedding.[22]

This is a beautiful reason to observe the fast, although I suspect that Sheryl's family might not appreciate it.

Avoiding Rift

Here is another very meaningful reason mentioned for the fast, although it is largely ignored by the later authorities: The Gemara states, "No *kesubah* is without an argument."[23] Unfortunately, it is common that differing opinions about wedding arrangements or setting up the couple's new home cause friction between the families making the wedding. Since this problem is common, the couple should strive their utmost to avoid any conflict at all, and they should also pray and fast that the wedding passes with no disputes.[24] Somehow, Sheryl did not think that her parents would appreciate this reason for her fast, and I agreed with her.

Daily Judging

Others explain that the origin for the custom is because the *chassan* is compared to a king, and we are taught by the *Talmud Yerushalmi* that a king is judged daily.[25] Thus, the *chassan* fasts because he is being judged on his wedding day.[26] Although we may not fully understand what this means, it is certainly a good reason to do *teshuvah* and fast.

Appreciating the *Mitzvah*

The abovementioned anthology *Hanesu'in Kehilchasam* mentions yet another reason, which he attributes to the *Rokei'ach*. Great *tzaddikim* were in such eager anticipation of performing rare *mitzvos* that they could not eat on the day that such an opportunity presented itself. Similarly, the *chassan* and *kallah* look forward to performing their *mitzvah* with such excitement that they cannot even eat! Sheryl decided that this was the perfect explanation for her family.

Let's examine several other issues pertaining to fasting:

Aneinu

Do the *chassan* and *kallah* say Aneinu in their prayers, even if they will end their fast before the day ends?

The *Rema* rules that the *chassan* recites Aneinu in his prayers, even if he is not going to complete the fast, such as when the wedding ceremony takes place during the daytime.[27] In this latter situation, where he will not be completing the fast, many recommend that he omit the three words *beyom tzom taaniseinu*, "on this day of our fast," since for him, it is not a full day of fasting.[28]

Accepting the Fast

Usually, someone intending to observe a voluntary fast must state at the end of Minchah of the previous day that he intends to fast the following day. Are the *chassan* and *kallah* required to declare that they accept the fast during Minchah of the previous day?

The halachic authorities recommend that the *chassan* and *kallah* make this declaration after Minchah on the day before the wedding, and recommend specifying that they intend to fast only until the ceremony. Nevertheless, even if they did not declare the day to be a fast, and even if they did not mention the stipulation, one may assume that they should fast, and that they are required to fast only until the ceremony.[29] If the ceremony is before nightfall, the *chassan* and *kallah* should *daven* Minchah before the wedding ceremony, so that they will be able to recite Aneinu, since once they break their fast, this prayer is inappropriate.[30] By the way, if they forgot to say Aneinu, they do not repeat Minchah.

No-Fast Days

Are there days when the *chassan* and *kallah* do not fast? Indeed, a *chassan* and *kallah* must refrain from fasting on the many days when fasting is prohibited. This includes weddings taking place on Chanukah or Rosh Chodesh. The *Magen Avraham* adds that they should not fast even on minor holidays, such as Isru Chag, Tu BeShevat, and the Fifteenth of Av.[31]

Preventing Intoxication

One can understand that the *chassan* and *kallah* are not allowed to fast – but if the reason for the fast is so that they should not become inebriated, how will this be prevented? To avoid this danger, they must be careful not to drink any intoxicating beverages before the ceremony.[32] Observing this precaution is an actual fulfillment of the custom to fast. If they choose to down a few drinks after the ceremony, they may do so on their own cognizance.

Lag BeOmer

Technically speaking, there is no halachic problem with fasting on Lag BeOmer or during the month of Nissan, even though the custom is not to fast. Since *halachah* permits fasting on these days, the custom is for a *chassan* and *kallah* to fast.[33] This also applies during the month of Tishrei or the first part of Sivan, even on days when we do not say *tachanun*.[34] There are some who record a practice that *chassanim* and *kallos* not fast on days when we do not say *tachanun*.[35] The *Elyah Rabbah*, who records this approach, rallies many proofs from earlier authorities that this is not the *halachah*, but concludes that one who chooses to be lenient and not fast on these days will not lose by his lenient practice (*hameikil lo hifsid*).

Second Marriages

Does someone marrying for a second time fast on his wedding day?

According to the rationale that the fast is out of concern that someone might be intoxicated, there is no difference between a first or second marriage, and one is required to fast. Similarly, according to the reason that this is a day of atonement, they should also fast, since the day of a second marriage also atones. This is obvious from the Biblical source that teaches us that this day atones. When Eisav married Basmas/Machalas, he was already married to two other women, yet the Torah teaches that the day atoned for him. Thus, we see that even a subsequent marriage atones, and someone marrying for a second or third time should fast on the day of his wedding.

Feeling Unwell

At this point, we can address the second question raised above: Yocheved asks, "I usually do not fast well, and I am concerned as to how I will feel at my wedding if I fast that day. What do I do?"

We should be aware of the fact that on the most minor of the required fasts, Taanis Esther, even someone suffering from a relatively minor ailment is not required to fast. The custom to fast the day of the wedding is certainly more minor than that of Taanis Esther, and therefore, if either the *chassan* or the *kallah* suffers from a minor ailment or could get weak or dizzy from the fast, they should not fast.[36] Of course, specific questions should be addressed to one's *rav*.

Conclusion

The Ashkenazic practice of fasting on the day of one's wedding is within the category of custom, *minhag*, and therefore, as we have seen, includes many leniencies. Indeed, when these reasons apply, there is no reason to fast unnecessarily. Thus, if one is a Sefardi, not feeling well, or marrying on a day when *tachanun* is not recited, one has a solid basis not to fast. However, when none of these reasons apply, one must follow the accepted *minhag*. The Gemara teaches that customs accepted by the Jewish People come under the category of *al titosh Toras imecha* (do not forsake the laws of your mother), and that one is obligated to observe them.

May the fasts of our *chassanim* and *kallos* contribute towards the increase of *shalom* and *kapparah*, and the creation of many happy marriages in Klal Yisrael.

NOTES

1. E.g., *Levush, Even HaEzer* 60:1; *Magen Avraham* and *Elyah Rabbah*, introduction to 573; *Beis Shmuel* 61:6; *Chochmas Adam* 129:2; *Aruch Hashulchan* 61:21.
2. *Levush, Even HaEzer* 60:1.
3. *Yevamos* 63b; *Yerushalmi, Bikkurim* 3:3.
4. *Shu't Divrei Yatziv* #259.
5. *Ben Ish Chai* 1: *Shoftim*: 13.

6. *Eishel Avraham* (Butchach) 573.

7. *Magen Avraham*, introduction to 573; *Elyah Rabbah* 573:2; *Beis Shmuel* 61:6.

8. *Rema, Even HaEzer* 61:1.

9. *Pischei Teshuvah, Even HaEzer* 61:9.

10. *Aruch Hashulchan, Even HaEzer* 61:21.

11. *Shu't Mahari Bruno* #93; *Aruch Hashulchan, Even HaEzer* 61:21.

12. *Eishel Avraham* (Butchach) 573.

13. 129:2.

14. *Pischei Teshuvah, Even HaEzer* 61:9.

15. *Shu't Mahari Bruno* #93.

16. *Bach, Orach Chayim* 562 at end; *Beis Shmuel* 61:6.

17. p. 198, note 56.

18. see *Birkei Yosef, Orach Chayim* 470:2; *Shu't Yabia Omer* 3: *Even HaEzer*: 9.

19. *Birkei Yosef, Orach Chayim* 470:2.

20. Rav Ovadiah Yosef rules that Sefardim who move to Eretz Yisrael should not fast on the day of the wedding, even if they come from communities where the custom is to fast. Although he respects this custom of the Ashkenazim, he contends that since this is a day of celebration, those who do not have the practice are not permitted to fast.

21. *Tashbeitz* [*Koton*] #465.

22. I am unaware of any *midrash* that mentions the Jews fasting on the day they received the Torah. Obviously, this source, the Tashbeitz, was aware of such a *midrash*. Perhaps this is why the later halachic authorities do not discuss this opinion or any halachic ramifications that result from it.

23. *Shabbos* 130a.

24. *Shu't Mahari Bruno* #93.

25. *Sanhedrin* 2:3.

26. *Shu't Mahari Bruno* #93.

27. 562:2.

28. Rav Shlomo Zalman Auerbach.

29. *Mishnah Berurah* 562:12.

30. Ibid.

31. 573:1.

32. *Pri Megadim, Mishbetzos Zahav* 573:1.

33. *Rema, Magen Avraham* 573.

34. *Magen Avraham* 573:1, 2.

35. *Elyah Rabbah* 573:3, quoting *Nachalas Shivah*.

36. *Aruch Hashulchan, Even HaEzer* 61:21.

8

Is Your *Kesubah* Kosher?

Important Halachos for Writing a Kosher *Kesubah*

The time before the *chasunah* is a very special one for both the bride and groom. Many elaborate preparations go into the wedding plans, and many hours are spent purchasing the items that will be necessary for setting up a new home. Since the *chassan* and *kallah* hope to build a *bayis ne'eman beYisrael*, of course care will be taken in acquiring all the proper Jewish appurtenances.

Some even will make an extra effort to buy a beautiful *kesubah* to embellish their home. It is important to remember, however, that the *kesubah* is more than a work of art: it is the legal document that underpins the whole marriage. Witness the problems that crop up in the following situations:

1. ***Custom-made.*** Chaim and Chani hired a renowned calligrapher, who was careful to use an approved text, to design their *kesubah*. Nevertheless, the *kesubah* still suffered from severe, nonartistic flaws.

2. **Silk-screen.** While shopping together before their wedding, Tamar Goldstein and her *chassan*, Avrohom Fishman, chose a beautiful silk-screen *kesubah*, without realizing that it was a Sefardic text, which is much lengthier than a standard Ashkenazic *kesubah*. When the *kesubah* was filled in, the sections that Ashkenazim do not use were crossed out and the witnesses were instructed to sign.

3. **Standard Hebrew bookstore.** Marcia and Yosef used an inexpensive *kesubah*, but some of the areas were left blank when the *kesubah* was signed at their wedding.

In all of the above cases, the person supervising the *kesubah* arrangements was apparently unaware of the complex laws involved in writing and signing *kesubos*. As a result, in some of the situations mentioned above, the couple married without a kosher *kesubah*. *Halachah* mandates that a married woman own a kosher *kesubah*,[1] so anyone planning a wedding would do well to learn how to avoid such problems.

A Husband's Responsibilities

The Torah places many responsibilities on a husband to guarantee his wife security in their marriage. In addition to his requirement to "honor his wife more than himself and love her as much as he loves himself,"[2] he is also responsible for supporting her at the financial level she is accustomed to, even if he comes from a more modest background; and at the comfort level of his family, if he comes from a wealthier lifestyle.[3] His support requirement allows her to devote her energies to maintaining a household and bearing and raising children without assuming responsibility for their daily bread. In return for assuming these responsibilities, her husband may use her earnings and the profits from her property to help support the family, although all property that she owned prior to their marriage remains hers, as does anything that she inherits during the marriage. She also has the option of electing to keep her earnings for herself and forgo his support.[4]

Furthermore, a husband's responsibility is not limited to supporting her throughout his lifetime, but includes maintaining her from his property after his passing.

The *Kesubah*

The *kesubah* is a legally binding prenuptial agreement whose purpose is to protect a woman's financial interests both during the marriage and after its termination. One of the differences between the Ashkenazic and Sefardic versions of the *kesubah* is that the Ashkenazic version omits many halachic details specified in the Sefardic text. Nevertheless, omitting the mention of these details does not change the husband's requirements to fulfill these obligations.

Although an Ashkenazic husband may specify these obligations in his *kesubah,* the usual practice is not to do so.

So far, there seems to be no reason why a Sefardic couple should not use an Ashkenazic *kesubah,* or vice versa. However, there are reasons why a Sefardic couple should not use the standard Ashkenazic *kesubah* without some modification. The Ashkenazic text states that the *kesubah* requirement of the husband is *min haTorah,* a minority opinion held by Rabbeinu Tam and some other early authorities.[5] However, many authorities contend that the requirements of *kesubah* were introduced by the early Sages, and some major authorities contend that stating that the husband is required *min haTorah* to provide a *kesubah* invalidates the *kesubah.*[6] Since the *Rema*[7] justifies the use of this *kesubah* by Ashkenazim, even though many Rishonim question its *kashrus,* Ashkenazim may continue this practice, whereas Sefardim should not, without revising the wording.[8] (An Ashkenazic man marrying a Sefardic woman may use an Ashkenazic *kesubah,* and a Sefardic man marrying an Ashkenazic woman should use a Sefardic *kesubah.*)

Documentary Details

A *kesubah* must be written following the rules established by Chazal for the creation of any *shtar,* a halachically mandated document. One may write it in any language,[9] yet the almost universal practice is to write it in Aramaic, which is written in Hebrew characters and is halachically considered a Hebrew dialect.[10]

Anyone may write a *kesubah*: man or woman, adult or child, Jew or gentile, human or machine. However, two people who have the status of kosher witnesses regarding all Torah laws must sign the *kesubah*. In addition, the custom in many places is that the groom also signs the *kesubah*, a practice that dates back at least to the thirteenth century and is mentioned by the Rashba.[11]

Writing a *Kesubah*

The halachos of writing *kesubos* are manifold. As I mentioned before, the *kesubah* is a *shtar*, a halachically binding document. Chazal established very detailed rules regulating how a *shtar* must be drawn, most of them to make it difficult to forge or alter. Because these details are highly technical, there is a likely chance that someone writing a *kesubah* who is unaware of these rules will produce an invalid document. It is therefore very important that the *kesubah* be supervised by someone well-versed in these areas of *halachah*. Here are some examples of Chazal's regulations:

Everything in a *shtar* must be written in a tamperproof way. For example, one must write the word *mei'ah* (hundred) so that it cannot be altered to *masayim* (two hundred). This is done by placing the word in the middle of a line, not at the end and by writing it close enough to the next word so that two letters cannot be inserted between them. A *shtar* may not be written on paper or with ink that can be erased without trace.[12] One may not write with numerals that can be easily altered. For example, one may not place the numbers *shalosh* (three), *arba* (four), *sheish* (six), *sheva* (seven), or *eser* (ten) in the margin, since these numbers can easily be altered.[13]

The witnesses must sign the *shtar* close enough to the text that one cannot insert other conditions or factors above their signature.[14] As an additional safeguard, no new conditions or details are derived from the last line of a *shtar*, just in case someone figured out how to sneak a line between the end of the *shtar* and the witnesses' signatures.[15] For this reason, the last line of every *shtar* simply reviews the basics of the transaction to which it attests; typically, the last line of a standard *kesubah* simply reviews the names of the bride and groom – all information previously noted.[16] The accepted practice today is to safeguard every *shtar* in an additional way, by closing it with the words *hakol sharir vekayom*, "and everything is valid and confirmed," since no supplements are allowed after these words.

Initialing Corrections

In addition to the above examples, a *shtar* may have no blank spaces, erasures or cross-outs. The common, modern practice of modifying a contract by initialing adjustments is halachically unacceptable for a very obvious reason – how does this method guarantee that one party did not tamper with part of the contract already initialed by the other?

Correcting a *Kesubah*

What does one do if one made a mistake while writing a *shtar*, or if one wants to adapt or modify a standard printed *kesubah* document? Must one dispose of the *shtar* and start over?

Not necessarily. *Halachah* accepts the following method of validating corrections. At the end of the *shtar*, one notes all the erasures and other modifications, closes with the words *hakol shrir vekayom*, and then the witnesses sign the *shtar*.[17] Thus, any irregularity is recorded immediately above the witnesses' signatures. If the witnesses mistakenly signed the *shtar* without verifying its modifications, they should place these modifications directly below their signatures and then resign the *shtar*.[18]

Mistakes

Does a mistake automatically invalidate a kesubah? If someone wrote a *shtar* that included a major error, is the *kesubah* valid? The Rishonim dispute whether the *shtar* is still valid, some contending that any *shtar* that does not follow Chazal's rules is invalid. Both the *Shulchan Aruch* and the *Rema* conclude that the *shtar* is still legitimate, although the *Rema* rules this way only when it is quite clear that the *shtar* has not been tampered with.[19]

Incorrectly Corrected

I was once at a wedding where the couple had purchased a beautiful, specially designed *kesubah*. While reading the *kesubah* before the wedding, someone noticed an error in the text of the *kesubah*. Can one correct this text immediately before the wedding ceremony? Fortunately for this couple, the *mesader kiddushin* (the rabbi overseeing the ceremony) admitted that he did not know the correct procedure for correcting text in a *shtar*, and instead, presented them with a kosher, although far less beautiful, *kesubah*, saving the artistic one as a beautiful memento. Had he attempted to correct the *kesubah*, they could have spent their married lives without a kosher *kesubah*!

One prominent *rosh yeshivah* I know will not be *mesader kiddushin*. He unabashedly tells his *talmidim* that he has never had the opportunity to study the laws of documents thoroughly, and therefore he is not qualified to preside at a wedding. He arranges for a prominent *talmid chacham* to be *mesader kiddushin* in his stead. I give him much credit, and consider his behavior worthy of emulation.

What if the Names Are Illegible?

Often, the names in a *kesubah* are written illegibly. These *kesubos* are invalid, since it must be clear who the marrying parties using this *kesubah* are.

At this point, we can already appreciate the problems that happened to the abovementioned *kesubos*:

Chaim and Chani's calligrapher used an approved text for the *kesubah*. Nevertheless, the *kesubah* still suffered from severe flaws – several words were written in such a way that they could be altered; numbers were placed at the end of the line in a way that they could be modified, and too much space was left in the middle of some lines. The result was a beautiful piece of art, but not a properly written *kesubah*, although technically it was still considered kosher.

Tamar chose a beautiful Sefardic *kesubah*, which in itself does not present a problem, provided that it was either fully filled out, or that the corrections were noted at the end. However, the person filling out the *kesubah* simply crossed out the remaining sections of the *kesubah* and then instructed the witnesses to sign. If it was indeed obvious that these parts of the *kesubah* were not tampered with after the signing, the *kesubah* is kosher, even though it was not filled in correctly.[20] However, he should have noted at the end of the *kesubah* which lines were crossed through and have the witnesses sign below this declaration.

Standard Printed *Kesubos*

If a standard *kesubah* is arranged properly, it will reduce the incidence of many of the abovementioned problems, but it is by no means foolproof. I have seen numerous standard *kesubos* improperly filled out. There are standard *kesubos* that have mistakes, such as placing certain information in the margin and leaving too much space between the *kesubah* and where the witnesses are expected to sign.

Blank Spaces

Marcia and Yosef used an inexpensive *kesubah* for their wedding, but some areas were still blank when it was signed at their wedding.

Obviously, one may not use a *kesubah* without filling in all blank spaces, since someone could subsequently tamper with the document. If areas were left blank without omitting vital information from the *kesubah*, then whether the *kesubah* is kosher or not depends on the abovementioned dispute between the *Shulchan Aruch* and the *Rema*. Sefardim who follow the *Shulchan Aruch* may assume that the *kesubah* is kosher, notwithstanding its flaws, whereas Ashkenazim must replace this invalid *kesubah* as quickly as possible.

Oh My Gosh

What does one do if, after reading this article, one checks one's *kesubah* and discovers that it has one of the abovementioned fatal flaws?

Don't panic. One should simply contact a local *posek*, telling him that one suspects that one's *kesubah* may be invalid. He will check it and rule whether it requires replacing or not. One should not replace a kosher *kesubah*, but an invalid one must be replaced. There is a special text to be used when replacing an invalid *kesubah*, called a *kesubah demishtakich bei ta'usa*, a *kesubah* in which a mistake was found, that is used in these circumstances. The *posek* fills in the corrected *kesubah*, which is then signed by two witnesses and given to the wife. The form for such a corrected *kesubah* is not difficult to obtain.

(Similarly, if a woman has misplaced her *kesubah*, the couple should have it replaced immediately. Replacing a lost *kesubah* is a simple procedural matter that takes a matter of minutes and should not involve any major costs. One should speak to one's local *posek*. Also, a couple who were originally not married in a halachic fashion and are now observant need to obtain a valid *kesubah*.)

Wrong Location

Datelining a *kesubah* with the wrong location does not invalidate it.[21] Thus, it is not of the highest importance to determine the exact legal location of a hotel or hall where a wedding is located.

Misspelled Names

Halachah has extensive rules regarding how to spell names, yet I have seen many *kesubos* with the names misspelled. Fortunately, this rarely invalidates a *kesubah*, and one should not rewrite the *kesubah* of a married couple because of this mistake.

Family Names

Many contemporary authorities feel that family names should be included in the *kesubah*. Including family names is usually dependent on local custom.

A Humorous Error

The *kesubah* states that the husband will support his wife *bikushta*, faithfully, with the "t" sound spelled with the Hebrew letter *tes*. I once saw a *kesubah* where the scribe misspelled the word with the letter *taf*, and therefore the word translates as "with a bow," thus committing the groom to support his wife "with the bow." For her sake, I hope that he was an expert archer or violinist. Fortunately, this *kesubah* is kosher, even if the groom is as talented in these areas as I am.

Conclusion

As we see, writing a *kesubah* correctly requires extensive halachic knowledge of the laws of documents, an area not as well known as it should be. Without question, this is the most common cause of so many people having invalid *kesubos*.

Many people place much effort into obtaining a beautiful *kesubah*, with stunning artwork and calligraphy. Indeed, there is nothing wrong with enhancing the *kesubah* in this way. One must, however, be careful that, whether beautiful or not, the *kesubah* fulfills its purpose as a valid *shtar*. After all, a nonkosher *kesubah* is not worth the paper on which it is written.

NOTES

1. *Shulchan Aruch, Even HaEzer* 66:3.
2. Rambam, *Hilchos Ishus* 15:19.
3. *Kesubos* 48a, 61a.
4. *Kesubos* 58b, 70b, 83a, 107b.
5. See *Tosafos* and *Rosh, Kesubos* 10a; *Shu't HaRivash* #66; *Shu't Tashbeitz* 2:182; 3:301.
6. *Ramban, Kesubos* 110b; *Ritva, Kesubos* 10a.
7. *Even HaEzer* 66:6.
8. *Shu't Yabia Omer* 3:*Even HaEzer*:12.

9. *Gittin* 11a.

10. See *Rema, Even HaEzer* 126:1.

11. Commentary to *Bava Basra* 175a s.v. *Miha.*

12. *Gittin* 11a; *Shulchan Aruch, Choshen Mishpat* 42:1.

13. *Shulchan Aruch, Choshen Mishpat* 42:4.

14. *Shulchan Aruch, Choshen Mishpat* 44:6, 7.

15. See *Shach* 44:23.

16. *Choshen Mishpat* 44:1.

17. *Choshen Mishpat* 44:5, 9.

18. *Rema, Choshen Mishpat* 44:11.

19. *Choshen Mishpat* 44:1, 5.

20. See *Shulchan Aruch, Choshen Mishpat* 44:5.

21. *Choshen Mishpat* 43:22.

9

The Torah and Derech Eretz

The Halachic Etiquette of a Good Guest

The Torah describes how Avraham Avinu treated his guests, and how his angelic guests behaved. From these interactions, Chazal derive many *halachos* pertaining to the behavior of a guest.

Some of these rules are fairly self-explanatory. For example, a guest should not bring another guest along with him.[1]

A guest should feel that whatever the host serves and prepares is in his honor. The Gemara explains, "What does a good guest say? How hard the host worked for me! How much meat he brought! How much wine he served! How many dainty dishes he prepared! And all this he prepared for me!"[2]

On the other hand, what does a bad guest say? "Did the host work for me? I ate only one roll and one piece of meat and drank only one cup of wine. All the work he did was performed for his wife and children!"[3]

A Strange Conversation

In the context of learning proper etiquette, the Gemara[4] records the following anomalous story. Rav Huna, the son of Rav Nosson, visited the house of Rav Nachman bar Yitzchak, where apparently Rav Huna was not known. His hosts asked Rav Huna, "What is your name," to which he replied "Rav Huna." They then offered him to sit on the couch, although everyone else was sitting either on the floor or on benches, and the couch was reserved for special guests. Rav Huna sat on the couch and did not decline the honor. Subsequently, they brought him a *kiddush*-sized cup full of wine, which he immediately accepted and drank in front of them, but he paused once in the middle of drinking.

Rav Nachman's household, which included *talmidei chachamim*, felt that Rav Huna's responses to their invitations were inappropriate and peppered him with questions about his behavior. (Since he had identified himself as a *talmid chacham*, his behavior became a halachic model from which others could learn. However, those present felt that he had not acted correctly; it was therefore appropriate to ask him to explain his behavior.) The conversation that ensued is the source of many *halachos*.

"Why did you introduce yourself as 'Rav Huna'?" they first asked. Is this an appropriate way to identify oneself?

Rav Huna responded, "That is my name."

"When we offered you to sit on the couch, why did you agree?" They felt that it would have been proper for him to politely refuse the honor and sit on the floor with everyone else.[5]

Rav Huna retorted by quoting the now famous halachic adage, "Whatever the host asks him to do, he should do."[6]

The hosts continued, "When we offered you the cup, why did you accept it the first time we offered it?"

To which Rav Huna replied, "One may refuse a small person, but one should not refuse the request of a great person."

The hosts then inquired, "Why did you drink the small cup of wine we gave you in two gulps, rather than drink it all at once?"

Rav Huna countered, "The earlier authorities taught us that only a guzzler drinks a whole cup of wine at once, and arrogant people drink a cup with three sips. The proper way to drink a cup of wine is in two swallows."[7]

Finally, his hosts asked, "Why did you not turn your face when drinking?" A *talmid chacham* should not eat or drink in the presence of many people.[8] To this, Rav Huna replied that only a bride should be so modest; for anyone else, this is not considered modesty.[9]

Understanding the Conversation

In the course of this puzzling conversation, Rav Huna taught his hosts (and us) several *halachos* germane to proper etiquette that require understanding. We will now dissect the conversation between these scholars, in order to understand its underlying lessons.

Introducing Oneself

He identified himself as "Rav Huna." Why would Rav Huna, a great Torah scholar and *tzaddik*, have introduced himself in what is considered a conceited manner?

The following Gemara is the source of this *halachah*.[10] Rava points out that two verses seem to contradict one another. In one verse, Ovadiah says to Eliyahu, "Your servant has feared Hashem from his youth,"[11] implying that it is appropriate to make a true statement about one's spiritual accomplishments. On the other hand, Shlomo Hamelech declares in *Mishlei*,[12] "Someone else should praise you, but not your mouth."

Rava explains that the *pasuk* in *Mishlei* applies only when there are people present who can notify others that this person is a *talmid chacham*. However, if no one present knows that he is a *talmid chacham*, he may notify people of his special status in order to receive his deserved rights, and so that people will not be punished for treating him disrespectfully.[13]

Since the members of Rav Nachman's household were unaware that Rav Huna was a *talmid chacham*, it was appropriate for him to bring this to their attention.[14]

It is noteworthy that when Rav Huna explained why he had identified himself as *Rav* Huna, the Gemara quotes him as saying *baal hashem ani*, which Rashi seems to explain as meaning, "This was always my name." However, this is not the usual manner, in either Hebrew or Aramaic, of communicating one's name or appellation. Alternatively, the words *baal hashem ani* can be interpreted as meaning, "I am well known by that name," which implies that he was a well-known personage, although he was apparently unknown by the members of Rav Nachman's household.[15] Thus, he was responsible for informing them of who he was, so that they would not treat him disrespectfully.

Sitting on the Couch

The hosts proceeded to inquire about his next act: "Why did you sit upon the couch when we invited you?" Apparently, they felt that it was inappropriate for him to sit on the couch, and he should have politely refused the honor. To this inquiry Rav Huna replied, "Whatever the host asks you to do, you should do."

Did the hosts indeed want him to sit on the finest seat in the house, or were they simply being polite? It is not unusual for a guest to face this type of predicament: is the host's offer genuine, or does he really prefer that the guest refuses the offer?

Rav Huna answers that when the host's intent is unclear, one should assume that his offer is sincere and do as he suggests.

There is a clear exception to this rule. If one suspects that someone has invited him but cannot afford his offer, one should refuse the invitation. Why would he invite anyone if he cannot afford to do so? It is possible that he is inviting a guest because he feels obliged to do so, even though he cannot afford to have company. This is referred to as a *seudah she'einah maspekes lebaalah*; literally, "a meal insufficient for its owner."[16]

Do What the Host Asks

Why should one do whatever the host requests? Here are two interpretations of this statement of Chazal:

1. A visiting (nonpaying) guest should carry out all of the host's requests, since this is a form of payment for services rendered. In return for free accommodations, the guest should reciprocate by performing the tasks and errands the host asks of him.[17]

In a sense, this parallels the modern practice of presenting the host with a gift.[18] The gift reciprocates the host's kindness. However, the host may often prefer a different favor, such as babysitting, rather than a box of chocolates that his waistline can do without, or an additional bouquet of flowers that will soon wilt. Therefore, one's reciprocation can consist of doing any appropriate favors for the host.

In a similar vein, if one has the opportunity to reciprocate hospitality, one should do so. However, neither host nor guest may specify in advance that the hosting will be reciprocal, because of concerns of *ribbis*, prohibited paying and receiving interest on a loan.[19] This is because the individual who hosts first has in essence extended his hospitality as a loan to the other!

2. Courtesy dictates that a guest should respect his host and fulfill his requests as master of the house (Levush). Rav Huna ruled that denying the host's request to honor his guest contradicts the host's authority as master of the house. By sitting on the couch and accepting the honor, the guest affirms his host's authority to honor whomever he wishes in his home.

In many societies, turning down a host's offer of a cup of tea or coffee is considered insulting. If one is unaware of local custom, one should follow Chazal's instructions as Rav Huna did.

Differing *Kashrus* Standards

What happens if the host and the guest maintain different standards of *kashrus*? Must the guest follow the host's request to join him for a meal?

If the guest follows a stricter halachic opinion than the host, the guest should apprise the host of his practices. The host may not serve the guest food that does not meet the guest's standard, unless the food is obviously something he may not eat.[20] For example, if the guest observes *chalav Yisrael* fully, and the host follows the *poskim* who permit unsupervised milk in modern Western society, the host may not serve anything to the guest that does not meet the guest's standards without informing him. However, he may place food on the table that is obviously not *chalav Yisrael*. Similarly, if the guest notifies the host that he uses only food with a specific *hechsher*, the host may not serve him food that violates this standard.

Once a *halachah*-abiding host knows his guest's standards, the guest may assume that the host is accommodating them and eat whatever is served without further question.[21] This is included in Chazal's adage, "Whatever the host asks him to do, he should do," since questioning the host's standards unnecessarily is offensive. Offending someone is always halachically reprehensible, and all the more so when the one he offends has done him a favor.

Personal *Chumros*

On the other hand, if the guest has a personal halachic stringency that he would rather not divulge, he should not violate his *chumra*, and he is not required to divulge it.[22]

Except Leave

Our editions of *Maseches Pesachim*[23] have two Hebrew words appended to the end of the statement "Whatever the host asks him to do, he should do." The additional words are, *chutz mitzei*, *except leave*, and therefore the passage reads, "Whatever the host asks him to do, he should do, except leave." It is unclear if these words are an authentic part of the text, as they are not mentioned in *Maseches Derech Eretz*, the source of the original statement. Some very authoritative commentators take exception to it, and the *Tur* and *Shulchan Aruch* both omit it. Meiri reports that these words are an incorrect textual emendation added by clowns and should be disregarded.

Nevertheless, other authorities[24] accept these words as part of the text and grapple with different possible interpretations.

I found numerous analyses of this text, including six different treatments in one *sefer* alone![25] Several of these approaches assume that performing whatever the host requests refers to reciprocating his favors, the first approach I mentioned above. According to these approaches, the words *chutz mitzei* mean that the guest is not expected to perform any inappropriate activity for the host. This would include the host asking the guest to run an errand for him outside the house, from which the guest may refrain, since it is unacceptable to ask someone to run an errand in a city with which he may be unfamiliar.[26]

Nevertheless, if the host asks the guest to do something that he would not ordinarily do because he considers it beneath his dignity, he should defer to his host's request.[27]

Refusing Requests

We now return to explaining the original conversation that transpired between Rav Huna and his hosts.

The hosts continued, "When we offered you the cup, why did you accept it the first time we offered it?"

To which Rav Huna replied, "One may refuse a small person, but one should not refuse the request of a great person."

It is interesting to note that this particular rule of etiquette is based on a passage in the Torah. When Avraham Avinu invited the angels to dine, they immediately accepted, whereas when his nephew Lot invited them, they initially turned him down. Only after he begged them repeatedly did they accept his invitation.[28] Why did they accept Avraham's invitation immediately and, initially, turn down Lot's offer? The Gemara answers, because of this rule: "One may refuse a small person, but one should not refuse a great person."[29]

This *halachah* has ramifications for other non-guest situations. When someone is asked to lead the services in *shul*, he should initially decline the offer as a sign of humility. However, if a great person, such as the *rav* of the *shul*, asks one to lead the services, one should immediately agree.

Two Gulps?

The hosts then inquired, "Why did you drink the small cup of wine we gave you in two gulps, rather than drink it all at once?"

Rav Huna countered, "The earlier authorities taught us that only a guzzler drinks a whole cup of wine at once, and arrogant people drink a cup in three gulps. The proper way to drink a cup of wine is in two swallows."[30]

A *reviis*-size cup of wine, which is about three ounces, should be drunk in two gulps; not all at once, and not in more than two gulps. It is preferable to drink about half the cup each time, rather than to drink most of it and leave just a small sip for afterwards.[31] If the cup is smaller, the wine is very sweet, or the individual drinking is very obese, one may drink the entire cup in one gulp.[32] When drinking beer, one may drink a greater amount in each gulp, since beer is less intoxicating than wine; certainly, this is true for nonalcoholic beverages.[33] On the other hand, if the drink is very strong, one may drink it much more slowly.[34] Thus, it is appropriate to sip whiskey or other strongly intoxicating beverages slowly.

Turning One's Face

Finally, his hosts asked, "Why did you not turn your face when drinking?" To this Rav Huna replied that only a bride should be so modest. What is the meaning of this conversation?

A *talmid chacham* should not eat or drink in the presence of many people.[35] The hosts felt that Rav Huna should not have eaten in their presence, without turning to the side so that they could not see him eat. Rav Huna held that the *halachah* that a *talmid chacham* should not eat or drink in the presence of many people does not apply when one is eating a meal together with other people. However, a bride should not eat in a way that other people see her eating, even if they are all participating together in a festive meal.[36] Therefore, Rav Huna replied that only a bride should be so modest; for anyone else, such conduct is not considered behaving modestly.[37]

The *halachah* is that one should not eat in the street or marketplace.[38] Nor should one stare at someone who is eating, or at the food that he is eating, so as not to embarrass him.[39]

As we can see, Chazal had tremendous concern for appropriate conduct in all circumstances. They were attentive to modes of behavior that those in today's generation don't even have minimal regard for. We can follow Chazal's example and apply this lesson to our daily lives, inspiring ourselves to behave in a way that reflects our lofty status as children of the King.

NOTES

1. *Bava Basra* 98b.
2. *Berachos* 58a.
3. Ibid.
4. *Pesachim* 86b.
5. *Tosafos,* ibid.
6. See *Maseches Derech Eretz Rabbah* 6:1.
7. *Maseches Derech Eretz Rabbah* 8.
8. Gemara and *Rashi, Bechoros* 44b.
9. *Rashi, Pesachim* 86b.
10. *Nedarim* 62a.
11. *Melachim* I 18:12.
12. 27:2.
13. *Rosh, Nedarim* 62a.
14. *Meiri; Maharsha,* ibid.
15. *Meiri,* ibid.
16. Rambam, *Hilchos Teshuvah* 4:4; also see *Chullin* 7b and *Rashi.*
17. *Bach, Orach Chayim* 170.
18. One can find halachic sources for this practice in *Orach Meisharim* 18:2.
19. *Rema, Orach Chayim* 170:13.
20. *Shach, Yoreh Deah* 119:20.
21. Ibid.
22. *Shaarei Teshuvah* 170:6; *Ben Yehoyada.*

23. 86b.

24. *Bach, Magen Avraham; Ben Yehoyada.*

25. *Ben Yehoyada.*

26. *Bach, Orach Chayim* 170.

27. *Birkei Yosef* 170:5.

28. *Bereishis* 15:1–5, 16:1–3.

29. *Bava Metzia* 86b.

30. *Maseches Derech Eretz Rabbah,* chapter 8.

31. *Magen Avraham* 170:12.

32. *Pesachim* 86b, as understood by *Magen Avraham* 170:13.

33. *Magen Avraham,* ibid.

34. *Aruch Hashulchan* 170:9.

35. *Bechoros* 44b and *Rashi* op. cit.

36. *Tosafos, Bechoros* 44b s.v. *Ve'ein.*

37. *Rashi, Pesachim* 86b.

38. *Kiddushin* 40b.

39. Rambam, *Hilchos Berachos* 7:6; *Shulchan Aruch, Orach Chayim* 170:4.

10
What Will the Neighbors Think?

Understanding the Halachos of
Maris Ayin

Most of us are familiar with the prohibition of *maris ayin*, avoiding doing something that may raise suspicion that one violated *halachah*. However, most of us are uncertain when this rule applies, and when it does not.

Here are some questions of *maris ayin* that people confront in modern life on a day-to-day basis:

1. My boss asked me to attend a lunch meeting with a new client in a nonkosher restaurant. May I attend the meeting, or do I violate *maris ayin* if I am seen in a *treif* restaurant?

2. When I serve coffee after a *fleishig* meal, I like to put non-dairy creamer on the table in a small pitcher, because the original container is unsightly. Recently, someone told me that I may not place the creamer on the *fleishig* table, unless it is in its original container. Is this true?

3. Hyman Goldman would like to retire and sell his business, Hymie Goldman's Bakery, to a non-Jew who will keep it open on Shabbos. Must he compel the gentile to change the store's name?

4. My not-yet-observant cousin is making a bar mitzvah in a Reform temple. We have a good relationship, and he is very curious about exploring authentic Judaism. May I attend the bar mitzvah?

Maris Ayin

We can see that modern life presents some vexing problems wrapped up in very quotidian issues. We might think that this is unique to our times. As it turns out, there are some very clear-cut cases of *maris ayin* mentioned already in the *Mishnah* and Gemara:

1. One may not hang out wet clothes on Shabbos, because neighbors might think that he washed them on Shabbos.[1] This is true, even when all the neighbors realize that he is a meticulously observant individual.

2. Officials who entered the Beis HaMikdash treasury did so barefoot and wearing garments that contained no hemmed parts or wide sleeves, and certainly no pockets or cuffs, so that it would be impossible for them to hide any coins.[2] The Mishnah states that this practice is derived from the *pasuk Vihyisem nekiyim meiHashem umiYisrael,*[3] which means that one should do things in a way that is as obviously above. Rav Moshe Feinstein, *ztz"l,* contends that some types of *maris ayin* are prohibited *min haTorah.*[4]

3. *Tzedakah* collectors should find other people to convert their currency for them and not convert it themselves, because people might think that they gave themselves a more favorable exchange rate.[5]

Curious Contradiction

The concept of it being a *mitzvah* to avoid a situation of *maris ayin* is a fascinating curiosity, because it contradicts another important Torah *mitzvah* – to judge people favorably. This *mitzvah* requires us to judge a Torah Jew favorably when we see him act in a questionable way.[6] If everyone were to judge others favorably at all times, there would never be a reason for the law of *maris ayin*. Yet, we see that the Torah is concerned that someone might judge a person unfavorably and suspect him of violating a *mitzvah*.

Indeed, a person's actions must be above suspicion; at the same time, people observing him act in a suspicious way are required to judge him favorably.

Entering a *Treif* Restaurant

May I enter a nonkosher restaurant to use the bathroom, to eat a permitted item, or to attend a professional meeting?

A prominent *rav* once gleaned insight on this *she'eilah* from early *poskim*, who discussed the kashrus issues of Jewish travelers. In the sixteenth century, there was a dispute between the *Rema* and the Maharshal as to whether a Jewish traveler would be allowed to eat herring and pickles prepared and served in nonkosher inns.[7] The *Rema* ruled that, under the circumstances, a traveler could eat these items on the inn's nonkosher plates, whereas the Maharshal prohibited using the inn's plates. However, neither sage prohibited either eating at or entering the inn because of *maris ayin*; from this the *rav* inferred that entering a nonkosher eating establishment does not violate *maris ayin*.

However, Rav Moshe Feinstein rules that entering a nonkosher eatery *is* a violation of *maris ayin*.[8] Why does he not compare this law to the inn of the earlier *poskim*?

The answer is that in the sixteenth century, the inn functioned as a place of shelter and lodging, not only as a place providing food. Therefore, someone seeing a person entering the inn would have assumed that he was looking for a place to sleep, and that he had no intention of eating nonkosher food there. Thus, the sixteenth-century inn is comparable to a twenty-first century hotel that contains nonkosher restaurants. There is certainly no prohibition of *maris ayin* in visiting a hotel, since a passerby would assume that one is entering the hotel for reasons other than eating nonkosher food. However, the primary reason people enter a nonkosher restaurant is to eat *treif* food. Therefore, Rav Moshe rules that it is prohibited to enter a *treif* restaurant, because of *maris ayin*.

Most Common Reason

This leads us to a practical question. May one do something that could be interpreted in different ways, one of which involves violating the Torah, and the other, not? Is this activity prohibited because of *maris ayin*? For example, someone hanging up wet clothes on Shabbos may have just washed them, or he may have just accidentally dropped them into a basin of water or used them to mop up a spill. Yet the *halachah* is that this is prohibited because of *maris ayin*. This implies that since the most common reason for hanging out clothes is that they were recently washed, the activity is prohibited because of *maris ayin*.

Similarly, there are many reasons why one might enter a *treif* restaurant: to attend a meeting, to use the comfort facilities, or to drink a cup of water. On the other hand, the most common reason people enter a nonkosher restaurant is to eat nonkosher food. This is why Rav Moshe prohibits entering a *treif* restaurant.

However, Rav Moshe rules that under highly extenuating circumstances, such as when one is famished and there is nowhere else to eat, one may enter a *treif* restaurant. This is based on another principle of Chazal that when one suffers a great deal, one may override a rabbinic prohibition to alleviate the pain.[9] For this reason, Rav Moshe permits someone who is famished to eat kosher food in a nonkosher restaurant. Based on his ruling, one could presumably permit entering a *treif* restaurant to use the restroom, if it is the only one readily available. A common example of this would be using the facilities in nonkosher restaurants at rest stops off of the highway.

The Company Cafeteria

Many workplaces have a cafeteria where one can purchase (nonkosher) food or bring in one's own food. Alternatively, some cafeterias have packaged kosher food available. In either of these situations, there is no concern of *maris ayin*, since people enter the cafeteria to eat kosher food as well.

Business Meetings

May I attend a meeting where they will serve nonkosher food? *Rabbonim* rule differently on this issue; therefore, one should ask a *she'eilah* to one's own *rav*. Personally, I believe that the answer depends on how secure one is at one's place of employment. If one feels that skipping the meeting might jeopardize one's employment, then one may attend, since losing one's job entails a great amount of suffering. However, if one feels that it will not jeopardize one's employment, one may not attend.

New *Maris Ayin* Cases

If a situation exists that could be a case of *maris ayin*, but is not mentioned by Chazal, is it prohibited because of *maris ayin*? There is actually an early dispute about this question between the *Rashba* and the *Pri Chadash*. A little explanation is necessary before we present this case.

Chazal prohibited placing fish blood, which is perfectly kosher, in a serving bowl since someone might confuse it with animal blood.[10] Based on this Gemara, the *Rashba* prohibited cooking meat in human milk, even though human milk is halachically pareve.[11] Similarly, the *Rema* prohibits cooking meat in "almond milk" – a white, milk-like liquid made from almonds, that probably looked similar to our nondairy creamer or soy milk – because of its similar appearance to cow's milk. One may cook meat in almond milk and serve it *only* if one leaves pieces of almond in the "milk" to call attention to its nondairy origin.[12]

The *Pri Chadash* disagrees with the *Rema*, contending that we should not create our own cases of *maris ayin*, and one should prohibit only those items that were prohibited by Chazal.[13]

The consensus of *poskim* is to prohibit these new *maris ayin* cases, following the position of the *Rashba* and the *Rema*.

Based on this ruling, some contemporary authorities contend that one should not serve pareve, nondairy creamer after a *fleishig* meal, since someone might think that something *milchig* is being served after a *fleishig* meal. They permit serving the "creamer" in the original container that clearly identifies it as a pareve product, similar to serving the meat cooked with almond milk, provided there are some almonds in the "milk."

However, other *poskim* contend that today, no *maris ayin* issue exists germane to these products, since the average person knows about the ready availability of pareve creamers, cheeses, ice creams, margarines, soy and rice milk, and the like.[14]

This leads us to a new discussion: perhaps *maris ayin* is not applicable anymore?

Maris Ayin in Our Times

If something was prohibited as *maris ayin* in earlier generations, does it become permitted if there is no longer a *maris ayin* issue? Is it correct that although, at one time, one could not cook meat in almond milk, today one may cook meat in soy milk, since pareve milk substitutes are readily available? Similarly, may one serve margarine at a *fleishig* meal?

We can begin to gather the necessary background information by examining the following case: One may not hire a gentile to perform work on Shabbos that a Jew may not do. However, a non-Jew may operate his own business on Shabbos, even if he rents his facility from a Jew.

The Gemara rules that a Jew may rent his field to a non-Jewish sharecropper, since the gentile is not his employee. However, a Jew may not rent his bathhouse to a gentile, since the non-Jew may operate the bathhouse on Shabbos.[15]

Bathhouse vs. Field

How is a bathhouse different from a field? Why may I rent the non-Jew my field, but not my bathhouse? What is the difference between the two?

At the time of the Gemara, it was common to rent fields, and thus someone seeing a gentile work a Jewish-owned field on Shabbos would assume that the gentile had rented it. He would not think that the Jew had hired the gentile to work for him, which would constitute a violation of the laws of Shabbos.

However, in antiquity, it was uncommon to rent out a bathhouse. The person who owned the bathhouse hired employees to operate the business for him. Therefore, someone seeing a gentile operate a Jewish-owned bathhouse on Shabbos might assume that the Jew hired gentiles to operate his bathhouse on Shabbos, which violates *halachah*. Because of this, Chazal prohibited renting a bathhouse to a gentile, because it would result in *maris ayin*, when people see the gentile operating the Jew's bathhouse on Shabbos.[16]

The *Shulchan Aruch*[17] rules that if it is common in a certain city for people to rent out their bathhouses, one may rent one's bathhouse to a gentile, despite the Gemara's ruling. There is no *maris ayin*, since people in this city will assume that the gentile rented the bathhouse from its owner. Thus, the *maris ayin* prohibition of the Gemara is rescinded in places and times when the concern of suspicion no longer exists. Similarly, we can conclude that nowadays, someone seeing nondairy creamer served at a *fleishig* meal will assume that it is a *pareve* milk substitute even if it's not served in the original container, and that there is no issue of *maris ayin*.

Selling to a Non-Jew

Let's examine the third *she'eilah*: Hyman Goldman would like to retire and sell his business, Hymie Goldman's Bakery, to a non-Jew, who will keep the business open on Shabbos. Must he compel the non-Jew to change the name of the shop?

Background

The *Rema* permits renting to a gentile a business that people do not associate with a Jewish owner.[18] Thus, according to the *Rema*, a Jew may buy the regional franchise of a non-Jewish company and rent or franchise out the individual stores to gentiles. However, the Acharonim dispute whether he may do this, even if the Jew is sometimes involved in the management of the stores.[19]

Similarly, a Jew who owns a shopping mall may rent the stores to gentiles, since people assume that each business is owned individually. However, if the rent includes a percentage of sales, he might thereby be receiving *sechar Shabbos*, profits from work performed on Shabbos. One should ask a *she'eilah*, since the *halachah* in this case depends on the specific circumstances involved.

However, although a Jew may rent his facility to a gentile tenant, it is unclear whether he may *sell* the business to a gentile who will keep the Jew's name on the business and have it open on Shabbos. Even if passersby realize that there are now exclusively non-Jews staffing Hymie's, they may think that Hyman still owns the shop and is hiring gentiles to operate the business for him. I discussed this *she'eilah* with several different *rabbonim* and received different answers.

Maris Ayin of *Yichud*

Here is another interesting *maris ayin she'eilah*:

> I will be working in a town with very few observant people. There is an observant woman in town who lives alone, and will be away the entire time I am there. She is very willing to let me use her house while she is away. Is there a problem that people may not realize that she is away, and they might think that we are violating the prohibition of *yichud* – being secluded with someone of the other gender to whom one is not closely related?

Rav Moshe Feinstein discusses this almost identical *she'eilah*. Someone wants to sleep and eat at a widow's house when she is out of town. Is there a concern of *maris ayin*, because people will think that he is staying at her house when she is home, and that they are violating the prohibition of *yichud*? Rav Moshe rules that it is permitted, reasoning that since there are many ways to avoid *yichud*, we need not assume that people will think that he is violating the *halachah*.[20]

Permitted Actions

Rav Moshe Feinstein notes that *maris ayin* does not include doing something permitted that people might mistakenly think is forbidden. *Maris ayin* means that someone thinks I violated something – he thinks that I misappropriated someone else's money, washed clothes on Shabbos, ate something nonkosher, etc. However, it does not include doing something permitted that people might mistakenly think is forbidden.

Thus, Rav Moshe discusses whether there is any prohibition in traveling a short distance by car on Friday evening after candle-lighting time, when one will certainly not come to desecration of Shabbos. He rules that one may do this, since there is no prohibition against someone who has not lit Shabbos candles performing work after candle-lighting time, even if people who are unaware of the *halachah* think that there is.

Entering a Reform Temple

Our fourth *she'eilah*: My not-yet-observant cousin is making a bar mitzvah in a Reform temple. We have a good relationship, and he is very curious about exploring authentic Judaism. May I attend the bar mitzvah?

Rav Moshe rules that one may not enter a Reform temple at the time people are praying there, because someone might think one prayed there, which is prohibited according to *halachah*. Alternatively, someone might erroneously learn from this person's example that it is permitted to pray with them. Someone faced with the above predicament should discuss with his *rav* how to develop the relationship with his cousin, without entangling himself in any halachic issues.

Conclusion

By examining the parameters of *maris ayin*, we become aware of the importance of the impression that our actions make. We cannot delude ourselves into thinking that it does not matter what others think of us. Our behavior must not only be correct, but also *appear* correct.

In general, our lives should be a model of appropriate behavior and *kiddush Hashem*. Let others look at us and say, "He is a *frum* Jew – he lives his life on a higher plane of honesty, of dignity, and of caring for others." As Chazal say in *Pirkei Avos:*[21] *Kol she'ruach habrios nochah heimenu ruach haMakom nochah heimenu* (One who is pleasing to his fellowman is pleasing to his Creator).

NOTES

1. *Shabbos* 146b.
2. *Shekalim* 3:2.
3. *Bamidbar* 32:22.
4. *Shu't Igros Moshe, Orach Chayim* 4:82.
5. *Bava Basra* 8b; *Shulchan Aruch, Yoreh Deah* 257:2.
6. For further information on the *mitzvah* of judging people favorably, see *Shaarei Teshuvah* of Rabbeinu Yonah, 3:218.
7. *Yam shel Shlomo, Chullin* 8:44; quoted by *Taz, Yoreh Deah* 91:2.
8. *Shu't Igros Moshe, Orach Chayim* 2:40.
9. See *Kesubos* 60a.
10. *Kerisos* 21b.
11. *Shu't HaRashba* 3:257.
12. *Rema, Yoreh Deah* 87:3.
13. *Yoreh Deah* 87:6.
14. *Shu't Yechaveh Daas* 3:59.
15. *Avodah Zarah* 21a.
16. *Avodah Zarah* 21b.
17. *Orach Chayim* 243:2.

18. 243:2.
19. See *Mishnah Berurah* 243:14.
20. *Shu't Igros Moshe, Even HaEzer* 3:19.
21. *Pirkei Avos* 3:13.

11
The Big Critic
Book and Restaurant Reviews

Ever wonder whether publishing reviews is permissible according to *halachah*? A while back, I received the following interesting series of *she'eilos*:

Dear Rabbi Kaganoff,

1. Is a person allowed to write balanced reviews of books? This question concerns hashkafic works, halachic works, self-help books, as well as novels.

Obviously, I realize that there are many halachic ramifications, including *lashon hora*, etc. I would specifically like to know if one is allowed to "pan" (unfavorably review) a work that the reviewer finds seriously lacking.

2. May one write and publish reviews of other products, such as wine or restaurants? I am concerned primarily about cases where the owner is Jewish.

3. If a person asks my opinion of a book, a wine, or a restaurant, may I answer truthfully, even

if my personal negative opinion may result in the individual choosing another product?

With much thanks in advance,

Aaron Bernstein

Before answering Aaron's questions, we must first examine the *halachos* of *lashon hora* that apply to this topic.

Lashon Hora

A true statement that may damage a person's professional or business reputation, or cause him financial harm constitutes *lashon hora* – even in the absence of negative intentions.[1] Thus, random schmoozing about the quality of different workmen's skills, the halachic prowess of various *talmidei chachamim,* or the quality of education provided by a particular school, all constitute *lashon hora.*

However, when one requires particular information, one is permitted to inquire of people who might know. For example, if one needs to do home repairs, one may "ask around" about other individual's experiences with various professionals. One should tell them why one needs to know, and they should respond with only what is relevant to one's needs.

Examples

1. Gila hired a home improvement contractor who was skilled and efficient, but inexperienced in certain plumbing work. Ahuva asks Gila whether the contractor was good. Gila should reply that he was skilled and efficient, but does Ahuva intend to include any plumbing? If the reply is negative, Gila should say nothing, since Ahuva understands that if she changes her mind and decides to include plumbing, she should discuss it with Gila first. If the reply is that there *is* plumbing work to be done, Gila should tell her that the contractor's work was excellent and efficient, but that he seemed to be somewhat inexperienced in plumbing. Gila can suggest that perhaps by now he has gained experience, or maybe Ahuva should mention to him that she would prefer if he subcontracts the plumbing to someone more experienced.

2. Yaakov moves to a new neighborhood and asks Michael who the local *poskim* are. Michael can mention one, some, or all of the local available *poskim*, but should not mention any disqualifying factors about them, such as, Rabbi X is curt, Rabbi Y is very *machmir*, or Rabbi Z's *shiurim* are unclear. Michael may ask Yaakov what qualities he is looking for in a *rav* and then provide recommendations based on Yaakov's answer.

The Dishonest Mechanic

Yitzchok and Esther just moved to the neighborhood and mention to Yosef that they are planning to bring their car, which is making unusual noises, to Gonif's Service Station. Yosef's personal dealings with Gonif's have been highly negative; Yosef found the proprietor to be very dishonest. May Yosef warn Yitzchok and Esther?

The *halachah* is that not only may Yosef say something to them, but he is obligated to do so.[2] This is because he is responsible for ensuring that Yitzchok and Esther are not hurt financially by the crooked repair shop. This *halachah* is included in the *mitzvah* of *Lo saamod al dam rei'echa* (Do not stand by idly while your friend is injured).[3]

However, the exact manner in which Yosef imparts this information to Yitzchok and Esther depends on the circumstances.

The Five Rules

In any situation where one must protect someone from harm, whether it is a potentially harmful *shidduch*, damaging *chinuch*, or a bad business deal, there are five rules that govern what one may say.

1. Is It Bad?

Be certain that what may transpire (if one does not intercede) is indeed bad. Often, one assumes that an issue is worse than it really is. Later in this essay I will describe a case that appears to be bad, but is not considered so halachically. In the case at hand, Yosef is responsible to see that Yitzchok and Esther are not deceived by the repair shop. By warning them, Yosef has complied with the first rule.

2. No Exaggerating

One may not exaggerate, describing the situation as worse than it really is. In this case, even if Yosef needs to describe Gonif's dishonesty (which he can probably avoid, as I will explain later), Yosef should describe only what he personally knows, and he must be careful not to embellish or include hearsay.

3. Appropriate Motivation

One's motivation must be to protect the innocent person from harm, not to bring retribution on the person responsible for causing the harm. In our case, this means that Yosef's goal is to protect Yitzchok and Esther from harm, not to "get back" at Gonif's. The reason for this condition is that one violates the prohibition of speaking *lashon hora* if one has evil intent, even in a case when one may otherwise transmit the information.[4]

4. No Other Choice

Can one accomplish what one needs to without speaking *lashon hora*? The answer to this question depends on the situation. What does one need to accomplish? In the case of the crooked repair shop, Yosef's goal is that Yitzchok and Esther should not be victimized by the shop. Yosef can accomplish this goal using several different approaches, some of which do not require tarnishing the repair shop's reputation. For example, if Yitzchok and Esther will heed Yosef's advice to take their car to Careful and Honest Repairs instead, then he has no need to tell them that Gonif's is a dishonest shop. In this instance, Yosef has accomplished his purpose without mentioning the dishonest acts that he witnessed.

5. Too Damaging

Will sharing the negative information harm the perpetrator more than what he should suffer according to *halachah*? For example, Levi knows that Reuven's professional work is sometimes of substandard quality, and he discovers that Shimon, who is known to back out on deals he has committed to, contracted Reuven to do work. Although under other circumstances, Levi would not only be permitted, but even required to notify others of Reuven's lack of professional skill, in this situation, Levi may not notify Shimon because he (Shimon) may back out on Reuven in a manner that contravenes *halachah*.

When Bad Is Not Really Bad

In condition #1 above, I mentioned that there are situations that a person considers bad, but are not considered bad according to *halachah*. The background behind this *she'eilah* will impact directly on our original *she'eilah* about reviewing books, wines, and restaurants.

An example of this type of situation is a retailer that charges high prices.

Chani sees Miriam, who is new in the neighborhood, about to enter a grocery store that Chani knows is expensive. May Chani tell Miriam that this store overcharges slightly? The Chafetz Chayim rules that one may not reveal this information;[5] he maintains that slightly overpaying for an item is not considered a "bad thing," provided that the storekeeper is within the halachic range of what he may charge.

Since the storekeeper who charges higher prices is not violating *halachah*, one may not hurt his livelihood by encouraging people to purchase elsewhere. Doing so would be considered *lashon hora*, which includes damaging someone's livelihood.

Thus, there is a major difference between a dishonest store and one that is more expensive. It is a *mitzvah* to steer someone away from a dishonest store, but it is forbidden to steer him away from a Jewish store that charges more.

What if someone new moves to town and asks someone where he can purchase kosher groceries?

One should tell him which local groceries sell kosher products that have the *hechsherim* he wants. One does not need to supply him with a complete list of the stores in the neighborhood, and it is permissible to mention only the stores that are less expensive. However, one may not tell him which stores are more expensive.

If an individual knows that a third party plans to purchase an item from a store that tends to be expensive, he should keep quiet. Even though the buyer could save money by purchasing elsewhere, the storekeeper is losing from his actions. One should not get involved in saving one person's money at someone else's expense.[6] However, if the proprietor of the store is not an observant Jew, one may warn the purchaser that his prices are high.

If the storekeeper is violating *halachah* in some way, such as selling defective or misrepresented products, one should warn a person intending to make a purchase.

Book Reviews

Now that we've acquired some background information, we can discuss Aaron Bernstein's first *she'eilah*: "Is a person allowed to write balanced reviews of books?"

The first question one must ask is – what does the review accomplish?

The answer depends on the type of book being reviewed. Let us begin by examining one particular category: Jewish novels.

Why do secular publications review novels?

They review so that people can decide whether they will enjoy the book, and whether they should spend the money to purchase it.

Is such a practice acceptable according to *halachah*? Is one protecting another from harm by telling him not to purchase a particular book? On the other hand, by warning people regarding the book, one is hurting the livelihood of those who have invested time and money into writing and publishing the book, expecting this book to provide them with *parnassah*.

Is this situation not parallel to the case where one Jewish storeowner, in his desire to make a living, charges a bit more than his competitors? The *halachah* in that case is that one may not advise others to avoid his store, since one is harming the storekeeper. Similarly, one may not advise people to save money by avoiding the purchase of a book. One may, however, publish a review that describes the positive aspects of a book.

However, if a work contains flaws in *hashkafah*, then one is required to refute the author's mistakes. Similarly, if a *halachah* work is flawed, one should write a review to clarify that the work contains errors. This is similar to warning a buyer not to purchase from a particular store because they sell defective merchandise.

Example

Many years ago, I was asked by a well-known Jewish publication to review a particular halachic work. When I read the work, I felt it to be sorely lacking in certain areas – particularly *hashkafah*. I was concerned that the book could easily be used as a resource for someone who would as a result behave in a questionable or non-halachic fashion. I pointed out these concerns of mine in the review, because in this situation it was very important to avoid serious halachic mishaps.

If the work reflects an approach to *halachah* that is different from one's own, then it depends – if the *halachah* quoted is reliable, one may draw the reader's attention to the fact that it reflects a different halachic approach.

Of course, this means that even the most standard book and other reviews common in secular circles contravene halachic guidelines. One may include a book review column only if it merely informs people of new publications, but does not provide a negative, critical review.

Other Reviews

Now we can examine the second question: May one write reviews of other products, such as wine or restaurants?

We already know the answer to this question. If the purpose of the review is to discourage people from buying a product or eating in a restaurant, one may not write the review. But, one may publish a review that covers the positive aspects of the product.

Specific Products

What if someone asks one's opinion of a particular wine or restaurant?

If one has a poor opinion of the wine, restaurant or book, one should inquire, "What are you looking for?" Based on the answer, one can direct them to the product that would most satisfy his needs and interests. If the wine or restaurant in question may not be what he wants, one should explain to him which aspects would meet his needs, and which might not. This is permitted, because they have come to ask for information about the item. However, one may not simply reveal this information in the media for everyone, including readers who have no need of or interest in the information.

For example, one does not have a positive opinion of a restaurant. Why? One feels that the service is poor. Would such information be a decisive factor for this person? If one is not certain, and believes that there are other redeeming factors that may induce this person to eat there anyway, one should convey the information in a way that does not reflect too negatively upon the restaurant, such as, "Once when I was there, the service was a bit slow. But I don't dine there very often."

One of the *rabbonim* to whom I sent this article for his opinion wrote to me the following: "I don't agree with what you wrote about restaurants. If one has a criticism that doesn't necessarily make it an undesirable place for the one asking, I think that it is better to just say that 'I don't go there too often.' The individual won't suffer by trying, and will decide on his own if he is happy with the place."

Consumer Reports

According to *halachah*, may one publish a magazine such *Consumer Reports*, a publication that features reviews and comparisons of consumer products?

Although the editors of that magazine have not sought my opinion, I think that they may publish the results of their research, if it is read only by people interested in purchasing these items, and not by a general audience.

Wine Reviews

Is a kosher wine review feasible according to *halachah*?

Possibly, but only if its readership was limited to people who are shopping for and seeking advice about wines.

In conclusion, we see that the halachic approach to this entire issue is very different from that of contemporary society. By examining our behavior through the prism of *halachah* and not from the point of view of modern civilization, we create a unique society that exemplifies remarkable interpersonal and business conduct, as mandated by the Torah. I'll toast to that!

NOTES

1. Rambam, *Hilchos Dei'os* 7:5.
2. *Chafetz Chayim, Hilchos Rechilus* 9:1.
3. See *Be'er Mayim Chayim, Hilchos Rechilus* 9:1.
4. See *Be'er Mayim Chayim, Hilchos Rechilus* 9:3.
5. *Be'er Mayim Chayim, Hilchos Rechilus,* 9:27.
6. See *Be'er Mayim Chayim, Hilchos Rechilus* 9:27 and commentaries.

12

Snitching on Your Coworker

Plagiarizing and Employee Responsibility

Recently, I received the following inquiry:

Hi, Rabbi Kaganoff,

While editing an article, I discovered that the author had "borrowed" large sections of the article from another source. This is plagiarizing!

I called the writer and informed her that I could not pass the article on for proofreading. She asked why – if I would tell her what the problem was, she said she could change it. When I explained that I had found much of the article under a different byline, the writer told me that she had been instructed that she could use material from the Internet, that she had been given an unrealistic deadline to write the article, that she had found no other sources on the subject, and other excuses.

I tried to sound sympathetic, and I patiently

explained that although it is perfectly fine to gather information from a previously published source, it is unethical to quote entire sections from someone else's writing. I am not sure that she understood, although she did rewrite the article, which I then edited and sent to the proofreader.

With this introduction, I can now ask my questions:

1. Am I required to notify our joint employer that the author originally submitted a plagiarized article?

2. If I am required to tell the employer, should I have told him about this problem *before* I told the writer? Although I sincerely hope that this problem never reoccurs, I would like to know the *halachah* for future reference.

Any additional comments and insights are welcome.

Sincerely yours,
Meirah Goldstein

Answering this *she'eilah* requires us to understand several halachic issues and some legal matters, as well. We need to clarify:

1. Did Meirah satisfy her responsibility to her employer by educating the writer?

2. Does the employer still have a right to know about the writer's shortcomings?

3. Is it considered *lashon hara* to inform him?

I will first outline the halachic issues involved, and then discuss their application to our situation.

Tochachah

The *mitzvah* of *tochachah* entails calling attention to the fact that a person has violated a *mitzvah* in the Torah and providing positive encouragement to perform *teshuvah*. To paraphrase the Rambam:[1]

One who sees a fellow Jew sin or act in a wrongful manner is required to influence him positively by speaking to him in a soft way, privately, elucidating to him that it serves his own self-interest to correct his ways, for this earns him *Olam Haba.*

Thus, Meirah's first step of explaining gently, patiently, and sympathetically to the writer that she had done something wrong fulfilled the Torah's *mitzvah* in an exemplary fashion.[2]

Is Plagiarism Evil?

Is a writer who is lifting paragraphs doing something wrong?

Although Meirah and most writers, editors, and publishers would be appalled at a writer for using extensive material from a source without crediting it, is this indeed halachically prohibited? Some might argue that there is no evidence that the Torah bans plagiarizing. They will argue that although the Gemara[3] states, "One who quotes his source brings redemption to the world, as we see from Esther, who told the king in the name of Mordechai," this quotation actually demonstrates the contrary – that although it is meritorious to credit one's sources, it is certainly not required.

If one were to make this assumption and contend that she has done nothing wrong, it may be forbidden to inform the employer, unless she is endangering him. As the Rambam teaches, "Communicating information that will damage someone else's person or property is *lashon hara.*"[4] If the writer's act is halachically justifiable, then jeopardizing her employment violates the *halachah.*

Nonetheless, there exist several halachic issues concerning the use of plagiarized material:

1. Since publishing norms prohibit the practice of copying without reference, the employer expects an original article. Therefore, submitting an article that someone has not written himself as an original work is deceptive and violates the laws of *Choshen Mishpat.*

2. Because plagiarizing is considered unacceptable to the outside world, it may be prohibited halachically, either as potential *chillul Hashem* (desecrating Hashem's name) or under the heading of *dina demalchusa dina* (the halachic obligation to obey the laws of one's country of residence). Although both of these subjects are very important, their details are beyond the scope of our current topic.

3. If a publisher of copyrighted or plagiarized material can be held liable, a writer submitting such material may be jeopardizing the publisher.

My Letter to an Attorney

In order to verify the answer to the last question, I penned some queries to an attorney I am acquainted with:

> I trust this letter finds you and yours well.
>
> I was recently asked a *she'eilah* for which I need some legal information.
>
> Is it considered illegal to copy paragraphs from an article on an Internet site and include them in an article published under one's own name? Is the magazine or newspaper liable, even if they are unaware this was done? What are the legal ramifications or penalties that could be involved for either the author or the publisher? Is this usually/ sometimes/never prosecuted?

The Attorney's Response

> Dear Rabbi,
>
> It is illegal to publish material written by someone else under your own name. Although there may be criminal penalties in the case of deliberate fraud, most of the cases are civil complaints. In cases of fraud, treble damages could be assessed.

In the United States, this is usually a misdemeanor punishable by fines of up to $50,000 and a year in jail. In some jurisdictions and under certain circumstances, it could be a felony, or even a federal felony punishable by up to $250,000 and ten years in jail.

In addition, both the magazine publisher and author can be held liable for damages resulting from the infringement. If a writer plagiarizes without the knowledge of the publisher, the publisher can still be held liable. The writer is his agent, and the acts performed under the scope of his duties make the publisher liable.

There are three different classes of damages – actual, ill-gotten-gains, and statutory. The prevailing party can also be awarded attorney's fees.

The frequency with which this is prosecuted depends on the level of outrage on the part of the infringed-upon author; also on the intent of the plagiarist. This case is actually worse, because it shows a deliberate effort to steal work.

I must admit that I did not realize that plagiarizing an article could involve such serious consequences. Although I do not plagiarize other authors' halachic writings, I now have an added appreciation of the importance of writing my articles myself!

Informing the Employer

Since we now recognize the liability of publishing plagiary, must Meirah notify the owner that he may have a plagiarizer on staff?

In general, if I am aware that a fellow Jew is being harmed financially, I am responsible to bring it to his attention. By doing so, I fulfill the following *mitzvos*:

1. **Lo saamod al dam rei'echa.** The *mitzvah* of *lo saamod al dam rei'echa* is defined as the prohibition of idly standing by while one's neighbor is in danger.[5] This *mitzvah* includes

not only saving a fellow Jew's life or limb, but even saving his money.[6] For this reason, if I see someone damaging another person's property, I am required to attempt to stop the person from doing the damage. (However, I am not required to do so if I may be injured or suffer a loss as a result.) Similarly, if I witness a fire on someone's property, I must call the fire department, even if there is no risk to anyone's life.

2. **Hashavas aveidah.** Alerting someone to a potential loss of property is also part of the *mitzvah* of *hashavas aveidah*, returning lost objects.[7] Therefore, if I see a parked automobile with its lights on, I am responsible for informing the owner so that he can turn them off and not waste his car battery. The same *halachah* applies if I discover that someone's employee is using company time for private matters, without permission.

3. **Ve'ahavta lerei'acha kamocha.** Loving your neighbor as yourself includes ensuring that other individuals do not suffer losses, given that I would certainly want others to forewarn me and protect my interests should the need arise.[8]

It would seem that one must inform an employer if his employee is not performing his job properly, whether he is lacking the necessary skills, is unaware of his responsibilities, or is behaving unethically. However, the details of these *halachos* are quite complicated. For example, several other requirements must be met, including the fact that the notifying person must be certain of the facts himself, and reasonably sure that he can rectify the problem by discussing it with the employer. In addition, he should ascertain that the employee will not suffer more than *halachah* permits in the situation.[9] For example, if the employee is less skilled than others, but can perform the task adequately, one may not inform the employer. This is because informing the employer may jeopardize the employee's job unjustifiably. Similarly, if the employee erred once and is unlikely to repeat the error, there is no reason to inform the employer. However, if the employee is likely to repeat the error and jeopardize the employer, it is a *mitzvah* to tell the employer.

Therefore, our question now becomes: Is the writer now aware of what she is expected to do? Is the employer still at risk, because the writer does not know or care?

Assuming that one is absolutely certain that the author now understands why she may not simply plagiarize someone's article, there is no reason to tell the employer. Since the writer feels remorseful for what she did and understands why it was wrong, there would be no reason to inform the employer of her misdeed. The author may simply have been unaware of these laws and misunderstood her instructions; one should be careful that she does not lose what is rightfully hers, since the employer may jump to conclusions and fire her unjustifiably.[10]

Judging Favorably

But what is the *halachah* if the editor is uncertain whether the author understands that it is wrong to plagiarize? In this instance, we should examine the *halachos* referred to as *dan lekaf zechus*, judging favorably.

In determining whether one is obligated to judge a person favorably, there exist three categories of people:

1. *A person who is known to be G-d-fearing.* One is required to assume that a G-d-fearing person did not do anything wrong, even if the situation implies that he did. Thus, if one sees a well-respected *rav* behave in a manner that appears to be dishonest, one should assume that there must have been a legitimate reason for his act, even if it seems very unlikely. Nevertheless, one may consider the possibility that a wrongdoing was performed in order to protect oneself from harm.[11]

2. *A person who is usually careful in* halachah, *but occasionally slips.*

A. If he behaved in a manner that can be interpreted either negatively or positively, one should assume that he acted in a correct manner.

B. If circumstances indicate that he did something wrong, one should regard the matter as unresolved.

3. ***A person who regularly does evil.*** One should assume that he will continue to do evil, even if the chances are more likely that he acted correctly.[12]

What Should Meirah Do?

In our case, the practical question is whether Meirah may and should assume that the writer now understands her responsibility and will be careful. If the writer was indeed a halachically meticulous person, one should mentally assume that she is now careful. However, one may double-check periodically to see that the material submitted is original.

Should she share her concerns with her employer?

Unless Meirah feels certain that the writer now fully understands her responsibility, she should still be concerned with the possibility that *maybe* the writer does not understand. If Meirah feels doubtful, she is required to tell the owner about the writer's indiscretion.[13] In the case at hand, if Meirah felt that the author did not take her admonition seriously, but was simply placating the editor, she should bring this matter to the attention of the employer.

Epilogue

Based on my halachic advice, Meirah apprised her employer of the situation, and advised the writer to discuss the matter with the employer. In her note to the employer, she wrote:

> I am worried, because neither shame nor remorse was expressed. I do not actually know if she understood the problem, or how she feels about it. After much thought and receiving halachic advice, I

sent her an e-mail that I think this matter should be discussed with you.

Kol tuv and *hatzlachah.*

The employer responded:

I think the lack of remorse stems from the writer not even realizing what she had done wrong. I have now made it clear to her that when researching articles, the writer must actually rewrite every single word of the information she is using. Furthermore, I gave her other clear and specific guidelines.

Meirah's final comments to me on the subject:

The employer gave no indication that he is planning to fire the writer, relieving one of my major concerns regarding this whole incident – a concern that may have been a reason not to report her actions to the employer in the first place. I hope we will continue working well together in the future, and that she now understands that her actions were wrong.

So do I.

NOTES

1. *Hilchos Dei'os* 6:7.
2. *Vayikra* 19:17.
3. *Megillah* 15a.
4. *Hilchos Dei'os* 7:5.
5. *Vayikra* 19:16.
6. See *Sefer HaMitzvos, Lo Saaseh* #297; *Shaarei Teshuvah* 3:70; cf., however *Shaar Mishpat* 28:2.
7. *Bava Metzia* 31a; *Shaarei Teshuvah* 3:70.
8. *Maadanei Yom Tov, Niddah* 9:5:6, quoted by *Be'er Mayim Chayim* 6:29.

9. *Chafetz Chayim*, chapter 10.

10. *Chafetz Chayim* 2:9:5.

11. *Chafetz Chayim* 1:6:10.

12. *Shaarei Teshuvah* 3:218.

13. *Maadanei Yom Tov* ad loc.

13

Double Jeopardy

Asking the Same *She'eilah* Twice

On the evening of the first night of Chol HaMoed in Eretz Yisrael (corresponding to the eve of the second night of Yom Tov in *chutz laaretz*), I received a curious phone call.

"Rabbi," the female voice began, "I am calling on behalf of my friend, Rivkah." After decades of rabbinic experience, I was convinced that this was the introduction to an embarrassing question. People often prefer pretending that they are asking for someone else – hiding behind the name "of a friend." But this time I was wrong.

Kiddush or Havdalah

"Rivkah is a student at Bnos Aliyah Seminary and is uncertain whether she should keep one day of Yom Tov or two. A few weeks ago, she visited a family for Shabbos and mentioned her predicament. The man of the house graciously told her that he answers halachic inquiries and ruled that she is only required to keep one day of Yom Tov. However, upon returning to seminary,

Rivkah was told by a teacher that she should not ask her *she'eilah* to *just anyone*, but must ask one of the seminary rabbis. Rivkah did so, and was told to keep two days. Subsequently, someone told her that she should not have asked the question a second time and must follow the first ruling she received. Now she is in a dilemma: Should she observe the second day of Yom Tov or not? Is she expected to find someone to recite Kiddush and Havdalah on her behalf?"

Although most people do not have a Yom Tov issue as Rivkah did, they could still stumble into a similar predicament by asking any query to two *rabbonim*. As I understood the *she'eilah*, the answer to Rivkah's query did not involve analyzing the laws of who must observe two days, but whether she must follow the first opinion or the second. Although the Gemara states that one may not ask the same *she'eilah* twice, perhaps this only applies if one receives a strict ruling that he or she is now trying to overturn. What is the ruling if one first receives a lenient ruling, and then receives a stricter response? In our instance, the first authority told Rivkah that is only required to keep one day of Yom Tov; most opinions consider this a lenient ruling since she may now perform *melachah* on the second day.[1] (For reasons beyond the scope of this essay, the *Shu't Chacham Tzvi*[2] contends that keeping one day is the stricter ruling.)

In order to resolve Rivkah's quandary, we must examine the following questions:

1. May one ask again after receiving a lenient answer?

2. If one did ask, and the second authority ruled strictly, whose reply is binding? Is one still bound by the first ruling, which was lenient, or the second, stricter ruling? Or, perhaps, should one now ask a third authority for a final decision?

3. Was the teacher correct in directing Rivkah to ask a second *she'eilah* after she had already received a *psak*?

Background Information

Before focusing on Rivkah's predicament, we must first understand the general principles of the topic.

The Gemara[3] teaches that someone who asked a *she'eilah* and receives a strict ruling may not subsequently ask the question from a different authority. I will refer to this principle as *hanishal lachacham* (one who asked a Torah scholar), based on the opening words of the Gemara's statement.

Tosafos[4] asks, "May one never question the *rav*'s decision? Let the different authorities debate the issue, and perhaps the second will prove to the original authority that his decision was incorrect." Tosafos concludes that the Gemara only prohibits asking a second *rav* without notifying him that one has already asked the question. However, if one notifies the second authority that the question has already been asked, the second authority may oppose the decision, if he considers it mistaken. Can he actually overturn the first ruling? This depends, as there are three levels of error.

1. Clear Mistake

If it is obvious to the second *rav* that the first *rav* erred, the second *rav* may inform the inquirer of the correct practice.[5] This is true only if the first *rav*'s ruling conflicts with accepted halachic practice or was based on inaccurate information.[6] In these instances, the first opinion is completely disregarded, since it is erroneous. Judaism does not accept a doctrine of rabbinic infallibility; on the contrary, the Gemara records several instances where great halachic authorities erred in specific halachic rulings.[7] For example, Rabi Tarfon ruled that a cow whose uterus was surgically removed is not kosher, as it will die shortly. The Mishnah records that when it was demonstrated that an animal can survive this surgery satisfactorily, Rabbi Tarfon acknowledged his error.[8]

2. Provable Error

If the second *rav* believes he can prove that the first ruling was mistaken, but the ruling is not an obvious error, the second authority may not say anything directly to the inquirer. Instead, he should contact the first *rav* to establish that the ruling was flawed. In the true style of intellectual honesty required of a Torah scholar, the first *rav* should carefully examine the second *rav's* approach to see if it has merit. It is now up to the first *rav* to decide whether to change his ruling.[9] If he still feels that his first interpretation is correct, or not proven to be in error, he should maintain his original position. According to some opinions, he may retract his position if he no longer feels it to be correct, even though he cannot establish that it is certainly incorrect.[10]

A similar scenario could result if the second *rav* knows that well-accepted authorities rule differently than the first *rav*, and he suspects that the first *rav* would accept their position.[11] In this situation, too, the second *rav* may simply notify the first *rav* of the variant opinion, and then it is up to the first *rav* to decide whether or not to rescind his original decision.

In all the cases we mentioned so far, the first *rav's* ruling is retracted, either because it was clearly erroneous or because he himself withdrew it.

3. Dispute in Interpretation

If the second *rav* disagrees with the first *rav's* conclusion, but cannot prove it incorrect, the second *rav* should say nothing to the questioner, who remains bound by the original decision. There is no halachic error here, but a diversity of outlook, and the first *rav's* verdict cannot be overturned. Even if the first *rav* himself subsequently reconsiders his decision, most authorities contend that he cannot alter his own original ruling, since the original approach cannot be disproved.[12] (However, note that the Levush[13] and the *Aruch HaShulchan*[14] rule that he can change his mind. They feel that the second *rav* should engage the first *rav* in debate, because this might change the first one's mind.)

How long does the ruling remain binding?

The *Rema*[15] rules that the *rav's* decision is binding only on this *specific instance* of the *she'eilah*. However, if the same *she'eilah* recurs, one may ask the same *she'eilah* again from either the same *rav* or a different *rav*. The same *rav* himself, and certainly any other *rav*, may rule differently when the question recurs. Therefore, if a person asked whether one may perform a certain activity on Shabbos, was told that it is forbidden, and subsequently discovers that the consensus of *poskim* permits this activity, he may be lenient in the future. Similarly, a *rav* who ruled one way and subsequently discovered that most *poskim* dispute his conclusion, may conclude differently the next time he is asked this question.

What if the First Scholar Was Lenient?

So far, we have assumed that the first *rav* ruled strictly. What happens if the first *rav* ruled leniently, and the questioner would like to ask someone else? This issue is germane to Rivkah asking her seminary rabbi about observing two days of Yom Tov, after the first rabbi permitted her to keep only one day.

The answer to this question depends on the reason one may not ask a *she'eilah* from a second authority. Here are two possible reasons.

Reason 1: Considering It Prohibited

Most Rishonim contend that when submitting a question to a *rav*, the inquirer accepts the *rav's* decision as binding and must then consider the item either permitted or prohibited.[16] This concept is called *shavya anafshei chaticha de'issura*, meaning that someone who asserts that something is prohibited is required to treat it as such. I will clarify this principle with a particular case I've dealt with in the past.

A man believes himself to be a *kohein*, even though there is insufficient evidence for his assumption. Since most Jews are Yisraelim and not *kohanim*, his halachic status is a Yisrael, and he has none of the rights of a *kohein* – he may not *duchen*, redeem a *bechor*, or receive the first *aliyah* to the Torah. However, since he considers himself a *kohein*, he must assume the *stringencies* that result from that esteemed status – he may not come in contact with corpses, nor marry a woman forbidden to a *kohein*. Since he believes that he is a *kohein*, he is *shavya anafshei chaticha de'issura;* meaning, he must consider himself as being prohibited, to the same extent as a *kohein*.

The Rishonim mentioned above maintain that asking a *she'eilah* requires accepting the *rav's* opinion as binding *halachah;* if he rules stringently, one must accept his verdict, and therefore one may not re-ask the question. (The exceptions mentioned previously where the ruling can be retracted are because the decision is considered an error and therefore not a valid decision.)

According to this approach, the principle of *hanishal lachacham* applies only when the first *rav* rules stringently. If he rules leniently, one is permitted to follow his ruling, but not obligated to, and therefore I may re-ask the *she'eilah* from a different *rav*.[17] Thus, Rivkah may ask her *she'eilah* from the seminary rabbi, notwithstanding the first ruling she received. We will soon discuss whether she is *obligated* to keep the second day of Yom Tov once she has received the second ruling.

Reason 2: Respect for a **Talmid Chacham**

Other authorities explain that re-asking a *she'eilah* from a second *rav* affronts the respect due the first *rav*, by implying that one is questioning his competence.[18] This rationale forbids re-asking a question, even if the first *rav* ruled *leniently*, as such conduct is offensive to the *rav's* honor. Following this approach, Rivkah should not have asked the seminary rabbi once she had already asked someone qualified to answer her *she'eilah*.

Should her teacher have instructed her to ask the *she'eilah* again? Certainly, her teacher should have asked her own *she'eilah* as to whether to instruct Rivkah to ask her *she'eilah* again.

Are there any other practical differences as a result of the dispute as to why one may not re-ask a *she'eilah*? Indeed there are.

A *Berachah* Dispute

Many halachic issues cannot be resolved as strict versus lenient rulings, but are simply judgments regarding correct procedure. For example, whether or not to recite a *berachah* in a certain instance, which *berachah* to recite, or whether to repeat a *tefillah* are all instances where there is no *stricter* or *more lenient* side to the ruling. Both options of the *psak* involve stringency, and therefore, the principle of *shavya anafshei chaticha de'issura* is not applicable.

Those who ban re-asking a question because of *shavya anafshei chaticha de'issura* should therefore permit re-asking any question of this type, in order to receive a more accurate or authoritative response. On the other hand, those who ban re-asking a question because it is offensive to a scholar's honor should prohibit it in this instance too, since asking again implies a lack of competence on the part of the first *rav* asked.

Before resolving Rivkah's dilemma, we need to explore one other fascinating point.

A Dispute between the Talmuds?

When the *Talmud Bavli*[19] cites the prohibition of re-asking a halachic inquiry, it refers only to cases where the first *rav* answers stringently, without mentioning any cases in which the first *rav* rules leniently. The implication is that the Bavli explains the reason for this prohibition in a similar way to the first approach – that one has accepted the prohibition of the *rav*.

However, the *Talmud Yerushalmi*[20] quotes the following anecdote:

> Rabi Simon permitted something, which Rabi Ami subsequently prohibited. Rabi Simon was upset; is it not said that if one sage permitted something, a second sage may not prohibit it?

This Yerushalmi appears to rule that one may not re-ask a question *even if one received a lenient ruling*, which is impossible according to the first approach. Thus, the Yerushalmi appears to understand that the reason one may not re-ask a question is due to the *talmid chacham*'s honor, corresponding to the second approach cited. This would imply that the two Talmuds dispute the answer to the exact question upon which our dear Rivkah and her teacher stumbled!

The Rishonim prefer to avoid stating that the two Talmuds disagree, suggesting different approaches to resolve this contradiction.

An Alternative Reading

Tosafos[21] suggests reading the last statement of the Yerushalmi rhetorically, as opposed to supporting Rabi Simon's position. The passage now reads: "Rabi Simon permitted something, which Rabi Ami subsequently prohibited. Rabi Simon was upset." The Yerushalmi now questions the validity of Rabbi Simon's reaction: "Does it say anywhere that if one sage permitted something, a second sage may not prohibit it?"

Following Tosafos's approach, the Yerushalmi rules exactly as the Bavli implies, that the prohibition to re-ask a question applies only when the first scholar ruled stringently. However, when he ruled leniently, a second scholar may rule freely on the case.

On the other hand, the Rosh[22] explains the Yerushalmi as I explained originally, that Rabi Simon objected to Rabi Ami's strict ruling as halachically objectionable after he (Rabi Simon) had permitted the matter. The Rosh quotes this approach as definitive *halachah*, meaning that *hanishal lechacham* is prohibited because of the honor of the first *rav*. The Rosh appears to hold that *both* reasons are true; the Bavli emphasizes one reason and the Yerushalmi the other. This approach maintains that one may indeed not seek out a second *rav*'s opinion (without telling him that one already asked someone), whether the first *rav* was lenient or strict.

How do we rule in this dispute?

Most halachic authorities rule that the law of *hanishal lechacham* applies only when the initial ruling was strict, but if it was lenient, one may indeed re-ask the *she'eilah*.[23] According to this approach, there was nothing wrong with Rivkah re-asking her question.

However, there are some who rule, like the Rosh, that *hanishal lechacham* applies whether the initial ruling was strict or lenient and forbid re-asking a question, even if one received a lenient ruling.[24]

Conclusion

Now that Rivkah has already re-asked the question, must she keep one or two days of Yom Tov? According to those who rule that *hanishal lechacham* is because one has accepted the stringent opinion, once Rivkah re-asked the question, she is bound to follow the second, stricter ruling. Since most authorities rule this way, one who re-asks the question from a second authority will be obligated to follow his opinion if he is stricter. No matter how many people one asks, one will always be required to follow the strictest ruling. Therefore, Rivkah should celebrate two days of Yom Tov.

The final *psak* Rivkah received only applies to the Yom Tov about which she asked. Before the next Yom Tov arrives, she may ask again whether to observe one day of Yom Tov or two. May she direct her question to a particular *rav*, knowing what answer she wants to receive? That is a topic for a different time.

NOTES

1. *Minchas Shlomo* 1:19:8.
2. #167.
3. *Avodah Zarah* 7a.
4. *Avodah Zarah* 7a s.v. *Hanishal*.
5. Ibid.
6. See *Mishnah Bechoros* 28b.
7. See *Horayos* 2a.
8. *Bechoros* 28b.
9. *Shu't Panim Meiros* #2; cf. *Shach, Yoreh Deah* 242:58; *Choshen Mishpat* 25:14:17.
10. *Levush, Yoreh Deah* 242:31; *Aruch Hashulchan, Yoreh Deah* 242:60.
11. See *Rosh, Sanhedrin* 4:6.
12. *Shach, Yoreh Deah* 242:58 and *Choshen Mishpat* 25:14:17; *Shu't Panim Meiros* #2; *Divrei Chamudos, Chullin* 3:24.

13. *Yoreh Deah* 242:31.

14. *Yoreh Deah* 242:60.

15. *Yoreh Deah* 242:31.

16. *Raavad* quoted by *Ran; Rosh.*

17. See *Tosafos, Avodah Zarah* 7a s.v. *Hanishal.*

18. Cited by *Ran* to *Avodah Zarah.* See there that he also quotes an additional reason.

19. *Avodah Zarah* 7a.

20. *Shabbos* 19:1.

21. Ibid.

22. Ibid.

23. *Shach, Yoreh Deah* 242:59; *Biur HaGra.*

24. *Rema, Yoreh Deah* 242:31.

14

To Buy or Not to Buy?

The Appropriateness of Purchasing Life Insurance

At times we have heard people opposing life insurance – claiming that it reflects a lack of *bitachon*, or that its acquisition could actually be to one's detriment. Indeed, are there halachic or *hashkafic* concerns about purchasing life insurance? From a Torah perspective, should this practice be encouraged or discouraged? Let's explore the issue through three real-life situations:

1. Chaim knows that, as the head of the family, he has the responsibility to care for his wife, Fruma, and their children. He feels that this responsibility obligates him to acquire an adequate amount of life insurance in case something should *chas veshalom* happen to him. Fruma's upbringing included the message that even discussing this matter can cause bad things to happen. Who is right – Chaim or Fruma?

2. Miriam calls her *rav* with a *she'eilah*. "My husband and I

would like to buy life insurance, but we are concerned that it might show a lack of *bitachon* that Hashem always does what is best for us. Is that correct?"

3. Tzadok is one of the city's biggest *tzaddikim*. He teaches, voluntarily oversees some local *tzedakah* projects, and maintains incredibly solid *kevi'us itim*. He is a *talmid chacham* and is raising his own large family. One of the *baalei batim* has offered to purchase a life insurance policy on his behalf, but Tzadok questions whether doing so might jeopardize him, since his family would no longer be dependent on his support. Is his fear founded?

Let us understand what the halachic authorities say about this subject. The three situations I presented above demonstrate three different issues that *poskim* discuss when analyzing if there is a halachic problem in purchasing life insurance:

1. ***Creating a devil's advocate.*** The Gemara[1] states that one should not say something that might cause evil to occur. *Al yiftach adam piv l'satan* – Do not create an opportunity for the Satan to mix in! Is purchasing life insurance considered encouraging the evil Satan to do something nefarious?

2.. ***In G-d we trust.*** If we really believe that Hashem provides for all of our needs, doesn't purchasing life insurance demonstrate that we are worried about the future and lack trust in Hashem?

3. ***Succeeding in Divine judgment.*** As opposed to a human court, Hashem's judgment and decisions are perfect, and take all ramifications into consideration. The Heavenly Tribunal will not recall someone unless all the consequences of his disappearance are calculated. Based on this, perhaps purchasing life insurance jeopardizes the insured, since his family is no longer as dependent on his support, thus minimizing his merits when judged by the Heavenly Tribunal.

Let's analyze each one of these issues individually, in order to determine whether or not purchasing life insurance should be allowed or even encouraged.

Issue 1: Creating a Devil's Advocate

Al yiftach adam piv l'satan literally translates as, "A person should not open his mouth for the Satan." One should be careful not to say something that might provide the Satan with ammunition. The Gemara[2] applies this rule to forbid a person from saying, "I sinned a lot, but Hashem has not punished me." The admission that one is guilty and deserves punishment gives the Satan a chance to prosecute him in the Heavenly Tribunal. According to the *Magen Avraham*,[3] the main concern here is that the words "Hashem has not punished me" imply that one anticipates the punishment, although this is clearly not what the speaker intends. However, when the Satan prosecutes, he might take the speaker's words out of context.

The question is whether purchasing life insurance provides the Satan with such an opportunity to prosecute.

A different Talmudic discussion implies that it is completely permissible to make arrangements for oneself in preparation for one's demise, and that doing so is not considered opening one's mouth to the Satan. The Gemara[4] discusses whether someone who prepares shrouds (*tachrichim*) for himself that are four-cornered is required to attach *tzitzis* to their corners, implying that it is, indeed, permissible to prepare shrouds for oneself. In other words, planning for one's death does not constitute violation of the warning *al yiftach adam piv l'satan* and does not provide Satan with any ammunition.

Indeed, this Gemara's discussion is rallied as a source in the following situation. Maury Bond is lying on his deathbed on a hot Friday afternoon. There is concern that if he dies before Shabbos, his corpse will begin to decompose and smell unpleasant before it can be buried after Shabbos, which would not be a *kavod* for the departed. (Remember that earlier generations did not have ready access to refrigeration.)

The authorities debate about whether it is permissible to dig

Maury's grave while he is still breathing, so that, should he die on Friday, he could be buried quickly before Shabbos. Most authorities[5] permit digging the grave while Maury is still living; the dissenting opinion prohibits it out of concern that Maury might find out that his grave is already dug, which will distress him, and this itself could lead to his premature demise.[6] However, none of the authorities debating this case is concerned that the efficacy of digging Maury's grave while he is still alive violates *al yiftach adam piv l'satan* and provides the Satan with the opportunity to clamor for Maury's swift departure. Some of the authorities who discuss this question state explicitly that it is perfectly acceptable for a healthy person to arrange the digging of his own grave and to prepare his own shrouds, as we see from the above-quoted passage in the Gemara. One highly respected authority expressly approves the practice of purchasing adjacent burial plots for a couple, the fact that at least one member is still alive notwithstanding.[7]

Thus, we see that it is not considered *al yiftach adam piv l'satan* when a healthy person makes funeral arrangements for himself, since he is not mentioning his sins and giving the Satan any reason to prosecute him. Based on this concept, several authorities rule that purchasing life insurance is also not a violation of *al yiftach adam piv l'satan*.[8]

However, I would like to note that there are two sources that seem to indicate that *al yiftach adam piv l'satan* does indeed apply even though one does not mention his sins. The Gemara[9] states that a person should not make the following declaration, "Many will drink the cup of mourning" because of the concern of *al yiftach adam piv l'satan*. This source implies that there is concern of *al yiftach adam piv l'satan* even when one's statement does not imply that one has sinned and deserves punishment.

Thus, we need to resolve why the halachic authorities who discuss making shrouds, digging a grave, or purchasing a burial plot for a living person do not prohibit these actions because of the principle of *al yiftach adam piv l'satan*, even though the statements "many will drink the cup of mourning" and "if something goes wrong, my death should atone for my sins" are prohibited for this reason.

The answer appears to be that these last two cases are a concern only because one is *expressing* the possibility of one's passing, which corresponds to the words of Chazal: "A person should not *say*, 'I sinned a lot, but Hashem has not punished me.' " Assuming our solution is correct, arranging plans for one's demise, including writing one's will and purchasing life insurance, do not violate *al yiftach adam piv l'satan*, provided that one does not verbally express the possibility of one's death.

Issue 2: In G-d We Trust – Exclusively

A Jew is obligated to believe that although he makes an effort to earn his *parnassah*, it is ultimately Hashem alone Who provides it. The question is whether there is a difference between working for one's daily needs and working to save money for future expenses. Is it a shortcoming in *bitachon* to save for the future? Does purchasing life insurance imply lack of confidence that Hashem will provide for one's family?

To answer these questions, we must first examine the halachic relationship between *parnassah* and *bitachon*.

Is There a Dispute in the Mishnah?

The Mishnah[11] quotes two ostensibly dissenting opinions. Rabi Meir is quoted first as saying: "A person should teach his son a livelihood that is easy [to learn] and free of potential sin. [At the same time, he should] pray to Him Who is the source of all wealth and property. [Always realize that] there is no profession that does not have its vicissitudes. Poverty and wealth are dependent on his merit." We see that Rabbi Meir advocates teaching one's child a livelihood, while simultaneously acknowledging that livelihood comes from Hashem and not from our efforts.

On the other hand, the very same Mishnah quotes Rabi Nehorai as saying, "I abandon all means of livelihood and teach my son only Torah."

Thus, we appear to have a dispute between two Tannaim as to whether one should or shouldn't take time from teaching one's son Torah in order to provide him with vocational training. However, this analysis cannot be accurate for the following reason:

The Gemara[12] teaches that Rabi Meir was an alternate name for Rabi Nehorai, because his teaching of Torah produced so much light. (Meir means "He who gives light," and the word Nehorai also means "light.") How could Rabi Nehorai disagree with himself?

Resolving the Dispute

One answer to this problem is that Rabi Nehorai's statement that he would teach his son nothing but Torah was personal – Rabi Nehorai himself had no worldly concerns, because he placed complete trust in Hashem. Someone at this spiritual level should indeed not teach his son any worldly occupation. However, most people do not reach this level of trust and must provide their sons with a livelihood, while emphasizing that *parnassah* is from Hashem.[13]

Rav Moshe Feinstein[14] presents an alternative answer to the contradictory statements of Rabi Meir. The two statements are discussing different stages of life, one before the son must begin supporting his family, and the other when he has to support his family. Rabi Nehorai's statement that "I teach my son only Torah" applies before the son needs *parnassah*. Until then, he should learn only Torah. The other statement refers to a son who has to earn a living. At that point, his father should teach him a livelihood that involves few halachic challenges and is easy to learn, while at the same time teaching him that his vocation is only *hishtadlus*, one's feeble, apparent attempt, and that *parnassah* comes only from Hashem.

There is a halachic difference between the two approaches. According to the first approach, someone with total trust that Hashem will provide for him, even if he makes no *hishtadlus*, should not make any effort toward *parnassah*. According to Rav Moshe's approach, even a person with total trust in Hashem is required to earn a livelihood. Rav Moshe brings evidence from several sources that it is inappropriate to rely on miracles for one's *parnassah*. Furthermore, he considers having no livelihood as equivalent to relying on miracles.[15]

On the other hand, Rav Wosner *shlita* rules,[16] similar to the first approach, that a pure *baal bitachon* is permitted to rely totally on Hashem for *parnassah*; however, he agrees that this applies only to rare individuals. There are stories about *gedolim*, such as Rav Yosef Chaim Sonnenfeld, who made no conventional *hishtadlus* to attain *parnassah*. These *gedolim*, too, must have had the same opinion as Rav Wosner. According to Rav Moshe's approach, one may not deliberately adopt such a lifestyle.

Both Rav Moshe and Rav Wosner rule that, generally speaking, people are required to have some type of *parnassah*, and that it is not a lack of *bitachon* to do so. Unless he is a great *tzaddik*, no one should assume that he has sufficient *zechuyos* (merits) or unshakeable *bitachon* to expect Hashem to provide his *parnassah* with no *hishtadlus* whatsoever on his part.

The *poskim* bring evidence from Tosafos that it is not a shortcoming to make arrangements to take care of one's financial future. The Gemara[17] rules that although technically, according to *halachah*, a father may marry off his daughter while she is a minor, he is prohibited to do so out of concern that when she grows up, she may not like her husband. In Tosafos's time, however, underage daughters were married off, which appeared to be a violation of this *halachah*. Upon what basis was there a practice contrary to the Gemara's ruling?

Tosafos explains that in his turbulent times (the Baalei HaTosafos lived during the period of the Crusades), a man who had sufficient means to provide his daughter with a dowry would arrange her marriage to someone appropriate. If the father delayed, he risked losing his money, which would have been tantamount to his becoming unable to marry off his daughter. Tosafos does not contend that a person should have *bitachon* that he will have the means to marry her off later.

Similarly, a person who can purchase life insurance, an annuity, or another means for causing his life or the lives of his dependents to be more secure, may do so.[18] *Bitachon* does not require someone to ignore future needs. *Bitachon* does require that a person realize that everything that happens is under Hashem's supervision and control.[19]

What Will I Eat Tomorrow?

But doesn't this approach violate the statement that "Someone who has [today's] bread in his basket, and asks, 'What will I eat tomorrow?' lacks faith"?[20] Aren't Chazal teaching us that someone who plans for tomorrow's livelihood lacks proper trust in Hashem?

The answer is no. This last passage is discussing people's beliefs. Everyone must believe that Hashem provides for him and that whatever happens is under His control. One may not say, "What will I eat tomorrow?" thereby ignoring Hashem's supervision. However, this does not mean that formulating practical plans for the future is a violation of *bitachon*, provided that one fully realizes that everything comes from Hashem and is dependent on Him.

The Manna

However, there is another passage of Gemara[21] that may indicate otherwise:

"Rabi Shimon ben Yochai's disciples asked him, 'Why did the manna not fall for Bnei Yisrael once a year [for the entire year]?' He answered them, 'I will give you a parable. A human king once provided his son with support on an annual basis. The son visited his father once a year to receive his allowance. Wanting to see his son more often, the father altered the system and began providing his son with support on a daily basis. Thereafter, his son visited his father every day. Similarly, the head of a large household worried that no manna would fall on the morrow; thus, he would pray daily for sustenance.'" Doesn't this Gemara imply that it is better for one's *parnassah* to arrive one day at a time than to be prepared in advance for the future?

The halachic authorities offer two answers to this question that are dependent on the dispute between Rav Wosner and Rav Moshe mentioned earlier. According to Rav Wosner, this Gemara reflects the ideal: A great *tzaddik* should, indeed, receive his *parnassah* one day at a time. However, most people are not at this level of faith and may plan for the future. According to Rav Moshe's approach, the Gemara means that a person should mentally acknowledge every day that Hashem provides for all his needs; however, he is permitted and required to make *hishtadlus*, which includes planning for future needs.

On a practical level, all the *poskim* that I have seen discussing this issue rule that purchasing life insurance qualifies as normal *hishtadlus*.

In this context, it is worthwhile to quote a *midrash* that demonstrates the obligation to make *hishtadlus*. Quoting the *pasuk* "*Lemaan yevorechecha Hashem Elokecha bechol maasecha asher taaseh*" (So that Hashem Your G-d will bless you in all your deeds that you will perform),[22] the Midrash points out that the last two words of the *pasuk, asher taaseh* (that you will perform), are seemingly superfluous, because the Torah already stated, *bechol maasecha* (in all your deeds). What is added with the words "that you will perform"?

The Midrash[23] explains, "The Torah states, 'Keep the *mitzvos*.' One might think that he should do nothing and expect his *parnassah* to come automatically. Therefore, the Torah repeats 'that you will perform.' If you work, you will receive blessing, and if you do not work, you will not receive blessing." This *midrash* proves that one has a responsibility to earn *parnassah*.

Issue 3: Succeeding in Divine Judgment

There is a third possible reason why someone should not purchase life insurance. What happens if a husband does not have the personal merit to guarantee longevity, while his wife and children do have the merit or the *mazel* (fortune) to live financially secure lives? In a case like this, the husband would live a long, productive life as their provider. By purchasing life insurance, which guarantees their sustenance even without his presence, he jeopardizes his life, since his dependents are now provided for, should something bad happen to him.

In the one halachic source I saw that mentioned this concern, the author, Rav Yitzchok Sternhell, *ztz"l*, quotes the exact opposite approach in the name of the Shinover Rav (Rav Yechezkel Shraga Halberstam, *ztz"l*, author of *Divrei Yechezkel*), who was one of the greatest halachic authorities of his day in Galicia. The Shinover contends that buying life insurance should provide longevity. He argues that since the *mazel* of the people who own insurance companies is to become wealthy, their *mazel* will prevail and prevent them from losing money by having to pay out life insurance policies. Thus, purchasing a policy actually rallies *mazel* to one's side and does not jeopardize one's life.[24]

Another counterargument runs as follows: If loss of merit is a concern, then there is valid reason to refrain from accumulating any wealth. The family members of a man who ekes out a daily existence are far more dependent on their breadwinner than are the wife and children of a wealthy man, since he will leave them with an appreciable inheritance, should something happen to him. Thus, one could argue that accumulating wealth is not in one's best interest, an approach that does not have too many advocates. I have never seen anyone refrain from accumulating wealth because of this concern, and neither have I seen any halachic authority suggest this as a reason to avoid affluence. Therefore, I conclude that this consideration is not a factor in the question of purchasing life insurance.

Conclusion

In conclusion, I am aware of thirteen written *teshuvos*[25] on the purchase of life insurance or annuities, written by authorities representing Litvishe, Chassidishe and, Sefardic approaches. All thirteen *teshuvos* permit purchasing life insurance, and some encourage the practice strongly.

Rav Meir Shapiro, the *rosh yeshivah* of Yeshivas Chachmei Lublin and progenitor of the *daf yomi* program, had a sizeable life insurance policy, even though he unfortunately had no children. His reason was that since fundraising for the yeshivah was completely on his shoulders, he was concerned that in the event of his premature death, the yeshivah would be forced to close. It is apparent that he was not concerned with any of the aforementioned issues and believed that purchasing insurance was an appropriate course of action.

May we all be blessed with long years and good health!

NOTES

1. *Kesubos* 8b.
2. *Berachos* 19a.
3. 239:7.
4. *Menachos* 41a.
5. *Beis Yosef, Bach* and *Biur HaGra* to *Yoreh Deah* 339; *Mishneh LaMelech, Hilchos Aveil* 4:5.
6. *Shu't HaRivash* #114 as explained by *Bach, Yoreh Deah* 339.
7. *Shu't HaRivash* #114.
8. *Shu't Be'er Moshe* 8:118, quoting *Shu't Lechem Shlomo* by Rav Shlomo Zalman Ehrenreich, #68; *Shu't Yechaveh Daas* 3:85.
9. *Kesubos* 8b.
10. *Berachos* 60a.
11. *Kiddushin* 82a.
12. *Eruvin* 13b.
13. *Sefer HaMikneh, Kiddushin* 82a. See *Kochevei Ohr* of Rav Yitzchak Blazer (colloquially called Rav Itzele Peterburger, because he once served as the Rav of St. Petersburg), the disciple of Rav Yisrael Salanter, chapter 11, for a description of the difference between these two types of people.
14. *Shu't Igros Moshe, Orach Chayim* 2:111; see also *Orach Chayim* 4:48.
15. We should note that Rav Samson Raphael Hirsch also follows this

approach numerous times in his commentary on the Torah.

16. *Shu't Shevet HaLevi* 4:1:2.

17. *Kiddushin* 41a.

18. *Shu't Yechaveh Daas* 3:85; *Shu't Kochevei Yitzchak* 1:22, both quoting several other authorities.

19. Both *Shu't Be'er Moshe* 8:118 and *Shu't Teshuvos VeHanhagos* 4:325 also reach the same conclusion and bring support to this conclusion from several other Talmudic passages and concepts. To keep this chapter reasonably small I have omitted his proofs. In addition, *Shu't Teshuvos VeHanhagos* provides sources that a person cannot selectively apply *bitachon* to medical issues. One should be consistent in how he bases his decisions on *bitachon*. The reader is encouraged to read their responsa on the subject.

20. *Sotah* 48b.

21. *Yoma* 76a.

22. *Devarim* 14:29.

23. *Midrash Shocher Tov*, cited by *Shu't Yechaveh Daas* 3:85.

24. *Shu't Kochevei Yitzchak* 1:22.

25. In addition to the above quoted sources and the sources that they quote, see letter from Rav Elyashiv to Rav Elya Svei and Rav Malkiel Kotler in *Kovetz Teshuvos* 1:19 encouraging Torah institutions to provide their educators with life insurance policies.

15

When There Is a Will, the Relatives Will Complain

Dealing with a Non-Halachic Will

Yonasan, who was originally adopted by nonobservant parents, called me with the following *she'eilah*:

> My parents, meaning the couple who adopted me, eventually divorced, and later my father remarried, although there was a halachic problem with his second marriage. My adoptive father was a *kohein*, and his second wife, Martha, was a divorcee. Recently, my father passed away. My father's final will, which was drafted when he was ill and very dependent on Martha, was completely different from his previous will, and left virtually all of his property to her. Uncle Jack, my adoptive father's brother, is very upset about the will, believing that this was certainly not my father's intention, and that it can be overturned in court. This would make me the legal heir to my father's estate, although halachically, I am

not his son. Uncle Jack wants to file a lawsuit over the matter; however, he has no legal recourse to do so, since civil law does not consider him my father's heir. May I file a lawsuit to overturn the will?

This *she'eilah* is indeed as complicated halachically as it sounds, and actually involves three different areas of *halachah*:

1. Who is the heir?

2. What is the halachic status of a will?

3. May one file the lawsuit in secular court?

In addition, there is a fourth halachic issue that must be addressed, a question of *yibum*, which I will discuss later.

I will explain each area of *halachah* mentioned above in order to explain the procedure I suggested that Yonasan follow.

Who Is the Heir?

Although civil law considers Yonasan the child of his adoptive parents for all matters, including his being their legal heir, the adoption did not make him their biological son. Indeed, the Gemara states that someone who raises a child is considered as if he had given birth to him;[1] however, the adopted child does not inherit, unless he receives the property as some form of gift, as I will explain.

Thus, although Yonasan is his father's legal heir (from a civil law perspective, if we ignore the will), *halachah* does not consider him an heir automatically, unless his father gave him the property in a halachically correct will. Since the existing will made other accommodations, Yonasan receives nothing from his father's estate halachically, neither as an automatic heir, nor as the receiver of gifts through his father's will. Thus, Yonasan cannot make a financial claim against his stepmother for his father's estate, since it does not belong to him. If the will is valid, then the property belongs to Martha, his stepmother. If the will is invalid, the property belongs to Uncle Jack.

Why Uncle Jack?

If a man dies without biological children and makes no halachic provisions for his estate, then his closest heir is his father, who, in this case, is already deceased. The next closest relative is any surviving brother. In this case, there is one biological brother of the deceased, Uncle Jack. Thus, he is the halachic heir of Yonasan's father, and if indeed the will is halachically invalid, the property halachically belongs to him, although he may not be able to take possession of it according to civil law.

Halachically, a woman does not inherit from her husband as next of kin. Instead, the *halachah* gives her the rights of the *kesubah*, including the right to live in her late husband's house and guaranteed income and support from his property. Martha is entitled to these financial rights if she was halachically married to Yonasan's father, even if the marriage fell into the category of a halachically prohibited marriage. (One method whereby Martha and Yonasan's father could have been halachically married in a prohibited marriage would be if they had deceived an Orthodox rabbi, dishonestly getting his agreement to perform their ceremony. There are others.) Thus, if Martha proves that she was halachically married to Yonasan's father, she will be entitled to this support, even though she was a divorcée and he was a *kohein*.[2]

Is the Will Valid?

According to civil law, a person has the right to choose his heirs and thereby to choose to whom he distributes his earthly wealth after passing on. However, according to the Torah, a person does *not* have the ability to choose his heirs, nor can he arrange to give away property after death. When a man dies, the Torah instructs us on how to distribute his assets, through the laws of *yerushah*.

How could a person bequeath his property to his adopted child?

There are methods whereby one can transfer his property to his adopted child, or to anyone else, for that matter, who is not a halachic heir. One method is to draw up a will, and then make a *kinyan* that transfers possession of the bequeathed property to the beneficiary of the will. (I mention this method as a possible illustration, since it does not work in all situations.) This can be performed in such a way that the person wishing to bequeath his property maintains ownership over it in the meantime and retains the right to change his bequest later. Some *poskim*, albeit a minority, contend that a legally valid will alone constitutes a *kinyan*. These authorities reason that arranging a legally valid will, knowing that the government will transfer property as a result, is halachically equivalent to making a *kinyan*.[3] However, most *poskim* maintain that a standard civil will is not halachically valid.

Yonasan's father was not observant and did not have his lawyer arrange a halachically valid will. (Unfortunately, many observant Jews do not attend to this important matter either. Just as it is important for a person to have a will drawn up, it is important to make sure that it is halachically valid.) Therefore, many *poskim* would consider Uncle Jack to be the halachic heir of the estate, yet he cannot file a civil suit concerning the property, since he is not an interested party according to civil law. But before dealing with this issue, we need to discuss whether the Torah permits Yonasan or Uncle Jack to sue in civil court.

Arka'os

A Jew may not litigate against a fellow Jew in civil court,[4] even if both parties agree.[5] This is known as the prohibition against using *arka'os*. Someone who uses a court system not sanctioned by the Torah commits a *chillul Hashem*, a desecration of G-d's Name, because he demonstrates his feeling that G-d's Torah cannot resolve his financial matters.[6] In the words of the Rambam,[7] "Whoever has his case judged by non-Jewish laws or courts, even if their laws are the same [as the Torah], is a *rasha*. It is as if he blasphemed and raised his hand against the Torah of Moshe Rabbeinu."[8] Someone who brought litigation to a secular court is invalidated from being a *chazzan* for the Yamim Nora'im.[9] In addition, he will probably transgress the violation of stealing (*gezel*), since the property he receives is not his according to *halachah*.

What if the other party refuses to go to *beis din*?

This problem is, unfortunately, neither uncommon nor recent, and apparently occurred even at the time of the Gemara.[10] If this happens, the halachically correct procedure is for the plaintiff to have *beis din* summon the defendant. If the defendant fails to appear in *beis din* or indicates that he will not appear, the *beis din* authorizes the plaintiff to sue in civil court.[11] Under these circumstances, the plaintiff has not violated the prohibition of going to *arka'os*, since he acted according to *halachah*.

(It should be noted that even if someone is authorized to sue in civil court, he is only entitled to receive what *halachah* entitles him. It could happen that the civil court awards him more money than he is entitled to according to *halachah*. Therefore, he should ask a *posek* after winning the litigation how much of the award he may keep. The balance he would be required to return to the other party.)

Applying these rules to our case means that Uncle Jack may file a suit in *beis din* against Martha. Although Uncle Jack would like Yonasan to sue in civil court, Yonasan may not sue according to *halachah* for two different reasons:

1. One may not sue in civil court without permission from *beis din*.

2. Yonasan has no halachic grounds to claim his adopted father's estate since he is halachically not an heir.

Yonasan explained the halachic analysis of the *she'eilah* to Uncle Jack. After hearing out Yonasan, Uncle Jack asked him if there would be any possibility of Yonasan proceeding with the claim in civil court, considering that Uncle Jack feels strongly that Martha took unfair advantage of his ill brother, and both he and his attorney believe that the will could be easily overturned in civil court.

Harshaah

Enter *harshaah*, the halachic equivalent of power of attorney, into the picture. A *harshaah* allows someone who is not an interested party in the litigation to sue as if he *is* an interested party. In this instance, Uncle Jack, as the halachic heir, can authorize Yonasan by means of a *harshaah* to sue Martha in *beis din*. If Martha ignores the summons or indicates that she will not respond to it, the *beis din* authorizes Yonasan and Uncle Jack to pursue the matter in civil court. The court will not accept Uncle Jack as a plaintiff against the will, since they do not recognize him as the heir. Although the court does not recognize Uncle Jack's claim, Yonasan may now sue in civil court, based on the *beis din's* authorization. Halachically, the basis of the civil suit is to save Uncle Jack the money that is his, even though neither the civil court nor Uncle Jack himself accepts that the money is his.

At this point in the discussion, Yonasan e-mailed me a further question:

> Dear Rav Kaganoff,
>
> In the event that my uncle does choose, with permission from a *beis din*, to sue my father's widow in civil court, *should* I or merely *may* I act on his behalf?

Indeed, this is a difficult question. In general, saving someone's money is a *mitzvah*, and therefore, if someone sued in *beis din* and was ignored, it is a *mitzvah* to help him save his money in civil court, providing that this approach was properly authorized by *beis din*. This act of *chesed* is included under the *mitzvah* of *hashavas aveidah*, returning a lost object to its proper owner.

In our instance, I was less certain if this is considered *hashavas aveidah*, since Uncle Jack does not consider the money his and is only planning to give it to Yonasan. Is Yonasan required to help Uncle Jack claim the money, knowing that Uncle Jack will probably reason that it belongs to Yonasan and give it to him? Furthermore, since there might be *poskim* who feel that the money is legitimately Martha's, one could certainly rely on their opinions to rule that it is not a requirement for him to be involved in the litigation. Thus, there are two different considerations as to why he may not be considered "saving someone's money":

1. Would Yonasan be saving someone else's money, when that person intends to give it to him?

2. According to some opinions, the money may not be Uncle Jack's, but Martha's. Although he is *permitted* to follow the opinion that the money is Uncle Jack's, is he *required* to?

Another Consideration: *Chalitzah*

At this point in the discussion, I introduced a new topic to Yonasan, that of the *mitzvah* of *chalitzah*. This requires some explanation. If a man dies without having biological children, there is a *mitzvah* for his brother to perform a religious procedure called *chalitzah*, which permits the widow to remarry. In addition, the *chalitzah* is a tremendous *tikun neshamah* for the departed. The *mitzvah* applies even if the widow is no longer of child-bearing age, and even if the couple married after she was beyond child-bearing age.

Many people do not realize that, if a couple has adopted children, but no biological children, the *mitzvah* of *chalitzah* still applies. Since Yonasan's father had no biological children, his widow (assuming that they were halachically married, as she claims) is a *yevamah*, who requires *chalitzah* from Yonasan's uncle to permit her to remarry.

I quote my letter to Yonasan:

> If your father's marriage to his last wife was halachically valid, then there is a requirement for your uncle to perform *chalitzah*,[12] even if your father's widow has no intention of remarrying and is not observant.

Yonasan replied:

> I'm surprised it didn't occur to me. I have a question, though: Even if they did marry with *chuppah* and *kiddushin*, she was a *gerushah*, and he a *kohein*, so the marriage was forbidden. He claimed to have asked a

rabbi, who permitted the marriage on the basis that since he was disabled, he would not be allowed to perform the *avodah*, even if the Beis HaMikdash was standing. I did not think this is correct [indeed it is not], but I didn't see any point in making an issue of it. Was he correct? Assuming that his marriage was halachically unacceptable, would that in any way impact on *chalitzah*?

To which I replied:

There is absolutely no halachic basis to any of the reasons he gave you for permitting this marriage. I presume that he mentioned these reasons to relieve his own conscience, and that he never asked a *she'eilah*. Halachically, he was prohibited from marrying a divorcée.

A *halachah*-abiding rabbi would not perform such a ceremony, unless he was unaware either that your father was a *kohein* or that his wife was a *gerushah*. However, even if there had been no proper halachic ceremony, they might have been considered married according to *halachah*, particularly since they considered themselves married. Thus, although this marriage was forbidden, if it was halachically valid then there is a requirement to perform *chalitzah*. The *mitzvah* of *chalitzah* applies even in the case of a *kohein* who marries a divorcée.[13] Is there anyone who lives near them knowledgeable enough to arrange this for them?

Yonasan responded to my inquiry:

There are some very prominent *talmidei chachomim* living near both my uncle and my stepmother. However, they live a considerable distance from one another. I doubt that the widow is aware of the need for *chalitzah*; I also doubt that she'll object to it if it's made easy for her. My uncle, however, is totally irreligious. How would I convince him to perform the ceremony and to travel the distance involved? He is unlikely to drop everything and fly to where she lives to perform what he would see as an unimportant religious ceremony, to help out a woman with whom he is upset. What if he were to appoint someone else as a *shaliach* over the phone? Would that be acceptable?

To which I responded:

> *Chalitzah* cannot be performed through *shelichus* [agency].[14] It sounds as if the most likely way for this to happen is to wait until a time that you know that they will be near each other and then plan carefully how to present it to them. Alternatively, simply mention to them that *chalitzah* is a big *tikun neshamah* for your father, whom they both liked (I presume), and ask if they can keep it in mind in future travel plans.
>
> By the way, the *mitzvah* is your uncle's *mitzvah* to perform, not hers.

As of this writing, I do not know if Yonasan decided to proceed with the litigation over the will, and I presume that no action has resulted concerning the *chalitzah*. However, this situation affords us the opportunity to discuss halachos with which many people are unfamiliar, and it provides a tremendous opportunity to foster awareness concerning a number of different *mitzvos*.

It is important to realize that legal rights and responsibilities are never governed by secular law. A Torah Jew realizes that Hashem's Torah is all-encompassing, and that *halachah* directs every aspect of one's life. Thus, *halachah* governs all financial aspects of our lives, and one should be careful to ask *she'eilos* about one's business dealings.

Indeed, through this entire halachic conversation, I was extremely impressed by Yonasan's ability not to be swayed by financial considerations, but to be certain that what he did would be the perfectly correct halachic approach. In fact, shortly thereafter Yonasan received a huge, and completely unexpected, financial windfall – no doubt as a reward for his adherence to *halachah*, despite the financial temptations.

NOTES

1. *Megillah* 13a; *Sanhedrin* 19b.
2. *Kesubos* 100b.
3. *Shu't Igros Moshe, Even HaEzer* 1:104.
4. *Gittin* 88b.
5. *Ramban*, beginning of *Parshas Mishpatim.*
6. *Midrash Tanchuma, Mishpatim* #3.
7. *Hilchos Sanhedrin* 26:7.
8. See also *Rashi's* comments on *Shemos* 21:1.
9. *Mishnah Berurah* 53:82.
10. *Bava Kama* 92b, as explained by Rosh.
11. *Shulchan Aruch, Choshen Mishpat* 26:2.
12. *Yevamos* 20a.
13. Ibid.
14. *Kesubos* 74a.

16

Monetary Mystery – A Drama in Real Life

Unpredictable Predicament of Lost Money

Hershel calls his *rav* one day, somewhat agitated and very excited, with the following *she'eilah*:

"While making an unusual household repair, I discovered a wad of hundred-dollar bills hidden in a secret place," he begins. The questions now come tumbling out. "I know this is not money I ever put aside. How do I determine who the owner is? May I trust any previous resident of the house who claims that the money is his? What do I do if I can't find the owner?"

In order to answer Hershel's questions, we need to clarify what the Torah's rules are for returning lost objects.

Hashavas Aveidah Basics

As we are all aware, there is a *mitzvah* to return a lost object to its owner.[1] There are actually two separate *mitzvos*, a prohibition against ignoring the lost object and a positive *mitzvah* to return it. A person who retrieves the lost object and successfully returns it fulfills both *mitzvos*. In addition, attempting to return the lost object is rewarded as if one actually succeeded in fulfilling the *mitzvah*.

There are several questions we must answer when confronted with a *hashavas aveidah* situation. Among them are the following:

1. Where did one find the item? Was it found in a location where the inhabitants do not observe the laws of *hashavas aveidah*, in which case the owner would assume that the finder would probably not return it? Or, perhaps one found it in a *shul* or another location where passersby observe the rules of *hashavas aveidah*.

2. Is it an object that the owner is likely to realize that he lost, such as a large amount of money? Or is it an item that he probably does not realize he lost, such as small change?

3. Does the item have an identifiable marking, namely a *siman*, or not?

4. Was the item placed in its location intentionally, or does it appear to have been dropped?

Yei'ush

An important principle governing the laws of lost objects is the concept of *yei'ush*, in which the owner does not expect to retrieve the lost item. Once the owner has given up hope of retrieving the object, he is considered according to *halachah* as though he has relinquished possession and the item no longer belongs to him.[2] At this point, there is no requirement to return the lost item, and one is certainly not obligated to try to locate the owner. Nevertheless, returning the lost object is still a *mitzvah lifnim mishuras hadin*, beyond the requirements of *halachah*.[3]

An example of such a case is a driver observing something blow out of his car window and not returning for it. In this scenario, we may assume that the owner was *meya'eish* (gave up hope of retrieving the lost object).

We are now prepared to discuss the first question we posed

above: was the item found in a place where the owner would assume that it will not be returned, such as a shopping mall, or in a place where it might be returned, such as a *shul*?

Based on the concept of *yei'ush*, there is no halachic requirement to return an item that was lost in a mall or other location frequented by people who do not observe *hashavas aveidah*. The finder may assume that the owner gave up hope of having the item returned, even if it had a *siman*. However, it is considered a *mitzvah lifnim mishuras hadin* to return the item.

Many *poskim* contend that there is no halachic requirement to return an item that is used by a child, such as a toy or child's garment. Since adults know that children lose things all the time, these items are categorized as *aveidah midaas*, items that the owner knows may be lost, since he gave them to someone who is not halachically responsible.[4] Therefore, when a parent gives a child these items, he is not surprised when they are lost – it is an assumption that children will periodically lose their clothes, toys, or school supplies.

This *halachah* does not apply to an item that might be used by a child over the age of *bar* or *bas mitzvah*, since they are halachically responsible.

Items the Owner Does Not Know He Lost

Until now, we have been discussing items that the owner *knows* he has lost. What is the *halachah* concerning items that the owner does not yet realize he has lost?

The Gemara discusses the rule governing *yei'ush shelo midaas* (literally, giving up hope without knowledge), which refers to items that someone will give up hope of retrieving as soon as he realizes he has lost them; however, he does not yet know that he has lost them. Are these items already considered ownerless? This question is probably the most famous dispute between the two great Talmudic scholars, Abaye and Rava, and it is often taught as an introduction to didactic Gemara study.

The Gemara concludes that *yei'ush shelo midaas* is not valid *yei'ush* until the owner realizes his loss. This means that although the owner will eventually give up hope of retrieving the item, until he realizes his loss, the item is still his property, and someone else may not take possession of it.

How does the finder know if the owner has realized his loss? In general, this depends on the item. If one finds a large item that the owner was probably carrying himself, one may assume that the owner has already realized his loss by the time one found it. Similarly, if one finds a large quantity of money on the street, one can assume that the owner is already aware of his loss, since one tends to check one's pockets frequently when carrying large sums of money. Therefore, the finder may assume that the owner was already aware of his loss by the time the finder found it, and gave up hope of retrieving it. It is therefore permitted for the finder to keep the item for himself.

On the other hand, if one finds an item that might go unnoticed for a while, such as small change, one should assume that the owner may not yet know of his loss, and one should not take possession of it.

What Is a *Siman*?

One of the distinctions I mentioned above was between items that have an identifying marking, called a *siman*, and those that do not. What is a *siman*, and why is it so significant to the *halachos* of lost objects?

Someone who lost an item in a *shul* or similar place, where most of the people are *halachah*-abiding, would assume that people would try to return the item. As we will explain shortly, to return a lost item, it is important that the item have a *siman* that the owner can use for identification. A *siman* may be a name tag or an unusual marking or blemish on the object – anything that the owner would know about, but that someone else probably would not.

Must the *siman* be something intrinsic to the item itself?

No. Placement of an item in an unusual manner or in an unusual location also constitutes a valid *siman*. Any person who knows this information would be demonstrating that he or she is the item's owner. For example, although money does not usually have a *siman*, placement of coins in a pile or in an unusual location constitutes a valid *siman*.[5]

The number of bills involved would also comprise a valid *siman*. Therefore, the number of bills in a wad of dropped money is a valid *siman*.[6]

Summary

Combining the the abovementioned rules, we arrive at the following conclusion: A person who finds a lost item in a *shul* or other place where the owner would assume that people observe *hashavas aveidah* should check whether the lost item has a *siman*. If it does, the owner will assume that he can still retrieve his lost item, and the finder is required to notify people that he has found such an item.

During the times of Chazal, different methods were utilized for this notification. For example, there was a well-known location near Yerushalayim from which vocal announcements were proclaimed during Yom Tov concerning items that had been found. A contemporary method is to hang up a sign on a nearby bulletin board or to bring the item to a "lost and found" depot run in a halachically approved fashion.

Upon finding a lost object that has a *siman*, one should not announce the object in such a manner that reveals its *siman*. Thus, if one found a watch in *shul*, one should announce (on the sign or bulletin board) that he found a watch, and leave it for the owner to describe the item by mentioning its identifying characteristics.[7]

An Item that Was Placed Intentionally

If the item appears to have been placed in a particular location and then forgotten, rather than dropped, one should leave the item where it is, since the owner will probably try to retrace his steps to find it.

I once left a *sefer*, one volume of a multivolume set of *Mishnayos*, in the coatroom of a wedding hall. Later that day, I realized that I had left the *sefer* behind, and I returned for it. Alas, the *sefer* had disappeared already! Had the finder of this *sefer* followed the *halachah*, I would still possess a complete set of these *Mishnayos*; instead, I need to borrow this volume whenever I need it.

If an item was placed in a very secure place, one should leave the item there, since it will not disappear.[8] However, if the item was left in a place where it will be thrown away, then one should try to return it to its owner.[9]

An Exception

There is one major exception to this principal, for which one should indeed take an item that was clearly left intentionally. This is when the forgotten item will disappear. The Gemara provides an example of this situation: someone found an item that had been placed in a garbage heap that is usually deserted, but the garbage is about to be cleared away.[10] Obviously, the owner is better off if the finder takes the item and announces it, than if the item disappears.

But, wait a minute – how will the owner be able to claim the item if it has no *siman*? Didn't I mention earlier that one may not return an item unless the owner proves his ownership with an identifying *siman*?

Knowledge Proves Ownership

The answer is that in this instance, the location of the lost item serves as its *siman*. Since no one but the owner knows where the item was hidden, this information validates his claim.[11] Therefore, one should take the item and announce it as a lost object.

When Should the Finder Not Return a Lost Item with a *Siman*?

One should not return the item without determining that the person can prove he is the owner. This is accomplished when the owner provides his *siman*, identifying himself as the legitimate owner of the lost item.

If the claimant is dishonest, one should not return the lost item to him, even if he seemingly demonstrates that he is the correct owner. This is because we are suspicious that he has deviously discovered proof that allows him to claim he is the owner, when in fact he is not.[12]

What if the Claimant Does Not Produce a *Siman*?

Under normal circumstances, one cannot return an item unless the claimant tells us about a *siman*, specific to the item in question, that would be known only to the owner.

When Should One Avoid Picking Up a Lost Item?

If the lost item has no *siman*, one is not obligated to pick it up, since one will anyway be unable to return it to the owner. Furthermore, there are two different circumstances in which one should *not* pick up the lost item, and if one did, one may not keep it, even though the lost item has no *siman*:

1. One case – which I mentioned above – is when the owner originally put the item in a certain place intentionally and subsequently forgot it there (*makom hinuach*). In this case, one should not pick up the lost item, because the owner might still be able to retrace his steps and find it, whereas if one picks it up he will be unable to claim it, since it has no *siman*.[13] However, if leaving the item in its place will cause it to disappear, then one should remove it and try to "announce" it, using its location as a *siman*.[14]

2. The second case where one should not pick up the lost item is when the owner does not yet know that he has lost it (*yei'ush shelo midaas*), and the item has no *siman*. As I explained above, since the owner does not yet realize his loss, he has not yet relinquished ownership. Therefore, the finder cannot keep the lost object.

May One Ever Keep an Item That One Has Found?

In both of the previous cases, if the item has been lost for a long enough time that one may assume the owner has discovered his loss, one may keep the lost item. This is due to the following reason: If the owner knows that he has lost the object and despairs of retrieving it, then the finder may keep it, provided he picked it up only after the owner gave up hope of ever get it back.[15] Therefore, if the finder can reasonably assume that the owner has already given up hope of retrieving the lost object, he may keep it.[16]

What Happened to the "Monetary Mystery"?

Having explored the basic laws of *hashavas aveidah*, we now return to the saga of Hershel's found money.

In our particular case, we can assume that previous tenants of the house lost the money. Therefore, we should be able to identify all the possible candidates, and then try to narrow down the list.

I asked Hershel if he knew who had lived in the house previously. He told me he would contact the previous tenants and find out what he could.

Hershel contacted the previous tenants; a fine, halachically-committed couple, Chaim and Rochel. Hershel asked them if they had hidden money in the house and forgotten about it. Without hinting to them where the hiding place was, so that he would not reveal the *siman*, Hershel asked them if the money might be theirs.

"No, I have no recollection of hiding money in the house that we left," responded Chaim, "I am sure the money is not ours."

From Chaim, Hershel found out the identity of the previous resident of the house, a not-yet-observant Jew, Phil. With a bit of luck, Hershel located Phil, and began to explain to him about the money.

"I hid money all over the house, in every hiding place you can imagine!" responded Phil, "I don't even remember all the hiding places I used. Indeed, I probably didn't take all the money with me when I left. I am sure the money is mine!"

Of course, this statement does not provide us with any help. Maybe the money is indeed Phil's, but he must provide us with a *siman*. His not remembering the *siman* does not allow us to give it to him. For all we know, Phil could be a dishonest person, and the money could belong to one of the residents before him. It could easily be that he was simply trying to acquire a few bucks without any effort, whether or not the money was legitimately his.

Unfortunately, this put Hershel in a very difficult position. As mentioned above, one may not return money to a dishonest person, even if he provides a *siman*, because of concern that he might have "guessed right."[17] Thus, if Phil is indeed dishonest, Hershel cannot trust him, even if Phil would indeed guess where Hershel had found the money.

Hershel attempted to explain to Phil that perhaps he could provide some more information about the money, such as where the money was hidden or how much money there was. Phil became very testy. "I am telling you the money is mine. What's the matter – don't you trust me?!"

Hershel called me back, a bit disappointed. He had tried to fulfill the *mitzvah* of *hashavas aveidah*, but unfortunately the trail ended here. We will never know whether Phil was the legitimate owner of the money, but the *halachah* requires us to be reasonably certain who the owner is before returning the lost item. Furthermore, there was no feasible method of tracing any tenants prior to Phil in order to try determining the money's owner. Hershel assumed that he would have to leave the money where he found it, hoping that perhaps, one day, someone would come by to identify the money properly by its *simanim*.

Failure to Return

In all likelihood, the owner could one day realize that he had left money in the house and come back to claim it. Failure to return for the money could only be attributable to two causes:

1. The owner has forgotten about the money. In this case, one may not take possession of it, since he never intentionally gave up hope of finding it. Furthermore, if at some time he remembers the money, he may remember where he put it and come back to claim it. Thus, the money is still the

property of the person who lost it. In this case, Hershel should leave the money in place as long as he continues to reside in the house.[18]

2. The owner remembers that he hid the money, but cannot remember where. In this case, we could assume that, at the moment he realized that he could not recall where he had put the money and finished searching all possible locations, he gave up hope of ever finding the money again, rendering the money as *hefker*, ownerless. In this scenario, Hershel is permitted to keep the money.[19]

Does the *halachah* allow Hershel to assume a particular scenario? It appears that the authorities have a dispute over which assumption one should make.

What Happened?

Hershel's *rav* believed that under these specific circumstances, one could not assume that the owner forgot where he put the money. One should assume that the owner did not remember placing the money in that particular location. In the latter case, one is required to continue holding the money for the owner, hoping that he may one day return for it.

NOTES

1. *Devarim* 22:1–3; *Shemos* 23:4; *Bava Metzia* 26b.
2. *Sefer HaChinuch* #538; *Shulchan Aruch, Choshen Mishpat* 262:5.
3. *Bava Metzia* 24b.
4. See *Bava Basra* 87b; *Mishpetei Torah* 3:44.
5. *Bava Metzia* 23b.
6. Ibid.
7. *Bava Metzia* 28b.
8. *Shulchan Aruch, Choshen Mishpat* 260:1.
9. *Bava Metzia* 25b.

10. *Bava Metzia* 24a.

11. *Bava Metzia* 22b.

12. *Bava Metzia* 28b.

13. *Bava Metzia* 25b.

14. Ibid.

15. *Bava Metzia* 22b.

16. *Sefer HaChinuch* #538.

17. *Bava Metzia* 28b.

18. *Sma* 262:12.

19. *Shulchan Aruch, Choshen Mishpat* 260:1, as understood by *Pischei Choshen* 1:282.

17

The Dry Cleaner and the Gown

Is the Dry Cleaner Liable for Damages?

The female voice on the other end of the line sounded very familiar. Her voice was full of anger and disappointment. It took me a few minutes to discern what she was trying to communicate.

Once I identified the voice, I realized that this was a woman I knew well who is usually very rational. I also began to understand why she was so upset. Mrs. Stein had been expecting to wear a specific, elegant dress for a family *simchah* and had brought it to the dry cleaner to get it ready. While she was there, she pointed out some stubborn spots on the delicate fabric.

"The dry cleaner managed to remove the stubborn stains," Mrs. Stein told me, "but my gown's color washed out in the process! The gown is now absolutely not wearable! I want the cleaner to pay for the damage in full!"

"I try not to judge a business dispute without hearing the other person's side of the story," I told her.

"That's fine," she responded. "I'll ask the cleaner to call you up to explain his side of the story."

"Are you willing to accept my ruling in this situation?" I asked her.

"Certainly!" she replied.

Precedents in the Torah

While awaiting the cleaner's call, I reviewed the appropriate *halachos*. If someone hires a workman or artisan to process or repair an item, and the workman damages it in the process, he is obligated to pay for its full value, and he does not receive payment for his work.[1] As an example of this *halachah*, the Mishnah discusses the case of someone hired to dye cloth who left the cloth too long in the dye vat and damaged the cloth. The dyer must pay for the value of the cloth he ruined.[2]

If one hired a builder to demolish a property and specified that one wished to reuse the stones in the subsequent reconstruction, if the builder destroyed building stones in the process, he must repay the value of the stones.[3]

If one hires a carpenter to repair a cabinet, and the carpenter breaks it, he must pay for the damage.[4]

Therefore, if the cleaner damaged the gown, he is indeed responsible to compensate Mrs. Stein for its full value. This is assuming that the cleaner does not have a notice posted in his shop that he is not responsible for garments that he damages. According to *halachah*, if the repairman notified his clients in advance that he does not assume responsibility for damage, he absolves himself of responsibility.

The Cleaner Version

The dry cleaner's phone call interrupted my research. His version of the events was somewhat different from Mrs. Stein's.

"Mrs. Stein pointed out the stains she wanted removed," he told me. "In retrospect, I regret that I did not specify to her that the solvents used to remove the stains could change the gown's color.

I do not remember whether the garment was wearable with the stains or not, but I know that people do not usually leave stains on their nice garments."

"Was the garment ruined?" I asked the cleaner. "Not at all," he answered, "I am willing to show it to any expert on women's clothes. We saw the stains and assessed that the best way to remove them was to clean the entire garment evenly with a specific solvent. This is a standard procedure in this type of situation. When you dry clean this way, if the color is affected, the entire garment changes to a consistent new color. I would love to show you the garment so you could see the masterpiece we created!"

The dry cleaner's interpretation of events had us dealing with a very different *she'eilah*! He contended that he used his best professional judgment in removing the stain, and the result was an altered, but perfectly satisfactory and useful garment. According to this understanding, he is entitled to full compensation for his efforts, since he did what Mrs. Stein hired him to do, and there was no damage to the gown, according to him, but rather, an improvement!

I now found myself in a predicament. I knew this dry cleaner well, and as far as I know, he was a very reputable person. Although he could have been covering up for his mistake, I had no reason to suspect him. On the other hand, Mrs. Stein was also a person I respected; a tremendous *baalas chesed* – a classic "pillar of the community." Should I suspect that one of them is not telling the truth?

Human Nature

The fact that I heard two very different versions of the events from the two parties did not mean that either one of them was, G-d forbid, lying or dishonest. Each of them viewed the events that transpired from their own perspective. This is human nature; we tend to see and color events through our own eyes, disregarding the fact that someone else's interpretation may vary considerably from ours.

This is the reason why it is very important for every person to have a good friend who gently challenges our assumptions. It is difficult, and maybe even impossible, for us to be objective about ourselves. A good friend can help us regain our objectivity when we become emotionally wrapped up in ourselves. In this case, if Mrs. Stein had asked a good friend for an honest evaluation, perhaps the friend could have helped her calm down. Similarly, the dry cleaner may have benefited by having someone point out to him that his interpretation of the events and facts may have been somewhat influenced by his personal involvement.

Although this helped me understand the human side of the dry cleaning interaction that took place, it did not help me establish the facts. The question still remained – did the cleaner damage the gown, or not?

Unsolicited Beneficial Work

There was indeed one other possibility: that both sides were right. The dry cleaner did what he thought was best, which was to clean the gown even though its color might fade slightly. To Mrs. Stein, this result was unacceptable. It is possible that had she been told that her gown might fade, she would have rejected this method of dealing with the problem.

If so, a third set of *halachos* applies – where the artisan did perfectly good work, but it was not what he was hired to do, and not what the person wanted. Perhaps, our case is comparable to the case in the Mishnah of someone who hired a worker to dye cloth red, and he dyed it black. In that case, the resultant product is worth more than it was when he started, but the owner did not want black cloth, just as Mrs. Stein did not want a faded gown.

Does the worker receive compensation in this case? Or is he liable for all damages?

In the aforementioned case, Rabi Meir rules that the worker compensates the customer for the value of the cloth that he received and keeps it, regardless of whether the finished product is worth more or less than the original cloth. Rabi Yehudah disagrees, contending that this arrangement benefits the negligent worker too much. Let us assume that the finished black cloth is worth far more than the original undyed cloth was worth. According to Rabi Meir, the dyer would benefit from all this profit. Rabi Yehudah contends that this is unfair – the worker should not benefit from his negligence. Instead, Rabi Yehudah contends that any benefits go to the owner, and this is the final *halachah*. (The actual formula whereby we determine how much, if anything, the worker gets paid is somewhat halachically complicated.)[5]

Three Possible Interpretations

Thus, we now have three possible interpretations of what happened.

1. The dry cleaner ruined the garment and should pay damages (Mrs. Stein's version).

2. The cleaner did the best possible job possible under the circumstances and made an unusable gown perfectly usable. Therefore, Mrs. Stein should pay him in full (the dry cleaner's version).

3. The cleaner exceeded what Mrs. Stein authorized him to do, in which case he would be entitled only to whatever increase in value there is. According to Mrs. Stein, there is none, the gown is not worth more than it was in its stained but non-faded state.

But I am a rabbi and not a prophet. What was I to do? How could I possibly determine what happened?

Making Shalom

Furthermore, there was a more important issue at stake. Whenever I am involved in these types of litigation, I am not satisfied with simply determining the *halachah*: I want the two parties to leave *beshalom*. To me, this is the most important result – that afterwards, there should be no lasting ill feeling.

I thought of a course of action that would accomplish this purpose. First, I asked my wife if she would be willing to look at

Mrs. Stein's gown to see whether she considered the garment unwearable. Of course, I realized that although I value my wife's opinion, she was not going to make the final halachic decision. However, I was looking to see what she thought, and consequently, which direction I might take in resolving this she'eilah.

In truth, this was the most difficult part of the she'eilah. How was I to determine whether the gown was now ruined goods or not? For one woman, a garment may be considered unwearable, whereas to another it can be perfectly fine. The halachah in such a dispute places the burden of proof on the person who wants to collect the money.

I also asked my wife the following question, after first explaining to her that there was a halachic reason why I needed the information (and therefore no lashon hora was involved). I asked her, "Is Mrs. Stein the type of woman who would be bothered by things that others would not notice?" My wife answered that Mrs. Stein is a very discerning dresser. Thus, I realized that it might be that even if the dry cleaner did what most people would consider the correct course of action, Mrs. Stein would not be happy with the results. On the other hand, it might be that the dry cleaner assumed that the garment was fine, but most people would consider it damaged.

Then I called Mrs. Stein to see if she would mind showing the damage to my wife. My wife studied the gown and felt that although it was definitely faded, most women would have worn the garment as is, although a discerning dresser like Mrs. Stein might find the new color unacceptable.

I called the dry cleaner and asked him whether he would be willing to bend over backwards to placate a customer.

"Of course," he responded, "I never gain anything from an angry customer. Do you know how many people might hear a story like this?"

I assured him that I would try my utmost to be sure that Mrs. Stein obeyed the rules of lashon hora. She is a very fine woman and meticulously observant of halachah.

Mrs. Stein agreed to come to my office to discuss the matter. First, I engaged her in some small talk, and then moved the conversation over to the matter at hand. I knew Mrs. Stein to be a woman who was cautious about avoiding *lashon hora*. I just hoped that she had not forgotten to be careful while she had been so agitated about her damaged gown.

Indeed, she told me that she had told only one person, other than me, about the ruined gown. She had deliberately decided to tell a friend who does not know where she takes her dry cleaning, so that there would be no question of *lashon hora*. I was extremely impressed with her care in observing *halachah* under highly stressful circumstances. *Baruch Hashem*, there had been no *lashon hora* said about this matter. And now, to make *shalom* …

I explained to her that I had spoken to the dry cleaner, and that he regretted having not asked her before he used the particular cleaning solution. I also told her that he had used it evenly on the entire garment, so that if it would affect the color of the garment, it would leave it in a pretty shade. I then added that I felt the dry cleaner was not guilty from a halachic point of view, but that he was eager to make some restitution anyway, because he did not want her to be angry with him.

Mrs. Stein stopped and thought about it. "You know, he has always been so accommodating," she mused. "I was just surprised and disappointed by him. I suppose not everyone is as fussy as I am. I would be very satisfied if he would make sure to hang up a note to himself in his shop to make sure that he asks every customer before he does something like this again!"

I had not expected that making *shalom* would be so easy. I guess that sometimes when one tries to do a *mitzvah*, Hashem makes it easier! And my wife tells me that Mrs. Stein wore a different outfit – which was absolutely stunning – to the *simchah*.

NOTES

1. *Shulchan Aruch, Choshen Mishpat* 306:2; 3.
2. *Bava Kama* 100b.
3. *Rema, Choshen Mishpat* 306:2.
4. Rambam, *Hilchos Sechirus* 10:4; *Shulchan Aruch, Choshen Mishpat* 306:2.
5. See Rambam and *Raavad, Hilchos Sechirus* 10:4; *Shulchan Aruch, Choshen Mishpat* 303:6.

18

How Do I Know that I'll Get It Back?

The Kosher Way to Collect a Loan

Although it is a very big *mitzvah* to lend money, some people are reluctant to do so, because they have heard stories of loans that were difficult to collect.

Must one lend someone money if one is not sure it will ever be repaid? What does one do if one lent money to someone who seemed very honest and sincere, but now that it comes time to repay, he informs the lender that he is penniless? What may the lender do, and what may he not do, in order to collect his money? How can he guarantee from the outset that one's money will be returned?

The *Mitzvah* of Lending Money

The Torah requires us to lend money to a poor Jew who needs it.[1] This is stated in the *pasuk* "Im kesef talveh es ami, es he'ani imach" (When you lend money to My people, to the poor person among you).[2] Chazal explain that the word *im* in this *pasuk* should not be translated as "if," which implies that it is optional, but as a commandment – "*When* you lend…"[3] The *poskim* even discuss whether we recite a *berachah* on this *mitzvah*, just as we recite one on *tefillin*, *mezuzah*, and other *mitzvos*.[4] Although the *halachah* is that we do not recite a *berachah*, the mere question shows us the importance of the *mitzvah* of loaning money.

It is a greater *mitzvah* to lend someone money, which helps him to maintain his self-dignity, than it is to give him *tzedakah*, which is demeaning.[5] There is a special *berachah* from Hashem to people who lend money to the poor.

One should not become upset if a poor person returns to borrow money shortly after repaying. One should have an attitude similar to that of a storekeeper: "Does one become angry with a repeat customer? Does one feel that he is a constant bother?" Similarly, one should not turn people away without a loan, but rather view it as a new opportunity to perform a *mitzvah* and to receive extra *berachos*.[6]

The Torah informs us that various levels of priority exist when it comes to giving *tzedakah*. Similar priorities apply to the laws of lending.

One should also lend money to wealthy people who need a loan, but this is not as great a *mitzvah* as lending to the poor. Someone with limited available funds who has requests for loans from both family members and non-family members should lend to family members first. Similarly, if one must choose to whom to lend, one should give priority to a closer family member over a more distant one.

The Unscrupulous Borrower

One is not required to lend money if one knows that the borrower squanders his money and does not repay.[7] In fact, it is better not to lend money if one knows that the borrower will probably not pay it back. A person who squanders money and therefore does not repay his loans is called a *rasha*.[8]

What Are the Responsibilities of a Borrower?

An individual who borrows money must make sure to pay it back. One may not borrow money that he does not think he will be able to repay.

The borrower must use whatever money he has available to pay his debts. He may not make significant contributions to *tzedakah*.[9] He may not purchase a *lulav* and *esrog* if he owes money; instead, he should borrow someone else's.[10]

Furthermore, he is required to pay his loans on time. If his loan is due and he cannot repay it, he is required to use his household items, if necessary, to meet his responsibility to the lender.[11]

It is strictly forbidden to pretend that he does not have money to pay his debts, or even to delay paying them, if he does have the money. It is similarly forbidden for him to hide money, so that the lender cannot collect his due. All of this is obligatory even if the lender is very wealthy.

Collecting Bad Debts

Most people who borrow are meticulous about repaying their debts – and doing so on time. However, it occasionally happens that someone who intended to pay punctually is faced with unexpected circumstances that make it difficult for him to repay the loan.

The Prohibition against Being a *Nosheh*

The prohibition in the Torah, *Lo sihyeh lo kenosheh*, commands the lender not to behave toward the borrower as a creditor. Included in this prohibition is demanding payment from a Jew when one knows that he cannot pay.[12] Also included in this prohibition is that the lender may not even stand in front of the borrower in a manner that might embarrass or intimidate him.[13]

However, if the lender knows that the borrower has resources that he does not want to sell, such as his house, his car, or his furniture, he may harass the borrower, since the borrower is halachically required to dispose of these properties in order to repay his loan.[14] Furthermore, the lender may sue in *beis din* for the rights to collect these items as payment.

(Technically, it is not the borrower's responsibility to sell the items and bring the cash to the lender; he may give them to the lender as payment. The lender must then arrange for a *beis din*, or a panel of three experts in Jewish law, to evaluate the property he has received. If he must hire experts to appraise the property, the expenses are added to the debt. Of course, the lender and borrower can agree to whatever terms are mutually acceptable without involving expert evaluation, provided that in so doing the lender is not receiving anything that the Torah prohibits as interest [*ribbis*]. The vast subject of *ribbis* is beyond the scope of this essay.)

The borrower is, of course, in a very unenviable position. He owes money that he would like to repay, but he is overwhelmed with expenses. He simply does not earn enough money to pay all his creditors. He knows that he could sell his house or his furniture to pay up, but he really does not want to humiliate or cause this level of discomfort to his family.

He should try to appease the lender in whatever way he can, such as asking for better terms or for a delay. He should certainly try to find additional sources of income and work on trimming his expenses. But, he should realize that he is obligated to sell even his household goods to pay off his creditors. Someone who uses his money to purchase items that are not absolutely essential, even *mitzvah* items, and does not pay back money that is overdue, demonstrates a lack of understanding of the Torah's priorities.

The lender may not enter the borrower's house to seize collateral or payment. Some *poskim* contend that the lender may seize property that is not in the borrower's house or on his person.[15] Furthermore, there are authorities who rule that if the borrower has the means to pay but isn't paying, the lender may enter the borrower's house and take whatever he can.[16] One should not rely on this approach without first asking a *she'eilah*.

If the borrower claims that he has absolutely nothing with which to pay, *beis din* can require him to swear to that effect.[17]

A lender who feels that the borrower is hiding money or property may not take the law into his own hands in order to collect, but he may file a claim in *beis din*. If the borrower does not submit to *beis din*'s authority, the lender may request authorization from the *beis din* to sue in secular courts. It is forbidden for him to sue in secular court without halachic approval.

Money-Back Guarantee

As most of us have no doubt experienced at one time or another, it is not pleasant to be owed money that is not repaid. The lender is entitled to get his money back.

Is there a way to lend money and guarantee that it will be returned?

First of all, the lender must ensure that he can prove that the loan transpired. This practice is actually a *halachah*. One is forbidden to lend money without witnesses or other proof, out of concern that this may cause the borrower to sin by denying that the loan exists.[18]

The above is only protection against a borrower denying that he borrowed, which is, fortunately, a rare occurrence. The question is whether there are feasible practices the lender can implement in order fulfill his *mitzvah* of lending to a needy person, yet ensuring that the loan does not become a permanent one.

By the way, one may lend money to a poor person, with the understanding that if the borrower defaults, the lender will subtract the sum from his *tzedakah-maaser* calculation.[19]

Cosigners

The most common method used to guarantee the repayment of a loan is by having someone with a reliable financial reputation cosign for the loan. In *halachah*, this person is called an *areiv*. In common practice, if the borrower defaults, the lender notifies the cosigner that he intends to collect the debt. Usually what happens is that when the lender calls the cosigner, the borrower suddenly shows up at his doorstep with the money.

Standard *Areiv*

There are several types of *areivim* recognized by *halachah*. The simplest type, a standard cosigner, is obligated to pay back the debt, but only after one has attempted to collect from the borrower. If the borrower does not pay because he has no cash, yet he does possess property, the *areiv* can legitimately claim that he is not responsible to pay. The lender would have to summon the borrower and the *areiv* to *beis din* (probably in separate *dinei Torah*), in order to begin payment procedures. Most people who lend money prefer to avoid the tediousness of this process.

Areiv Kablan

Some of this difficulty can be avoided by having the cosigner sign as an *areiv kablan*. This is a more compelling type of cosigning, whereby the lender has the right to make the claim against the cosigner, without suing the borrower first in *beis din*.

The primary difficulty with this approach is that the borrower may be unable to receive a loan, since many potential cosigners do not want to commit themselves to be an *areiv kablan*.

Another Approach

Is there another possibility whereby one can still provide *chesed* to the potential borrower, and yet be reasonably certain to get the money back?

Indeed, there is. The Chafetz Chayim[20] suggests that if one is concerned that the proposed borrower may default, one can insist on receiving an item as collateral, a *mashkon*, to guarantee payment.

Having a loan collateralized is a fairly secure way of guaranteeing that the loan be repaid, but this method is not totally hassle-free. There are two drawbacks that might result from using a *mashkon* to guarantee the repayment of the loan:

    1. Responsibility for the *mashkon*.

    2. Evaluation and conversion of the *mashkon*.

1. Responsibility for the Mashkon

When the lender receives the *mashkon*, he becomes responsible for taking care of it. If it is lost or stolen, the value of the collateral will be subtracted from the loan.[21] If the collateral is worth more than the loan, the lender might be required to compensate the borrower for the difference.[22] The creditor is not responsible for the *mashkon* if it is lost and damaged due to circumstances that *halachah* considers beyond his responsibility.

2. Evaluation and Conversion of the Mashkon

If the collateral is used for the purpose of collecting the debt, in order to protect the borrower's rights, the *mashkon* must either be evaluated by a panel of three experts before it can be sold,[23] or alternatively, sold with the involvement of *beis din*.[24] Some creditors find this step tedious.

However, there are methods whereby one can use a *mashkon* to guarantee a loan and avoid having to evaluate it afterwards:

When arranging the loan, the lender informs the borrower of the following condition: if the loan is not paid when due, the buyer agrees to rely on the lender's evaluation of the *mashkon's* value.[25]

An alternative method is for the lender to inform the borrower: If you do not pay by the day the loan is due, then retroactively, this transaction is not a loan, but rather a sale. The collateral becomes mine, immediately, for the value of the loan money. Such an approach is permitted even if the *mashkon* is worth far more than the loan, without any violation of *ribbis* (prohibited charging of interest), since retroactively, not a loan, but a sale took place.[26]

At times, lenders have asked me for a method whereby they can be certain to receive their money back, and I have suggested the collateral method. Sometimes, I receive the following response: I don't want to be bothered with selling the *mashkon* to get my money back. If I think the borrower is a risk, then I would rather not lend to him.

Do we have the same attitude towards other *mitzvos* we perform? Do we say that we only want to perform *mitzvos* when they are without complications? Certainly not! However, the *yetzer hara* convinces us that lending money is a good deed that one need only perform when it is convenient and one feels like being benevolent, and not when it is going to result in a hassle.

Shlemiel, the Borrower

Nachman once came to me with the following *she'eilah*:

Shlemiel used to borrow money from Nachman regularly, and although Shlemiel always paid him back, he often did so long after the due date. Nachman wanted to know what he could do about this situation. He wanted to perform the tremendous *mitzvah* of lending money, but he wanted his money back within a reasonable period of time.

I suggested to Nachman that he tell Shlemiel that the loan was available, but only if Shlemiel produced a *mashkon* and agreed to the above conditions. Since my suggestion, Nachman has been *zocheh* to fulfill the *mitzvah* of lending money to Shlemiel many times, and not once has a loan been late! Think of how many *berachos* Nachman has received from Hashem, because he is willing to subject himself to the "hassle" of transporting the *mashkon* to a secure place and risk having to sell it, should the need arise!

Why do people view loaning money as an optional "good deed," rather than as a commandment? The Chafetz Chayim[27] raises this question and lists several excuses that people use to avoid lending money. After listing the reasons, the Chafetz Chayim proceeds to refute each one of them. Simply put, the answer to this question is the old Yiddish expression, *Ven es kumt tsu gelt, es iz an andare velt* (When it comes to money, it is a different world).

Truthfully, people find it difficult to part with their money, even temporarily. This is precisely why one receives such immense reward for lending. As Chazal teach us, *lifum tzaara agra* (The reward is proportional to the difficulty the challenge entails).[28]

NOTES

1. Rambam, *Hilchos Malveh Veloveh* 1:1.
2. *Shemos* 22:24.
3. *Mechilta*.
4. *Shu't HaRashba* #18.

5. Rambam ad loc.

6. *Ahavas Chesed* 1:7.

7. *Shulchan Aruch, Choshen Mishpat* 97:4.

8. Rambam, *Hilchos Malveh Veloveh* 1:3.

9. *Sefer Chassidim* #454.

10. See *Pischei Teshuvah, Choshen Mishpat* 97:8.

11. *Nesivos HaMishpat* 86:2; Graz, *Hilchos Halvaah* 1:5.

12. Rambam, *Hilchos Malveh Veloveh* 1:2.

13. *Bava Metzia* 75b; Rambam, *Hilchos Malveh Veloveh* 1:3.

14. See *Shulchan Aruch, Choshen Mishpat* 97:23 for a list of what items he must sell to pay his debt.

15. See *Pischei Choshen*, vol. 1, p. 96.

16. *Shu't Imrei Binah, Dinei Geviyas Chov* chapter 2; *Pischei Choshen* vol. 1, p. 100.

17. Rambam, *Hilchos Malveh Veloveh* 2:2.

18. *Bava Metzia* 75b.

19. *Pischei Choshen*, vol. 1, p. 4.

20. *Ahavas Chesed* 1:8.

21. *Shulchan Aruch, Choshen Mishpat* 72:2.

22. See dispute between *Shulchan Aruch* and *Rema* ibid.

23. *Shulchan Aruch, Choshen Mishpat* 73:15 and *Ketzos HaChoshen*.

24. *Shach.*

25. *Pischei Choshen*, vol. 1, p. 145.

26. *Shulchan Aruch, Choshen Mishpat* 73:17.

27. *Ahavas Chesed* 2:8.

28. *Avos* 5:22.

19

How Not to Do a *Chesed*

Constructive Advice for the Kindhearted

Sometimes, performing *chesed* can lead to unexpected financial distress. However, a little bit of prevention can go a long way in avoiding such unplanned mishaps.

1. ***The automobile deliveries.*** Mrs. Rosenberg's son, Yanky, a trustworthy and serious *yeshivah bachur*, sometimes returns home from yeshivah driving cars that are not his own. He explained to his mother that he is performing a favor for a businessman who needs the cars to be transported from place to place. Mrs. Rosenberg would like to know whether Yanky is running any risk should something happen to the cars while in transit.

2. ***The money couriers.***

   A. Shifrah commutes to work along a route that passes two branches of a local business. The owner asked her if she would transport money back and forth between his two offices. Shifrah asked me whether she bears any halachic liability while performing this favor.

B. Yosef is traveling to Eretz Yisrael, and Mrs. Goldstein asked him to bring some Chanukah *gelt* to her nephew. Rabbi Friedman asked Yosef to bring some money to his daughter there, and Mr. Gordon requested that he transport money to his son. Although Yosef initially combined all the money, he later decided to separate it during the trip, for added security. Upon arrival in Israel, he discovered that some of the money had been stolen. Must Yosef replace the stolen funds? If he is not required to, how do we determine whose money was stolen?

3. ***The wonderful women of* N'shei.** The local *N'shei* chapter conducted one of its wonderful activities to raise money for *tzedakah*. For table décor, they borrowed some expensive vases. Sarah picked up the vases, and brought them to the hall. Rivkah was in charge of placing them on the tables, and Rochel was responsible for returning them. Leah, who was in charge of final clean-up, discovered that Rochel had forgotten to take the vases and now finds herself in a predicament. It is too late at night to call anyone, discover the intended destination of the vases, and return them. If Leah abandons the vases, no one will return them, and they will certainly be lost or broken. There is no room in her small, cramped apartment to keep the vases safe from her frolicking children, even until she arranges for someone to collect them in the morning. What should she do? Feeling that she has no choice, she brings them to her own house, hoping for the best. She calls me the next day, reporting that, unfortunately, some of the vases were broken before she could return them. Is Leah liable? If not, who is?

In all of these cases, the person doing a big *chesed* may have unwittingly stumbled into a major liability. Should one avoid performing *chesed* because of such fears? Of course not! But one should be aware of one's liabilities and how to limit them.

Shomrim

In each of the above cases, the person performing the *chesed* became a *shomer*, because he or she assumed responsibility for someone else's property. We must first review the basic rules of *shomrim*, and then see how these rules apply in each of our cases.

The Torah presents us with three basic categories of *shomrim*:

1. **Shomer chinam.** This *shomer* takes care of an item without receiving any financial benefit at all, even indirectly, and is not permitted to use the item. Although he is unpaid, this *shomer* is still responsible to pay for the item if it was damaged due to his negligence, or if he used it for himself. He is not responsible if he took appropriate care, yet the item was damaged or disappeared.[1] However, even if the *shomer chinam* guarded the item responsibly, the owner can still request that the *shomer* take an oath, swearing that he was indeed careful, did not use, and is not in possession of the item.[2]

2. **Shomer sachar.** This refers to a person who watches over an item in return for some financial or other benefit. This includes a person who rents an item, as well as a craftsman who repairs an object, since in both of these cases the individual is responsible for taking care of the object and receives benefit for his work.[3] Unlike a *shomer chinam*, a *shomer sachar* is responsible to reimburse the owner if the item is lost or stolen, although he is not obligated to pay if the item became lost or damaged through an accident beyond his control.[4]

3. **Sho'el.** This *shomer* borrows an item and receives benefit without paying. He is responsible to pay for any damages to the item, even if the damage is beyond his control. Since he is receiving benefit *gratis*, he must ensure that he returns the item to its owner, even replacing it if necessary. Although beyond the scope of this essay, please note that there are two cases wherein the *sho'el* is not obligated to pay.

Having discussed some of the basic *halachos*, let us consider their effect on the cases I mentioned at the beginning of this essay.

Case 1: The Automobile Deliveries

When Yanky Rosenberg travels long distance, he often drives cars for a car dealer with whom he is acquainted. This arrangement appears to benefit both parties – it provides Yanky with free transportation, and provides the dealer with an inexpensive driver.

Mrs. Rosenberg, however, is concerned about Yanky's potential liability. Her concerns are very valid, because Yanky has the halachic status of a *shomer sachar*, since he receives transportation, which is definitely worth money, in exchange for transporting the vehicle. Therefore, if the car is stolen during the trip, Yanky is fully responsible for the automobile. He is also liable for any damage caused by his negligence. For example, if the car is involved in an accident while Yanky is driving, he is responsible for the damages, if the accident could have been prevented had he been more careful.

After grasping the ramifications of the scenario, Mrs. Rosenberg became very concerned, as she does not want Yanky to maintain halachic responsibility for the automobiles. I told her that there is a simple solution. Yanky can simply inform the car dealer that he is not assuming any responsibility for the vehicles. Although the Torah rules that a *shomer sachar* is *usually* responsible for theft and similar losses, the two parties can negotiate a different arrangement, if they both agree.[5]

Thus, every *shomer* has the right to negotiate his own deal to assume either less or more responsibility than the Torah usually assigns. If Yanky tells the automobile dealer that henceforth he is assuming no responsibility for the cars he drives, and the dealer agrees, Yanky will no longer be responsible for any loss, theft, or damage caused by his negligence.

Of course, the owner may no longer want Yanky to transport the automobiles under such an arrangement. Alternatively, Yanky and the dealer may decide to negotiate an arrangement that limits

Yanky's responsibility. Whatever they decide, at least all parties will know what to expect in the event that there is an unfortunate incident.

Case 2: The Money Couriers

A neighborhood business owner asked Shifrah to transport money for him from one location to another. If Shifrah receives any compensation for this favor, such as the business owner paying for her gas, she becomes a *shomer sachar*, who is obligated to pay for any theft or any loss resulting from her negligence. If she receives nothing for her kindness, she is still a *shomer chinam*. Although her liability is far less, she is still responsible for the loss of the money if she is negligent, and the halachic definition of negligence here is quite broad, as I will explain shortly. Furthermore, should the money be stolen, she may be obligated to take an oath, swearing that she was not negligent. Since most religious people are hesitant to swear, this could present a problem for Shifrah.

Should Shifrah avoid the entire issue and refuse to transport the money?

I advised Shifrah to inform the business owner that she assumes no responsibility for his money in any way. He must absolve her of any obligation to swear if the money is lost or stolen, even if she is negligent. Shifrah explained to the business owner what I had told her, and he agreed that she carry absolutely no responsibility whatsoever for the money. Now, Shifrah can transport the money as a *chesed*, secure in the knowledge that she will incur no liability, no matter what happens.

Yosef, who transported money for people on his trip to Eretz Yisrael, did not inform Mrs. Goldstein, Rabbi Friedman or Mr. Gordon that he was not assuming responsibility for transporting their funds. Thus, he was a *shomer* when the theft occurred. We must determine whether he was a *shomer chinam* or a *shomer sachar*, who receives some benefit for being a *shomer*. For example, if Mr. Gordon gave Yosef a ride home one day in the course of bringing Yosef the money, Yosef might have become a *shomer sachar* for the entire sum of money entrusted to him by Mr. Gordon – if the ride was partially in exchange for transporting the money.

Even if Yosef qualifies as a *shomer chinam*, this does not indicate that he bears no liability. First, we must determine that he was not negligent according to the definition of *halachah*. The halachic definition of negligence for those taking care of money is very stringent. For example, the Gemara rules that one who is responsible for money must hide it in a place where a thief would almost certainly not find it, even if he does not hide his own money so securely. In the time of the Gemara, this meant that a *shomer* had to dig a deep hole in the floor of his house (remember that the floors were made of earth) and bury the money there, thus creating a hiding place that was almost impossible to locate. Storing the money anywhere else constituted negligence and rendered a person liable. Later, when burglars began digging beneath houses in search of hidden valuables, Chazal ruled that burying valuables was considered negligent, and the only responsible way to hide them was in certain specific hiding places in the wall of the house, where one could not tell that the wall was hollow![6]

When a person is transporting money on behalf of someone else, the *Shulchan Aruch*[7] rules that one must keep the money tied in a bundle in his hand, or in another place that is never out of one's sight. Placing someone's money for safekeeping in a seemingly secure place that is behind you, such as in a zipped-closed back pocket, is considered negligent.

Presumably, today we would apply different definitions as to what constitutes a secure place. Thus, it is possible that transporting money for someone without securing it in a money belt or some other very safe location may be considered negligent.

Even if Yosef is not halachically negligent, he still might be required to take an oath, swearing that he secured the money appropriately, and that it was stolen.

Assuming that Yosef is not responsible, we need to determine whose money was lost. This may depend on several factors. Where was the money placed? Did Yosef store each person's money in a different location? Did he keep his money together with their money?

At this point, I advised that all four parties (Yosef, Mrs. Goldstein, Rabbi Friedman and Mr. Gordon) should agree to submit the *she'eilah* to one *rav*, who could then rule whether Yosef is obligated, and if he is not, how to divide the remaining money among the three claimants. Since they did not choose me to be their arbiter, I do not know what the final decision was.

Incidentally, this *she'eilah* could have been resolved very easily – if Yosef had informed Mrs. Goldstein, Rabbi Friedman and Mr. Gordon that he was not assuming any responsibility for the money, as I advised Yanky Rosenberg and Shifrah to do. In such a case, one would only have to resolve the manner in which the recipients divide the remaining money.

Case 3: The Wonderful Women of *N'shei*

Let us determine which, if any, of the wonderful *N'shei* ladies is responsible to pay for the broken vases.

To review the case: Sarah borrowed vases for a *N'shei* function and transported them to the hall. Rivkah was responsible for placing them on the tables, and Rochel was supposed to return them, but she forgot. Leah discovered the forgotten vases, took them home, against her better judgment, and some of them were broken before she could return them. Who is liable for the vases?

Here, too, a bit of advance planning would have been very helpful. When Sarah went to borrow the vases, did she clarify that she was borrowing them on behalf of *N'shei*? Did *N'shei* authorize her to render the organization responsible? Who, within *N'shei*, can authorize assigning responsibility to the organization for borrowing an item?

If we can determine that Sarah was authorized to borrow the vases on behalf of *N'shei*, and the lender understood this and agreed to it, then Sarah would not be personally responsible for the vases. However, if no one clarified these issues, Sarah is the legal borrower of the vases.

Did Sarah have permission to give the vases to someone else? If she did not, then she is responsible, regardless of who was subsequently negligent with the vases. However, if the lender understood that other people would be using the vases, then Sarah is not the only party responsible, and Rivkah would become responsible, as soon as she began placing the vases on the tables.[8]

But then, you'll tell me, Rochel should be responsible for not returning the vases!

However, here we have an interesting problem. Although Rochel forgot to pick up the vases and return them, she technically never became responsible for the vases. This is because of the following *halachah* in the laws of *shomrim*: according to most opinions, a *shomer* becomes responsible only when he or she picks up the item, or if someone places the item in his or her jurisdiction. This transfer of responsibility is referred to as the *shomer* making a *kinyan* on the object. Since Rochel never picked up the vases and never made a *kinyan* on them, she never became responsible for them.[9]

There is a dissenting opinion that contends that the *shomer* can assume responsibility without making a *kinyan* on the object, but only in the following way: the *shomer* assumes responsibility for the item, and the person who owns it or was previously responsible for it stops assuming responsibility for the item. According to this opinion, the fact that the *shomer* assumes responsibility for the item and the owner walks away, shifts responsibility to the *shomer*.[10]

However, this did not occur in our case, since Rochel did not assume responsibility for the vases at the time that Rivkah relinquished responsibility.

Thus, at the time that Leah found the vases on the table, no one was assuming responsibility for them. The responsible party at that moment was either Sarah, who originally borrowed them, or Rivkah, who was the last person to take responsibility. Who the *shomer* is would depend on whether the lender of the vases assumed that several people would be in charge of them. If the lender understood this, then the responsibility transferred from Sarah to Rivkah, and if not, Sarah remains the responsible party.

Thus, when Leah found the vases, she was doing a favor either for the organization, the owner of the vases, for Sarah, or for Rivkah. In any of these instances, she did not want to assume responsibility, but simply wanted to save them from certain loss or damage. Does this release Leah from legal responsibility?

I have been unable to find clear sources that discuss this particular *she'eilah*. I discussed it with some prominent *poskim*, and received differing opinions. One contended that Leah is indeed responsible for the vases, notwithstanding her hesitation to take them. Another *posek* assumed that Leah is not responsible, since they would have certainly lost had she not taken them, and she took them only because she felt that maybe this way they would not be destroyed.

I suggested to these wonderful women that they establish a future policy of the organization assuming responsibility for any items borrowed on its behalf, and arranging that any losses of this type be subtracted from the profits of the benefit.

Careful *Chesed*

As we can see, the laws regarding responsibility for possessions are very complex and sometimes lead to surprising conclusions. In our cases, each participant was performing a *chesed* that could easily have created a substantial financial responsibility. These *halachos* help us highlight the importance of taking care of another's property. While we certainly shouldn't hesitate to perform acts of *chesed*, recognizing and preparing for the halachic ramifications of our actions is undoubtedly worthwhile. Of course, if one's act of kindness results, unfortunately, in an unexpected predicament, he or she should not regret the act of *chesed* performed, but rather resolve to better protect himself in the future.

NOTES

1. *Shulchan Aruch, Choshen Mishpat* 291:1.
2. *Shulchan Aruch, Choshen Mishpat* 295:1–2.

3. *Bava Metzia* 80b.

4. *Bava Metzia* 93a.

5. *Bava Metzia* 94a.

6. *Bava Metzia* 42a.

7. *Choshen Mishpat* 291:20.

8. See *Shulchan Aruch, Choshen Mishpat* 291:22.

9. *Shitah Mekubetzes, Bava Metzia* 98b, quoting Raavad; *Shulchan Aruch, Choshen Mishpat* 303:1.

10. *Rosh, Bava Metzia* 8:15; *Rema, Choshen Mishpat* 340:4; see *Shulchan Aruch, Choshen Mishpat* 291:5, who cites both opinions.

20

Anyone for a Buffalo Burger?

The Debate Whether Animals Require a *Mesorah*

Reb Yehudah, a respected Israeli *talmid chacham*, calls me with the following question: His grandparents have retired and moved to Israel. Now, they have invited the entire family over for a *chanukas habayis*, where Zeide is proudly planning to serve barbecued "buffalo burgers" that he brought from America. Reb Yehudah cannot figure out how his grandfather can serve buffalo, or more accurately, bison meat, and Zeide, a *frum* man all his life, cannot figure out what the problem is – after all, he specially purchased meat with the finest *hechsher*. I was called upon to mediate.

Before discussing the halachic issues regarding giraffe burgers and buffalo steaks, we will need some background information.

Some Basic Animal Facts

The Torah writes: Hashem spoke to Moshe and to Aharon to say: "Speak to the children of Israel, to say, 'These are the beasts from which you may eat: from the animals that are upon the ground, whatever has a split hoof that is separated completely and ruminates (chews its cud) among the animals, those you may eat.'"[1] Thus, the Torah defines any land animal with a totally split hoof that chews its cud as kosher. These two signs, or *simanim*, indicating that their proud owner is kosher, are possessed by sheep, goats, the many varieties of deer and antelope, as well as the entire bovine family, including Western domesticated cattle, Indian zebu cattle, Asian water buffalo, African cape buffalo, European bison (also called the *wisent*), American bison (colloquially and inaccurately referred to in North America as *buffalo*), and Himalayan yak. On the other hand, although a camel chews its cud and has a split hoof, since its hoof is only partially split and not fully separated, it is not kosher.[2] Although I have read articles claiming otherwise, visual inspection of giraffe feet shows that they have fully split hooves.

Land Animals vs. Birds

There is a major halachic difference between land animals and birds in determining whether a species is kosher. Unlike kosher animals, which are identified by the above two *simanim*, birds are determined to be kosher if they are omitted from the Torah's list of twenty-four nonkosher birds. Since many thousands of bird species exist, it is obvious that most are kosher. The question is: how does one identify the nonkosher varieties?

Simanim vs. *Mesorah*

The Gemara[3] specifies four identifying features (*simanim*); any bird species that possesses all four features is kosher. However, many Rishonim contend that we do not rely on our understanding of these *simanim* and eat only fowl for which we have an oral tradition, a *mesorah*, attesting to its kashrus.[4] The *Shulchan Aruch*[5] rules that one may rely on *simanim*, while the *Rema*[6] cites the custom of not eating any species of bird without a *mesorah*.

In addition to our basic background in identifying kosher species of land animals and of birds, we need to distinguish between two categories of kosher animals.

Beheimah vs. Chayah

Kosher land animals are divided into two categories, *beheimah* and *chayah*. Although *beheimah* (pl., *beheimos*) is often translated as *domesticated species* and *chayah* (pl., *chayos*) as *wild species*, these definitions are halachically inaccurate, as we will see.

There are three halachic differences between a *beheimah* and a *chayah*.

1. Cheilev – *Forbidden Fat*

The Torah forbade consuming certain fats called *cheilev*, most of which protect the stomachs and kidneys.[7] Eating *cheilev* is a very serious halachic prohibition, *kareis*, similar in severity to eating on Yom Kippur![8]

The prohibition of *cheilev* applies to all species of *beheimah*, but does not apply to *chayos*.[9] Thus, someone eating the fat protecting the kidney of a properly slaughtered kosher sheep or calf has violated *kareis*, whereas the greatest *tzaddik* may eat the *cheilev* of a deer, which is a *chayah*. Thus one may enjoy a sumptuous venison roast, without concern that he is eating any forbidden fat!

2. Kisui Hadam – *Covering the Blood*

Another *mitzvah* that is affected by whether a species is a *chayah* or a *beheimah* is the *mitzvah* of *kisui hadam*, covering the blood immediately after *shechitah*. This *mitzvah* applies to *chayah* species (and to fowl), but not to *beheimos*.[10] Prior to covering this blood, we recite a *berachah*, as we do when fulfilling most *mitzvos*.

Thus, if a species is a *chayah*, one is required to cover the blood spilled during *shechitah*. So, after performing *shechitah* on our deer, one recites a *berachah* and then covers the blood with dirt or sawdust. If it is a *beheimah*, there is no requirement to cover the blood.

3. Korbanos

A third *mitzvah* affected by whether a species is a *chayah* or a *beheimah* is the offering of *korbanos*. One may not offer *chayos* on the *mizbei'ach* in the Beis HaMikdash; only *beheimos* are kosher for this purpose.[11] Thus, although deer are kosher, we may not use them as *korbanos*.

Koy – An Animal without a Sense of Identity!

The Mishnah[12] discusses a species called *koy* (sometimes pronounced *kvee*), whose status is unclear. Although it is certainly a kosher species, we do not know whether it is a *beheimah* or a *chayah*. Due to this uncertainty, it has the stringencies of both categories: its fat is forbidden and one must cover its *shechitah* blood, but without a *berachah*. We omit the *berachah* because we are uncertain whether the Torah requires covering its blood. If there is indeed no *mitzvah*, reciting a *berachah* before covering its blood would be a *berachah levatalah*, a *berachah* recited in vain. As a result, we cover the blood, which *may* be a *mitzvah*, but do not recite a *berachah*, since perhaps it is not.

We have established that one can have kosher venison roast and need not be concerned about its *cheilev*, and that, as a self-respecting *chayah*, it is not acceptable as a *korban*. Serving venison on Pesach would be a welcome change of pace and provide a conversation piece, but one may not eat roast venison at the Seder, since the custom is not to eat any roast meat that night.[13]

Since there are several halachic differences between *beheimah* and *chayah*, we need to define which species are *beheimos*, and which are *chayos*. After all, no one wants to eat kidney fat of a *beheimah* thinking that it was a *chayah*!

What Is a *Chayah*?

The Written Torah did not indicate the defining characteristics distinguishing *beheimos* from *chayos*, leaving these rules to the Torah Shebe'al Peh, the Oral Torah. The Gemara[14] mentions several characteristics, mostly dependent on the animal's horns: a branched horn is indicative of a *chayah*, whereas nonbranched horns may indicate either a *chayah* or a *beheimah*, depending on whether they grow in layers, are grooved, and whether their tips are curved or straight.[15] Therefore, any species possessing branched horns or antlers, like those found on most deer, is a *chayah*, whereas those with straight horns may be either a *chayah* or a *beheimah*, depending on the other criteria. Since all antelope (a general category that includes several dozen species) have unbranched horns, one would need to examine the horns of each species to determine whether it is a *beheimah* or a *chayah*. (Technically speaking, the difference between deer and antelope is that deer have antlers that shed and re-grow annually, whereas antelope have permanent unbranched horns.)[16]

Note that whether a species is categorized as a *beheimah* or as a *chayah* has no bearing on whether it is domesticated or not. Reindeer, although domesticated, are clearly *chayos*, since they have branched antlers, whereas there are nondomesticated species that are almost certainly *beheimos* according to *halachah*.

Buffalo

The *Shulchan Aruch*[17] rules that one does not perform *kisui hadam* for a buffalo; this ruling renders it a *beheimah*. (He is presumably referring to the Asian water buffalo, which was domesticated in Southern Europe hundreds of years before the *Shulchan Aruch*. He is certainly not referring to the American bison, considering that the *Shulchan Aruch* was compiled before American bison were brought to Europe.) If there was any uncertainty regarding its status as a *beheimah*, the *Shulchan Aruch* would require *kisui hadam* without a *berachah* – after all, we would not ignore this *mitzvah*, particularly since it is easy to perform. However, the *Rema*[18] rules that the status of the buffalo is uncertain and contends that one should cover its blood, but without a *berachah*. According to both opinions, the *cheilev* is forbidden – according to the *Shulchan Aruch*, definitely, as the *cheilev* of a *beheimah*, and according to the *Rema*, because of doubt.

A Second Introduction

According to what we have so far explained, the North American bison, which ruminates and has clearly split hooves, is without doubt a kosher species. Referring to our opening question: what made Reb Yehudah, our Israeli *talmid chacham*, think that bison is nonkosher?

The controversy that erupted in Reb Yehudah's family centered around how to interpret the words of the major halachic authority, the *Shach*. Commenting on the *Shulchan Aruch's* definition of the differences between a *beheimah* and a *chayah*, the *Shach*[19] writes, "I did not elaborate … since today we only use that for which we have a *mesorah*." He then concludes with a reference to the laws of kosher birds. The *Shach's* comparison of the laws of animals to that of birds implies that accepted practice is to eat only land animal species that have a *mesorah* of being eaten, and not to rely on the *simanim* and presume that they are kosher, even when these *simanim* are obvious! This seems to run counter to the Gemara's ruling that *simanim* are adequate for establishing an animal's kosher status.

The *Pri Megadim*, the major commentary on the *Shach*, discusses this difficulty and concludes that the *Shach* meant something else: since the defining distinctions between a *chayah* and a *beheimah* are sometimes unclear, we do not eat the *cheilev* of any species unless we have a *mesorah* that it is indeed a *chayah*. In practical terms, this means that the only land animals whose *cheilev* we permit are deer, since they are the only *chayah* species for which we have a definite *mesorah*. Therefore, according to the *Pri Megadim*, if someone moves to an area where he encounters a new species that has branched antlers like a deer, has split hooves, and chews its cud, he may eat the meat of this animal (after properly *shechting* and salting it), but he may not eat the *cheilev*, even though it is certainly a *chayah*.

Another Interpretation of the *Shach*

Not all halachic authorities interpret the *Shach* as the *Pri Megadim* does. The *Chazon Ish*[20] explains the *Shach* literally and also understands the rulings of other authorities[21] as agreeing with his interpretation. In his opinion, the *Shach* is referring to a *minhag*, established in his generation or earlier, not to eat any animal species for which there was no *mesorah*. The *Chazon Ish* suggests several reasons why such a *minhag* may have begun, including the possibility that people would not know how to check whether this unfamiliar animal is a *treifah* (has some flaw that renders it nonkosher), or that they may assume that it is a *chayah* when it is not and mistakenly permit its *cheilev*.

On the other hand, several other prominent *poskim*[22] were unaware of such a *minhag*, and, in addition, many authorities question why early *poskim* never clearly mention such a practice.

Controversial Results – 1950 in Madagascar

In 1950, there was an attempt to import Madagascar beef from a variety of cattle called *zebu* into the new State of Israel. The zebu, the common cattle of India, has some features noticeably different from those of the common European beef cattle, including a large hump between its shoulders, and a very large hanging fold of skin under its throat called a dewlap. It definitely ruminates and has fully split hooves.

A dispute developed between the Chazon Ish and Rav Herzog, the first chief rabbi of the State of Israel, regarding whether this meat could be considered kosher and be imported into Eretz Yisrael. Rav Herzog contended that there was no need to have a *mesorah* that a species of beef is kosher, and the Chazon Ish objected. To avoid a major dispute within the fledgling country, Rav Herzog did not allow the beef into the country.

1990s in South America

More recently, a major controversy developed in Eretz Yisrael regarding the origin of the kosher beef raised in South America. Land in Israel is scarce, making it impractical to raise large quantities of cattle, whereas much of South America is perfect for raising beef cattle. In recent years, even the *hechsherim* with the highest standards have arranged for *shechitah* in South America, significantly lowering the price of beef.

A question arose regarding the common breeds of South American beef cattle, because they included animals crossbred from different varieties, including the zebu. Rav Elyashiv contended that one should not slaughter these cattle for kosher use without verifying that they are not descended from zebu cattle. Other Eretz Yisrael *poskim* were not concerned about this possibility, contending that even if a *minhag* exists not to eat zebu, the practice does not include beef varieties that look like European cattle, even if their ancestral background may include zebu.

Giraffe Burgers

Certainly the Chazon Ish would not approve of giraffe meat, even though, contrary to a common misconception, a giraffe has fully split hooves and ruminates. Other than the Chazon Ish's concern about *mesorah*, there is only one halachic reason to ban giraffe meat – the opinion of the *Beis Yaakov*, quoted above, that a *chayah* must have horns. Although a giraffe has boney protrusions on the top of its head, some might argue that these are not true horns, thus concluding that a giraffe is nonkosher, according to this opinion of the *Beis Yaakov*. However, since most authorities reject this approach, the giraffe can safely be regarded as a kosher species because of its *simanim*.

Actually, to the best of my knowledge, no one has ever *shechted* a giraffe because of several practical concerns. Giraffe meat is so tough that even non-Jews are not tempted to eat its meat. Also, giraffes are very expensive zoo animals, and are extremely powerful creatures, difficult to convince that they should cooperate with the *shochet*. However, there is no truth to the persistent rumor that no one knows where to *shecht* a giraffe. The area of its neck appropriate for *shechitah* may run up to seven feet long, certainly many times the length of the corresponding *shechitah* area of a dove.

Buffalo Burgers

At this point, we will return to our original discussion. Reb Yehudah, an Israeli *avreich*, has been invited to a bison barbecue hosted by his grandfather. Reb Yehudah follows all of Rav Elyashiv's rulings, and certainly those of the Chazon Ish, to the letter. Someone like him may not eat from a species such as bison, which obviously cannot have a long-standing *mesorah*, since it is a native American. Reb Yehudah could not comprehend how someone could provide a *hechsher* for a product that the Chazon Ish would prohibit.

On the other hand, not all *chareidi* Eretz Yisrael *poskim* accept the Chazon Ish's ruling in this matter. In a responsum addressed to some Chassidic *poskim* in North America, Rav Wosner[23] ruled that one may slaughter and eat species that do not have a *mesorah*. He was uncertain whether the *Chachmas Adam* and the *Shach* ever meant that land animal species require a *mesorah*. However, Rav Wosner ruled this way only for *chutz laaretz* and alluded to the possibility that one should be stringent in Eretz Yisrael, out of deference to the Chazon Ish.

Creating Shalom

With this background, I will explain how I mediated the family feud that had developed between Zeide and Reb Yehudah. Reb Yehudah called me first. I explained to him that although Rav Elyashiv and the Chazon Ish would clearly prohibit bison because of *minhag*, many prominent *poskim* dispute that such a *minhag* exists, contending that one may eat a species that is identifiably kosher. Thus, someone who follows Rav Elyashiv or the Chazon Ish in halachic decisions should indeed not eat a species that has no *mesorah*. On the other hand, one who follows other *poskim* is entitled to rely on those opinions who consider these species to be kosher based on *simanim*.

I then spoke to Zeide, who was perturbed that his grandson did not consider him kosher enough, and that "Yehudala" was going off the deep end with his *chumros*. I explained that although American *poskim* rule bison to be kosher, once the Chazon Ish holds that a *minhag* exists to eat animals only with a *mesorah*, the people among whom Yehudah lives will not be lenient, especially as doing so would be against the Chazon Ish's position. I assured Zeide that Yehudah was not hunting (no pun intended) for *chumros*, but that in his circle, this was accepted *halachah*. Although Zeide was disappointed that

Yehudah would never enjoy "buffalo," he accepted my explanation and served beef steak, presumably not zebu, in addition to his buffalo burgers.

NOTES

1. *Vayikra* 11:1–3.
2. *Vayikra* 11:4.
3. *Chullin* 61b.
4. *Rashi, Chullin* 62b s.v. *Chazyuha*.
5. *Yoreh Deah* 82:2.
6. 82:3.
7. *Chullin* 93a.
8. *Kerisos* 2a.
9. *Chullin* 89b.
10. *Chullin* 83b.
11. *Zevachim* 34a; Rambam, *Hilchos Issurei Mizbei'ach* 5:6.
12. *Bikkurim* 2:8-11.
13. *Shulchan Aruch, Orach Chayim* 476:2.
14. *Chullin* 59b.
15. *Rashi,* ibid.; cf. *Rabbeinu Chananel.*
16. The *Shu't Beis Yaakov* #41, quoted by *Pischei Teshuvah, Yoreh Deah* 80:1, contends that a *chayah* without horns is not kosher at all, but this approach is rejected by other *halachic* authorities (see *Pischei Teshuvah, Yoreh Deah* 80:1).
17. *Yoreh Deah* 28:4.
18. Ibid.
19. *Yoreh Deah* 80:1.
20. *Yoreh Deah* 11:4, 5.
21. *Chochmas Adam; Aruch Hashulchan.*
22. *Kaf HaChayim* 80:5; *Darchei Teshuvah* 80:3.
23. *Shu't Shevet HaLevi* 10:114.

21

Beeing Kosher

The *Kashrus* of Bee Products

There is a general halachic rule that products derived from nonkosher creatures are nonkosher. Therefore, eggs of nonkosher birds and fish, and milk from nonkosher mammals are not kosher. Honey is an exception, its production by the bee, which is itself nonkosher, notwithstanding. Why is honey kosher? And what about other byproducts produced by animals, like shellac and beeswax?

1. *A BEE C's.* Insightful Devorah asks me: "If honey comes from bees, why is it kosher – whereas camel milk, ostrich eggs, and sturgeon roe are not?"

2. **Beenah Yeseirah.** Beena calls with the following question: "I have heard that there is a halachic controversy about the *kashrus* of resinous glaze and vegetable coatings. Could you please clarify the subject for me?"

3. *Vitamin Bee.* Malka is a health food devotee and asks me if beeswax is kosher.

Bee Aware

Regarding our first question, the Gemara records a dispute between an anonymous scholar, called the Tanna Kamma, and Rabi Yaakov.[2] The Tanna Kamma contends that honey is not *produced* by bees, but is simply modified plant nectar, unlike milk and eggs that are produced by the nonkosher species. To produce honey, bees suck nectar from flowers and deposit it into special honey-sacs. Inside the sacs, enzymes contained in the bee's saliva convert the nectar into honey, which the bees store in the honeycomb until they need it for food, or until the hive is raided by a two-legged forager. The nectar is never "digested" by the bee, but rather, is transformed into honey. For this reason, the Tanna Kamma rules that honey is kosher.

Rabi Yaakov permits honey for a different reason. He contends that honey is not included in the universal rule prohibiting extracts of nonkosher species. He derives his decision from the word *zeh* in the verse *ach es zeh tochelu mikol sheretz ha'of* (only this may you eat from among small flying creatures).[3] Although the bee itself is forbidden, what it produces is permitted.

According to Rabi Yaakov, the method bees use to produce honey would not exclude it from the prohibition; it is kosher only because the Torah provided it with a unique status. His approach is referred to as *gezeiras hakasuv*, a special Biblical ruling.

Bee Different

Do any practical differences arise from this dispute between the Tanna Kamma and Rabi Yaakov? The Gemara states the following distinction: Two non-bee insects, *gizin* and *tzirin*, produce a honey through the same process as bees. (The exact identity of these species is unclear. Modern science knows of several species that produce sweet substances from nectar, although none are as popular as bee honey, and to the best of my knowledge, none of them are commercially produced.)

Whether this "honey" is kosher depends on the dispute between the Tanna Kamma and Rabi Yaakov. According to the Tanna

Kamma, these honeys should be kosher just like bee honey, since they are merely processed flower nectar.

According to Rabi Yaakov, however, only bee honey has a unique kosher status, because that is the common honey that the Torah permits. The Torah never permitted *gizin* honey and *tzirin* honey, even though they are very similar to the bee product. Therefore, according to Rabi Yaakov, "honey" produced by any insect other than the honeybee is not kosher.

At this point, we can answer Devorah's question: "If honey comes from bees, why is it kosher, whereas camel milk, ostrich eggs, and sturgeon roe are not?" To answer succinctly: According to the Tanna Kamma, honey is not a product of the bee. According to Rabi Yaakov, the Torah specifically permitted honey.

Bee Analytic

Before we proceed to answer Beena's question about the halachic controversy concerning resinous glaze and vegetable coatings, we need to analyze the opinion of the Tanna Kamma. Even though honey is basically converted nectar, bee saliva concentrated the nectar and transformed it into honey. Why, then, is honey not forbidden, either because of the admixture of bee saliva, or because it requires the bee's processing?

This question is, indeed, not a recent one. An early Torah authority, the Ohr HaChayim, in his work on *Yoreh Deah* entitled *Pri To'ar*, already noted that the bee does more than simply gather and concentrate flower nectar, because concentrated nectar is very different from honey. The Ohr HaChayim explains that since the main ingredient in the sweetness of honey is the nectar, *halachah* ignores the contribution of the bee and treats this food as kosher.[4] We will soon analyze more thoroughly the significance of the Ohr HaChayim's point.

Bee Decisive

Does the practical *halachah* follow the more lenient approach of the Tanna Kamma and permit the "honey" of *gizin* and *tzirin*, or does it abide by the stricter ruling of Rabi Yaakov, forbidding these "honeys"? The Rishonim discuss this question, and disagree as to whether the other honeys mentioned are kosher or not. The *Shulchan Aruch* quotes the lenient approach as the primary opinion, although he also mentions the more stringent position of Rabi Yaakov.[5] This means that the *Shulchan Aruch* himself concludes that one may eat the honey produced by the insects other than the honeybee, provided that local custom is not stringent.[6] However, there are other authorities who feel that one should follow the stringent position.[7]

Are there any other contemporary foods that may have the same *heter* that applies to honey? In other words, are there any other foods that derive from a nonkosher creature, and yet, are considered kosher? Indeed, there may be.

Beeing Shellacked!

Shellac is used both to provide the hard coating on certain candies and also as an ingredient in the coatings that are sprayed onto fresh produce to increase shelf life and make the produce more appealing. Shellac, also called resinous glaze or confectioner's glaze, is a glandular secretion of the female lac insect, *Kerria lacca*, a native-born citizen of India and Thailand that lives and reproduces on the branches and twigs of its host tree. These South Asian scale insects secrete hard layers of resin as a protective covering for their larvae. The word shellac is derived from the Indian word *laksha* and is used to identify the refined, or processed, lac resin. Seemingly, this product presents a *kashrus* concern, since it is produced by an insect, and it is not honey. Is there any halachic literature discussing the *kashrus* of shellac?

Bee Coated

Indeed, several responsa discuss the kosher status of shellac or glaze. In 5725/1965, Rav Nachum Kornmehl, a *talmid chacham* of note, and at that time the *rav hamachshir* of the Barton's Candy Company, asked Rav Moshe Feinstein if this glaze may be used to coat kosher candies. For a variety of reasons, Rav Moshe concluded that the shellac glaze is kosher. First, Rav Moshe assumed that according to the Tanna Kamma, shellac is kosher, for the same reason that honey is kosher: The lac insect imbibes sap from its host tree and converts it into shellac. Thus, we should consider the shellac not a product of the insect, but transformed sap. Rav Moshe then suggested that the same scriptural source that Rabi Yaakov cites to permit honey may also permit shellac. (Why shellac is different from *gizin* honey and *tzirin* honey, both of which Rabi Yaakov forbids, is beyond the scope of our essay.) Rav Moshe added other reasons to permit the shellac glaze, including that the percentage of shellac used in the coating is extremely small and it is therefore *bateil* (negligible), and that shellac is inherently tasteless.[8]

I found a different responsum on the use of shellac by Dayan Yitzchak Weiss, where he suggests that it may be permitted, since it is used only to allow the product to maintain color, a function in which its role is secondary to the coloring and sheen agents.[9]

Based on these responsa, most supervisory organizations in the United States treat shellac as kosher. Although there are other potential concerns about coatings, as of this writing, the consensus of the major kashrus organizations in the United States is that there is sufficient halachic reason to permit the consumer to use coated produce.[10]

However, in Eretz Yisrael, Rav Moshe's approach was less accepted and, as a result, none of the *mehadrin hechsherim* treat glaze as kosher. These *hechsherim* monitor which coatings, if any, are used on produce sold under their supervision. Indeed, there have been instances of fruit exported from the United States to Israel that the *mehadrin hechsherim* in Israel barred from the produce departments under their certification.

Bee Perceptive

The basic criticism of the Eretz Yisrael *hechsherim* of Rav Moshe's position is that honey is unusual – the Gemara states that the bee does not produce the honey, whereas one should at least suspect that shellac is produced by the lac insect. Rav Moshe, on the other hand, assumes that shellac is permitted according to the Tanna Kamma; most of his discussion centers on whether Rabi Yaakov would also be lenient. Why does Rav Moshe assume that shellac is to the lac, as honey is to the bee? Perhaps shellac is to lac, as egg is to ostrich, or milk is to camel?

Rav Moshe makes no reference to the comments of the *Pri To'ar*, but perhaps we can assume that he applied the same logic as is found there. Although there is a clear difference between the nectar that enters the bee and the honey that exits, nevertheless, we say that honey is plant nectar with minor modification. The *Pri To'ar* notes that the contribution of the bee is not significant enough to render honey nonkosher. Similarly, Rav Moshe understands that the lac's contribution to shellac is insignificant: the lac ingests sap from its host tree and then modifies this sap into shellac. Therefore, the resultant glaze is obviously kosher, according to the Tanna Kamma.

We can now answer Beena's question regarding the controversy about resinous glaze and vegetable coatings. American *hechsherim* treat fruit and vegetable coatings as kosher, whereas Israeli *mehadrin hechsherim* insist on verification for the sources of the coatings.

In my opinion, a consumer has the right to be lenient following the accepted local practice. To quote the Gemara, *nahara nahara upashtei*: literally, each river follows its own course, or, there are different halachic customs, each with a valid halachic source.[11] The equivalent English expression is: There is more than one way to skin a bee.

Beeswax

Beeswax is the substance bees use to construct the chambers of their hive, in which the young are raised and the honey and pollen are stored. To stimulate the production of beeswax, the honeybees feed themselves with honey and huddle together to raise the temperature of the cluster. Producing one pound of wax requires the bees to consume about *ten pounds* of honey! Although beeswax is not usually considered food, it is sometimes used as a polish for candies, fruits or nuts, and also as a flavor ingredient. It has a subtle, natural aroma – the fragrance of honey intermingled with the other scents present in a beehive. It is pleasant enough that some honey lovers chew it like gum or swallow it as roughage.

Is beeswax kosher? One early authority, the Levush, understands that beeswax is indeed kosher, stating that it consists of the ingredients removed from the nectar during honey production.[12] Thus, whichever rationale permits honey will also permit wax. (It should be noted that contemporary science assumes that glands on the sides of the bee's body secrete beeswax.)

I have seen sources that rally support for the Levush's position from a statement in the Rambam's commentary on the *mishnayos*,[13] which implies that earlier generations extracted honey from a hive by simply heating the entire hive until its contents melted. This would imply that the entire contents of the hive is kosher, not only the honey. (In actuality, it seems that the beeswax was probably removed by boiling the honeycomb in water and skimming the wax off the top, which could still be used as evidence that the wax is kosher, because otherwise heating the honeycomb would probably be prohibited.)

Others feel that this description by the Rambam does not demonstrate that beeswax is kosher, for the following reason: A melted hive will definitely include bees, larvae, and bee-parts in the honey. Obviously, these insect parts are not kosher. If so, how could they melt the entire hive and disregard the obvious nonkosher components? The answer is that these bee parts become *bateil* in the final product. There is no problem here either of *ein mevatelin issur lechatchilah*, that one may not intentionally attempt to nullify a prohibited substance, since one's intention here is to remove the honey in an easy way; one is not trying to include the bee parts.[14]

In practice, most, but not all authorities rule, as the Levush does, that beeswax is kosher.[15]

Bee Careful

May honey be purchased without a *hechsher*?

All commercially available honey today is bee honey, and

all *should* be kosher. The different varieties of bee honey, such as wildflower, clover, peach blossom, orange blossom, etc., are produced from different types of nectars, and are all products of the honeybee. Since honey is basically concentrated flower nectar, the source of the nectar obviously has a great impact on the taste.

However, some companies add flavoring to their honey. For example, they add orange flavor to honey and label it "orange honey." Any reputable company will clearly mention this on the label. However, how does one know for certain that the Brand X honey one has purchased is from a reputable company?

Bee Truthful

Every year prior to Rosh Hashanah, Israeli newspapers contain reports about unscrupulous companies selling adulterated honey. Certainly, one should be careful to purchase honey and not an adulterated product, particularly since one has no idea what the manufacturer may have added to it. However, from a strictly halachic point of view, the various cheap sweetening ingredients used to adulterate honey, such as sugar, corn sweetener, and molasses, are kosher. It is difficult to imagine serious *kashrus* problems resulting from this unscrupulous practice, although there is no way one can know what an unprincipled vender may add.

Bee Sweet

Every Rosh Hashanah, when we dip our *challah* and our apple in honey and wish ourselves a sweet and good year, we should remember what honey represents. Honey originates from stationary blossoms that were visited by the busy bee, whose industry is so vital for the plant world to reproduce. At the same time, this bee creates the sweet and kosher food we use to bless ourselves for a wonderful New Year.

NOTES

1. *Bechoros* 7b.
2. *Vayikra* 11:21.
3. *Pri To'ar* 81:1.
4. *Yoreh Deah* 81:9.
5. See *Shach, Yoreh Deah, Hanhagos BeIsur VeHeter.*
6. *Pri Chadash, Yoreh Deah* 81:28.
7. *Shu't Igros Moshe, Yoreh Deah* II:24.
8. *Shu't Minchas Yitzchak* 10:65.
9. *Daf HaKashrus*, Vol. 10 #10, article by Rabbi Gavriel Price; *Kashrus Kurrents, Facts on Wax*, article by Rabbi Dovid Heber.
10. *Chullin* 18b; 57a.
11. *Levush, Yoreh Deah* 81:8. It seems that one can infer this position from several other sources, including *Rashi, Bava Metzia* 40b, s.v. *Chafu; Magen Avraham*, 433:5.
12. The basis of *Levush*'s comments are in *Shabbos* 20b, although no mention is made there of any *kashrus* ramification.
13. *Uktzin* 3:11.
14. *Shach* and *Taz* comments to *Shulchan Aruch, Yoreh Deah* 84:13.
15. See *Tzefunot, Nissan*, 5752, article by Rabbi Shalom Brander; OU Document I-92, article by Rabbi Yoni Robinson.

22
The Chocolate Riddle

The Proper *Berachah* to Recite over Chocolate

Everyone knows that we say *shehakol* prior to eating chocolate bars. However, the question is, why? After all, chocolate is the product of the bean from the cocoa tree. Shouldn't its *berachah* be *borei pri ha'eitz*? As we will see, many *poskim* indeed contend that the correct *berachah* on chocolate is *ha'eitz*, the accepted custom notwithstanding.

Our investivation of this question holds a lot of interest for chocolate aficionados: we will take a tour of chocolate's history and the places where it is grown and produced; we will describe the tree it grows from, and follow a cocoa bean as it goes through the process of becoming a chocolate chip; and we will compare chocolate to other tree-borne food products, and ascertain how their different qualities affect the *berachos* we make on them. As a bonus, we will also investigate whether there is a difference between the *berachah* on dark chocolate and white chocolate.

The History of Chocolate

Chocolate is native to southern Mexico and Central America,

where the Maya Indians, and later the Aztecs, cultivated the cocoa (also called the cacao) tree for hundreds, possibly thousands of years. In fact, the word chocolate originates from an Aztec word meaning "warm liquid." In their society, the royal family drank warm, unsweetened chocolate from golden goblets, and cocoa beans were used as currency. Thus, if a Jew had accompanied Hernando Cortez on his trip to the New World, he might have recited Kiddush and Havdalah over hot chocolate, since it qualified there as *chamar medinah*, a beverage used to honor guests!

The Spaniards planted cocoa trees all over the tropical parts of the New World. Later, industrialists developed vast plantations of cocoa trees in Africa, Indonesia, and other tropical areas.

The Native Americans drank their chocolate unsweetened, whereas the Spaniards added sugar to it. This created two industries in the New World, the cocoa industry and the sugar industry. By 5340 (1580), hot chocolate flavored with sugar and vanilla was a common Spanish drink, and from there it eventually spread to the rest of Europe.

As long as chocolate was drunk as a beverage its *berachah* was certainly *shehakol*, since, except for grape juice and wine, we recite *shehakol* on all beverages, even if they are made from the five grains (such as beer and whiskey).[1]

Chocolate in the Nineteenth Century

Two major nineteenth-century developments vastly changed the way people consumed chocolate. In 1847, an English company introduced the first solid, edible chocolate. Until this time, chocolate had never been eaten.

The second development occurred in 1876, when the Swiss devised a method of adding milk to chocolate, thereby creating what we know today as milk chocolate. Prior to this invention, all chocolate was *pareve*. (By the way, some European manufacturers currently add animal fat to chocolate, obviously making it nonkosher.)

How Does Cocoa Grow?

The cocoa tree grows with large, colored fruits the size of melons or small pineapples that hang from the branches and trunk of the tree. Each huge fruit contains a sticky pulp that holds about twenty to fifty almond-shaped seeds, that are commonly called cocoa beans. The growers separate the beans from the pulp, ferment the beans for about a week, dry them in the sun, and then ship the semiprocessed cocoa beans to a chocolate maker.

Chocolate Production

The chocolate maker roasts the beans to bring out the flavor, and then removes the shell from the bean, leaving the kernel. The kernel is ground and becomes a thick, viscous liquid called chocolate liquor. The bean turns into a liquid when it is ground, because it contains over 50 percent fat.

Chocolate liquor contains no alcohol – that is simply the name for the ground, liquefied chocolate. Chocolate liquor is pure, bitter, unsweetened chocolate, similar to what the Aztecs drank in their time.

The chocolate maker now separates the cocoa liquor into its two main components: the fat, or cocoa butter (nothing to do with the butter that we eat made from milk), and cocoa bean solids. The solids are ground into cocoa powder. The chocolate we eat consists of a mix of chocolate liquor, cocoa butter, and cocoa powder, along with several other ingredients: notably sugar, and usually milk. This product is finely ground in a machine called a "conch" to give it a smooth consistency and taste. The chocolate is then tempered, which means that it is heated slowly and then cooled slowly, to enable the chocolate to harden properly, and to prevent the cocoa butter from separating from the chocolate. Finally, the chocolate is flavored and shaped into the final product.

Thus, before being ready to eat, chocolate has been separated, fermented, dried, roasted, shelled, ground, liquefied, separated, ground again, mixed with milk and/or cocoa butter, ground yet again in a conch, tempered, flavored, and shaped.

White chocolate is made from cocoa butter, sugar, and sometimes milk. There are no cocoa solids in white chocolate, and that is how it maintains its light color. Some "white chocolate" products are, in reality, made of vegetable oil and chocolate flavoring instead of cocoa butter.

The *Berachah* on Chocolate

With our newly acquired knowledge of what chocolate is and how it is made, we now turn our attention to the *halachos* of fruit and vegetable products that no longer have their original consistency, such as date butter, applesauce, jam, fruit puree, mashed potatoes, tomato paste, and peanut butter. What determines whether the correct *berachah* on these items is *borei pri ha'eitz* (*borei pri haadamah* in the case of some), or *shehakol nihyeh bidvaro*? By understanding these *halachos* we can begin to unravel the dispute among the authorities as to what the correct *berachah* on chocolate is.

The Rishonim dispute this question, many contending that even fruit that is completely pureed is still *borei pri ha'eitz*, whereas a minority rule that the *berachah* on a fruit or vegetable that no longer has its original consistency is *shehakol*.

The Ruling

The *Shulchan Aruch* rules that the *berachah* on date butter is *ha'eitz*, and this is the ruling followed by most Sefardim.[2] Ashkenazim follow the ruling of the *Rema*, who contends that one should recite *shehakol*, because of the *safek* as to which opinion we should follow. In practice, Ashkenazim usually recite *borei pri ha'eitz* when eating a product that has some of the consistency of the original product, as is the case of jam with recognizable fruit pieces in it or "chunky" applesauce, but recite *shehakol* before eating a completely smooth applesauce, or a smooth jam, where the fruit has completely lost its consistency.[3]

However, since the reason Ashkenazim recite *shehakol* is because it is a *safek*, several halachic differences result. For example, someone having a snack of applesauce and a beverage should make sure to recite the *shehakol* on the applesauce rather than on the beverage. If one recites the *shehakol* on the beverage without specifically including the applesauce, one now has a *safek* as to whether he has fulfilled the obligation to make a *berachah* on the applesauce. This is because, according to the opinions that the *berachah* should be *ha'eitz*, one does not fulfill the *berachah* by reciting *shehakol* on something else.

Similarly, someone eating a fruit and applesauce at the same time who recited *ha'eitz* on the fruit should not recite *shehakol* (and certainly not *ha'eitz*) on the applesauce. This is because, according to the *poskim* who contend that applesauce is *ha'eitz*, he has already fulfilled his duty to recite a *berachah* by reciting *ha'eitz* on the other fruit. In this situation, he should first recite *shehakol* on the applesauce and then *ha'eitz* on the other fruit.[4]

Some *poskim* are stricter, ruling that one should not eat an item that is definitely *borei pri ha'eitz* together with an item that is questionably *borei pri ha'eitz*, such as applesauce. This is because there isn't any way to fulfill the need for reciting a *berachah* on both items without creating an unnecessary *berachah*. If one recites the *berachah* on the fruit first, then one has a *safek* as to whether he can recite a *berachah* on the *safek* item. However, if one recites the *shehakol* on the *safek* item first, then, according to the opinions that the *berachah* is *ha'eitz*, one has now recited an unnecessary *berachah*.[5]

What about Chocolate?

The average person looking at a chocolate bar does not recognize the cocoa beans, since the producer ground, liquefied, and reconstituted them into a solid in the process. Can one still recite *ha'eitz* on the finished chocolate product, or does it become *shehakol*?

Many assume that the *berachah* on chocolate products is *shehakol*, based on the rulings of the *Divrei Yosef* and other authorities quoted by the *Shaarei Teshuvah*.[6] However, since all of these authorities lived at the time when chocolate was only drunk, it is difficult to base any halachic conclusion on what *berachah* to recite before eating chocolate, since we recite *shehakol* on all beverages, as mentioned above.

Among the more recent authorities who discuss which *berachah* one should recite before eating chocolate, the two most respected *poskim* to discuss this issue are Rav Shlomo Zalman Auerbach and Rav Moshe Feinstein, who reach diametrically opposite conclusions. In his *Minchas Shlomo*, Rav Shlomo Zalman suggests that one should recite *ha'eitz* before eating chocolate.[7] He compares chocolate to a case of spices ground so fine that their source is no longer identifiable. The *berachah* recited on them is whatever would have been the appropriate *berachah* on the particular spice, had it been edible before grinding (usually *haadamah*), even if the spice is mixed with sugar (and even if it is mostly sugar).[8] Let me explain this case with an example.

Cinnamon Sugar

Cinnamon is the bark of a tree, and its *berachah* is therefore *borei pri haadamah* (we do not recite *borei pri ha'eitz*, since we are eating the bark and not the fruit). "Cinnamon sugar" is a blend of cinnamon and sugar, in which the cinnamon cannot be identified by appearance, although it is clearly the more pronounced flavor. Based on the above-quoted ruling by Rav Shlomo Zalman Auerbach, one should recite *haadamah* before eating cinnamon sugar.

Why are spices different from finely ground fruit and vegetables, over which Ashkenazim recite *shehakol*?

Since this is considered the way that one "eats" spices, they do not lose their *berachah*, even though they can no longer be identified.[9]

The *Berachah* on Sugar

There is a thousand-year-old dispute over whether the correct *berachah* on cane sugar is *borei pri ha'eitz*, *borei pri haadamah*, or *shehakol*. The *Shulchan Aruch* concludes that we recite *shehakol* on sugar.[10] However, someone who recited either *borei pri ha'eitz* or *borei pri haadamah* on cane sugar should not recite a new *berachah*, since the correct *berachah* is disputed.[11]

Originally, sugar was produced only from sugar cane. Today, a large percentage of the world's sugar crop is extracted from the sweet white root of the sugar beet. However, mass cultivation and production of sugar beets did not begin until the nineteenth century and was a result of the Napoleonic Wars. When the British blockaded Napoleon's Europe, one of the products that was made unavailable was cane sugar, which does not grow in Europe's cold climate. Out of concern that his subjects might revolt over the unavailability of imported sugar, Napoleon built sugar refineries throughout Europe. He even awarded a medal for perfecting the production of white sugar from the white root of the sugar beet, which thrives in cold climates.

Although Napoleon was not worried about it, *rabbonim* were concerned about whether the *berachah* over the new type of sugar was also *shehakol*, just as the *berachah* over cane sugar. (The two types of sugar cannot be distinguished one from the other.) The *Mishnah Berurah* rules that one should recite *shehakol* over beet sugar, although if someone recited *borei pri haadamah*, he should not make another *berachah*.[12]

Thus, we see that there is a halachic difference between spices that are ground up and cannot be identified, whose *berachah* remains *haadamah*, and beet sugar, whose *berachah* is *shehakol*. We must now analyze the difference between these two foods and figure out where chocolate fits into the picture.

Beating a Beet

After the sugar beets ripen, they are harvested, washed thoroughly, and then sliced into thin chips. The beets are then soaked in hot water for about an hour, which extracts the sugar from them and creates a strong sugar solution. Chalk is added to the sugar solution, which causes the non-sugar parts of the solution to clump together, so that they can be filtered out. The sugar solution is then evaporated to concentrate the sugar. Eventually, the sugar concentration is great enough to form crystals, which are then removed from the solution.

An important fact affecting our halachic discussion is that in the case of both cane and beet, the sugar is extracted, or removed from the stem or root, rather than simply being processed.

Spices or Sugar?

Now our question is, do we compare chocolate to spices, which maintain their *berachah* even after they have been ground until they are no longer identifiable, or to sugar, which, we rule, loses its *berachah* and becomes *shehakol*?

Rav Shlomo Zalman compares chocolate to the case of ground spices that maintain their original *berachah*, although they are no longer recognizable.[13] Apparently Rav Shlomo Zalman felt that chocolate, which is refined from the cocoa bean, should not be compared to sugar, which is extracted from the cane or beet.

(In my opinion, those *poskim* who contend that the *berachah* on chocolate is *borei pri ha'eitz* should agree that the *berachah* on *white chocolate* is *shehakol*, since this product contains no cocoa solids. Cocoa butter should have the *halachah* of a liquid that is pressed out of a fruit, whose *berachah* is always *shehakol*.)

On the other hand, when Rav Moshe Feinstein, *ztz"l*, discusses which *berachah* to recite before eating chocolate-covered raisins, he assumes that the *berachah* on chocolate is *shehakol* and does not entertain the possibility that its *berachah* might be a *safek*.[14]

(This brings up another *she'eilah* altogether, and that is the correct *berachah* to say over chocolate-covered raisins. The question revolves around which part of this delicacy is the *ikar* and which is the *tafel*. However, this is a discussion reserved for a different occasion.)

Royal Food

As we mentioned above, the Aztecs considered chocolate a royal food. By studying the *halachos* of the *berachos* on this food, we truly elevate it to the stature of royal food – since we are determining which *berachah* the *mamleches kohanim vegoy kadosh* (the holy nation that is a kingdom of priests) should recite.

NOTES

1. *Tosafos, Berachos* 38a s.v. *Hai.*
2. *Orach Chayim* 202:7.
3. *Mishnah Berurah* 202:42.
4. *Ben Ish Chai, Pinchas* #16.
5. *Maamar Mordechai* 203:3.
6. 202:19.
7. Vol. 1, 91:2.
8. *Shulchan Aruch, Orach Chayim* 203:7.
9. *Mishnah Berurah* 203:12.
10. 202:15.
11. *Tur, Beis Yosef, Mishnah Berurah,* and *Biur Halachah, Shulchan Aruch,* ibid.
12. 202:76.
13. Dayan Gavriel Krausz, formerly the *av beis din* of Manchester, devotes a lengthy essay to advocate this position in his *sefer Mekor Haberacha.*
14. *Shu't Igros Moshe, Orach Chayim* 3:31.

23

Kindler on the Roof

The Ins and Outs of Lighting Shabbos Candles

On a recent Friday, someone phoned me with the following *she'eilah*:

> We are at a Shabbaton. My wife was planning to light Shabbos candles in our room, but there is a posted sign stating that the management does not permit lighting in the rooms, because it is a fire hazard. There is also a huge smoke detector in the room that will probably begin sounding as soon as someone lights candles. Tonight, we are eating the meal on a windy rooftop, where I am sure the candles will blow out. Where do we light Shabbos candles and how?

To answer this question, we need first to explain the background to the *mitzvah* of kindling Shabbos lights.

Why Do We Light Shabbos Candles?

The authorities provide several reasons for kindling lights before Shabbos.

1. It is a *kavod*, an honor, to have ample lighting for the Shabbos meal, just as one expects proper illumination in a place of honor.[1]

2. To enjoy the Shabbos meal.[2] One does not enjoy a meal when one cannot see what he is eating.

3. It is unpleasant and depressing to sit in the dark; this conflicts with the Shabbos atmosphere, which should be happy and dignified.[3]

4. If the house is dark, someone might stumble or collide with something and hurt oneself, which is certainly not conducive to enjoyment of the Shabbos.

It should be noted that there are circumstances when some of the reasons mentioned above apply, and others do not. For example, according to the first two reasons, in order to treat the Shabbos meal with honor and to enjoy it, one is required to have light only where one is eating; however, one would not necessarily need to illuminate an area that one traverses, but does not use for eating. On the other hand, the fourth reason, preventing a person from hurting himself, requires illumination even in parts of the house that one walks through during the course of Shabbos. (Chazal did not require kindling Shabbos lights in an area where one walks outdoors.) Therefore, one should kindle lights in all areas of the house that one uses in the course of Shabbos.[4]

Who Must Light?

Who is required to kindle the Shabbos lights? Most people are surprised to discover that the *mitzvah* of kindling Shabbos lights is incumbent upon every individual. To quote the Rambam: "Everyone is required to have a lamp lit in his house on Shabbos."[5] Although it is usually only the lady of the house who kindles the Shabbos lights, she does so as the agent for the rest of the family and their guests.[6] If she is away for Shabbos, her husband or someone else must kindle the candles instead. Similarly, a man living alone is obligated to kindle Shabbos lights every week, as are students in a dormitory, whether in a yeshivah or a seminary.

Kindling or Illumination?

Is the *mitzvah* to kindle lights, or to have an illuminated room? I am posing a question that appears technical, but which has several halachic ramifications: Chazal were concerned that one not remain in the dark on Shabbos. Did they simply require everyone to be certain that his house is illuminated, or did they enact an active requirement to kindle a lamp? The Rishonim dispute this question, some holding that Chazal were satisfied that one make certain that he have adequate lighting for Shabbos, whereas others contend that we are required to kindle a light specifically for this purpose.

Several halachic differences result from the abovementioned dispute:

Rekinding Lights – or, Keep Those Candles Burning!

If lights are already burning Friday afternoon shortly before Shabbos, is there a *mitzvah* to extinguish and rekindle them for the sake of fulfilling the *mitzvah* of kindling Shabbos lights? If the *mitzvah* is to make sure that there is illumination, then I am not required to rekindle lights, but may simply leave the lights burning on into Shabbos. However, if there is a special *mitzvah* requiring me to kindle the lights, then I must extinguish the burning lights and rekindle them!

The Rishonim dispute regarding whether or not one is required to extinguish the lights and rekindle them. Those who contend that one may leave the candles burning maintain that it is sufficient if there is adequate illumination for Shabbos, and one has no responsibility to extinguish the light and rekindle it. Other Rishonim, however, maintain that Chazal require kindling lights especially for Shabbos. Thus, leaving lights kindled is insufficient, if I did not light them especially for Shabbos.[7] We rule according to the second approach.

Later authorities rule that we satisfy the requirement to kindle a special light in honor of Shabbos by kindling just one light. Thus, if there are many lights burning around the house, one is not required to extinguish all of them and relight them all for the sake of Shabbos. It is sufficient to kindle one light for this purpose and leave the other lights burning.[8] Similarly, if one's house is situated in a way that street lighting illuminates one's hallway, one is not required to leave lights on to provide additional illumination.

Reciting a *Berachah*

Does one recite a *berachah* on the *mitzvah* of kindling Shabbos lights?

A second dispute that results from our original inquiry (on whether the *mitzvah* is to kindle lights or to have illumination) is whether one recites a *berachah* when kindling the Shabbos lights. According to those opinions that the *mitzvah* is simply to see that the house is illuminated, one would not recite a *berachah* when kindling Shabbos lights, even if one needs to kindle lamps before Shabbos. This is because, in their opinion, there is no special *mitzvah* to kindle lights.[9] However, the conclusion of the *poskim* is that there *is* a *mitzvah* to kindle Shabbos lights, and that even if one has lights kindled already, one should extinguish and rekindle them.[10]

Gentile Light

A third result of this dispute is whether one can fulfill the *mitzvah* by having a non-Jew kindle Shabbos lights on one's behalf. What happens if one is unable to light the Shabbos lights oneself? May one ask a non-Jew to kindle them on one's behalf? If the *mitzvah* is to kindle the lights, then one has not fulfilled a *mitzvah* this way, since a non-Jew cannot be one's agent to fulfill a *mitzvah*. On the other hand, if the *mitzvah* is for the house to be illuminated, having a gentile kindle lights fulfills the *mitzvah*, since the house is now illuminated.

Since we follow the second approach, one may not have a non-Jew light on one's behalf.

Electrifying Our Lives!

The main illumination in our modern houses is provided by electric lights. Does turning on our electric lights fulfill the *mitzvah* of kindling Shabbos lights? After all, all four reasons for the kindling of Shabbos lights are fulfilled by lighting with electricity: it makes the meal dignified, we can now see our food, it creates a pleasant Shabbos atmosphere, and we will avoid stumbling into items on Shabbos.

May we fulfill the *mitzvah* with electric lights? And if electric lights fulfill our obligation, why do people light candles or oil to fulfill the *mitzvah*, when electricity is so much simpler and cleaner?

Indeed, most authorities contend that one fulfills the *mitzvah* of kindling Shabbos lights with electric lights.[11] There are some authorities who disagree, because they feel that the *mitzvah* requires kindling with a wick and a fuel source that are at hand, both requirements that preclude using electric lights.[12] Others contend that one must use a lamp that is special for Shabbos. According to this latter approach, one could kindle a special electric Shabbos light to fulfill the *mitzvah*, but should not use the regular electric lights.[13] The consensus of most authorities is that in an extenuating circumstance, one may fulfill the *mitzvah* with electric lights.[14] Therefore, someone who is hospitalized for Shabbos should recite a *berachah* on electric lights, since hospitals usually forbid lighting an open flame.

Providing Significant Light

Some contemporary authorities have pointed out the following: The main illumination in our houses is electric lighting, which was not turned on specifically for the *mitzvah* of kindling Shabbos lights. Often, the illumination provided by the Shabbos candles is so insignificant that one hardly notices their light. Thus, if the primary purpose of kindling Shabbos lights is to provide illumination, the Shabbos candles are not really fulfilling their role. For this reason, the Shabbos lights should be placed where they provide illumination. Alternatively, one should turn the electric lights off immediately prior to kindling the Shabbos lamps, turn them on again for the sake of fulfilling the *mitzvah* of kindling Shabbos lights, then kindle the Shabbos oil or candles and recite a *berachah*, which now includes both the electric lights and the oil or candles. (I have assumed one is following Ashkenazic practice of reciting the *berachah* after kindling the lights. Most Sefardim recite the *berachah* before kindling the lights.)

Sleeping or Eating?

If one is sleeping in one place on Shabbos and eating elsewhere, where should one kindle Shabbos lights? Based on our previous discussion, we can reach four conclusions:

1. One is required to ensure that there is light in both places. One of the reasons for kindling Shabbos lights is to prevent stumbling. This reason applies also to the house where one is sleeping.

2. If there is adequate lighting in both places, one is required to kindle Shabbos lights only in one place.

3. It is more important to kindle where one eats than where one sleeps. This is because two of the four reasons cited above apply only to the place where one eats the Shabbos meal.

4. One should kindle preferably oil or a candle to fulfill the *mitzvah* of lighting a Shabbos lamp, but if these cannot be used, one may kindle an electric light.

Therefore, if no one else is kindling either where one is eating or where one is sleeping, one should light the Shabbos lights where one is eating, and, in addition, make sure there is adequate lighting where one is sleeping. If another person is already lighting where one is eating, then one should kindle one's Shabbos lights in the house where one is sleeping, to fulfill this part of the *mitzvah*.[15]

In this instance, one should make sure that the lights one kindles will still be burning when one returns after the meal, because otherwise, the Shabbos candles will not have accomplished anything. One should light longer candles or make sure to light sufficient oil so that it will burn until his return. If one is concerned about the safety of leaving Shabbos candles burning in a house with no one home, one should kindle the electric lights and recite a *berachah* on them, instead of kindling candles.

If one is uncertain whether the candles will still be burning when one returns, one should first kindle the Shabbos candles, then the electric lights, and then recite a *berachah* on both the electric lights and the Shabbos candles. One will then be fulfilling the *mitzvah* of lighting Shabbos lights primarily with the electric lights that one knows will still be burning when one returns.

Thus, if one is visiting family for Shabbos and sleeping in a house whose residents are away, one's primary kindling should be where one sleeps. Similarly, someone who sleeps in a dormitory and will be eating his Shabbos meals with a family should kindle where he sleeps.

What should I do if I am eating in one house and sleeping in another, but someone else will be lighting in both places?

If someone else is kindling in both places, then it is preferable to kindle where one is eating. In this situation, it is preferable to kindle in a way that one's lights add some illumination – or, alternatively, to turn off one of the electric lights and then turn it back on for the sake of Shabbos. Certainly, once one has kindled the candles and recited a *berachah*, one may not turn on the electric lights.

Shabbos in a Hotel

If one is at a family *simchah*, a conference, or a Shabbaton in a hotel, where should one light?

If there are already people lighting where one will be eating, then one should light where one will be sleeping. However, if one is going to rely primarily on the electric lights in both places, then one should light candles where one will be eating.

Sometimes, hotels set up candles in a place that is convenient for them, but is nowhere near where people are eating, sleeping, or traversing. Lighting these candles does not fulfill any *mitzvah*, and therefore one may not recite a *berachah* upon kindling them.[16] Under these circumstances, one should try to light near where one is eating. If this is not possible, and it is unsafe to leave unattended lights burning in one's room, one should recite the *berachah* on the electric lights in one's room, and should turn those electric lights off and on again prior to reciting the *berachah* on them.

We can now return to the original, actual inquiry concerning the hotel prohibiting lighting in one's room and eating on a windy rooftop, and analyze the options.

In the Room

First, even if there is no smoke detector, one may not light candles if the owner does not permit it. It is prohibited *min haTorah* to use someone's property in a way that he does not allow – and the owner specifically does not allow lit candles in the room. This is true even in a situation where there is no danger whatsoever in leaving unattended candles burning in the room. If it is a fire hazard to leave unattended candles, it is prohibited *min haTorah* to light candles, because of the *mitzvah*, "*Ushmartem me'od linafshoseichem* (You should guard your lives very [carefully])." Thus, kindling in the room is not an option. However, since there is a halachic requirement to make sure that the room has some illumination, one should leave an electric light on in or near the bedroom.

On the Roof

What about lighting Shabbos candles where one is eating? In this case, lighting candles where one is eating does not fulfill the *mitzvah*, since the candles will blow out before one has opportunity to have enjoyment from them. In the case at hand, I recommended that the person asking the question obtain a box that is used commonly in Eretz Yisrael to light a Chanukah menorah outdoors. These boxes protect the lights from the elements, yet allow one to benefit from the lamps. If it is possible to acquire one of these boxes, the person should recite a *berachah* on the Shabbos candles inside the box.

Otherwise, since he cannot kindle lamps or candles in either place, he has no choice but to recite the *berachah* on the electric lights. In this case, he should preferably recite the *berachah* on the electric lights that are kindled where they are eating.

The Gemara[17] teaches that someone who kindles Shabbos lights regularly will merit having sons who are Torah scholars. Let us hope and pray that in the merit of observing these *halachos* correctly, we will have children and grandchildren who light up the world with their Torah!

NOTES

1. Rambam, *Hilchos Shabbos* 30:5; *Rashi, Shabbos* 25b.
2. *She'iltos* #63.
3. *Rashi, Shabbos* 23b.
4. *Magen Avraham,* 263:1.
5. *Hilchos Shabbos* 5:1.
6. See *Levush* 263:3; *Graz, Kuntres Acharon* 263:2.
7. *Tosafos, Shabbos* 25b, s.v. *Chovah.*
8. See *Ketzos HaShulchan* 74:1.
9. See *Tosafos* ad loc.
10. *Tosafos* ad loc; *Rambam* 5:1; see *Mordechai, Shabbos* #294.
11. For example, *Shu't Beis Yitzchok, Yoreh Deah* 1:120; *Edus LeYisrael,* p. 122.
12. See, for example, *Shu't Maharshag* 2:107.
13. *Shu't Tzitz Eliezer* 1:20:11.
14. *Shu't Yechaveh Daas* 5:24; *Shu't Kochevei Yitzchak* 1:2.
15. *Graz* 263:9.
16. See *Graz* 263:14.
17. *Shabbos* 23b.

24

The *Chol HaMoed* Outing Saga

The Issues Involved in a Kohein Visiting a Museum

My sister and her family are coming for Yom Tov for the very first time, which has us all very excited! But, we need to figure out all the logistics of having everyone together for Yom Tov – where everyone will sleep and how to arrange sufficient seating space and chairs. After all, they have a very large family, and our two boys are each accustomed to having their own room.

We want to make sure that the visiting family is comfortable. In truth, there have been some sticky situations in the past. Well, let me put it this way. We are *frum*, but we do not keep all the *chumros* that they do. This has created some uncomfortable moments during their previous visits. What we realized is that to have an optimal relationship with them, we need to be very accommodating of their needs, which is sometimes complicated since we are not always certain what their needs are. To complicate matters, we have discovered that they don't trust the opinions of our rabbi. But they are really wonderful people, and in addition, *mishpachah* is *mishpachah*!

We already know that when they come we should make sure to have plenty of *chalav Yisrael* products available and to double-check what *hechsherim* they accept. And we know that they will not use the *eruv*, which our rabbi himself uses. So, I guess, each to his own. But I want to make sure that they are comfortable; we really want to have a nice Yom Tov together, and so do they.

Since they have never been here for such an extended stay, we would really like to show them the sites of our town. Our city is blessed with numerous, really nice museums, many of them extremely child friendly. Hopefully, these will help make the Yom Tov memorable for all.

Calling Rabbi Katz

Hold on a second. Muttie, my brother-in-law, is a *kohein*, and he has told me that he is very careful about checking museums before he goes. It would be really nice if I can figure out in advance which museums he can visit so that we can plan the Chol HaMoed itinerary.

But maybe we can take his under-bar-mitzvah boys to the Children's Museum without any concern? I am going to call the rabbi. After all, he is also a *kohein*.

I reached Rabbi Katz on the first try. He told me that the prohibition of making a *kohein tamei* also applies to a *kohein* who is too young to be obligated in *mitzvos*. An adult Yisrael may not bring a child or baby who is a *kohein* into a place where he would become *tamei meis*, such as a cemetery or funeral home. He told me that some *kohanim* are extremely careful not to visit people in hospitals – even in places where most of the patients are not Jewish – not that we are planning any hospital visits during this Yom Tov.

While on the phone, I asked Rabbi Katz if there is any problem with a *kohein* going to a museum. He answered me that he himself goes, but he knows of *kohanim* who refrain from going. I asked him what the issue was, to which he responded that he would check it out and call me back.

Rabbi Katz Comes Through

A day later Rabbi Katz called me back, having spoken to the city's *av beis din*, Rav Gross. The senior rabbi had explained that there is a dispute about whether a *kohein* may enter a museum in which there are human remains inside a glass-enclosed display area. He explained that whereas Jewish remains certainly convey *tumah* whether they are touched, carried, or are simply located in the same room (sometimes even the same building) as a person, it is disputed whether gentile remains convey *tumah* when they are in the same room if they are not touched or carried.

Rabbi Katz explained that the *tumah* that spreads throughout a room or building is called *tumas ohel*. This does not affect non-*kohanim* today, since everyone is *tamei* anyway, and to remove this *tumah* requires the ashes of the *parah adumah* which is, of course, not yet available in our times. However, a *kohein* must be careful not to enter the same *ohel* as Jewish remains.

Furthermore, Rabbi Katz explained that Rav Gross had told him that the remains of a non-Jew convey *tumah* if they are touched or carried, but it is unclear if there is a problem whether a *kohein* may enter a building containing the remains of a non-Jew.

Rabbi Katz added:

> When a museum contains parts of human bodies, we do not usually know whether these are from Jewish bodies or not. We may assume that since most of the world is not Jewish, the body parts are from non-Jews. In addition, the remains in a museum are usually inside glass displays that can be opened when necessary. Some authorities contend that this glass enclosure is halachically equivalent to having the remains in a different room; in their opinion a *kohein* may enter a museum.[1]

Thus, Rav Gross had concluded that a *kohein* wanting to visit a museum where all the remains are inside display cases has a basis to be lenient because of these two reasons.

A Bone to Pick

Although I was glad to discover that my *kohein* friends who visit museums have a basis for their conduct, I realized that Muttie would probably not accept the lenient approach. I remembered a time that we were visiting them and they had taken us to a neighborhood children's museum with many "hands-on" science exhibits perfect for children. Upon turning a corner of the museum, we discovered an area described as a "Native American Burial Ground," complete with bones for realistic effect. Assuming that the bones were artificial, Muttie had casually asked the receptionist, "Are these bones authentic?"

The receptionist answered casually, "Actually, we have no reason to assume that the bones are from Native Americans; they were acquired from a medical school, which receives them as donations. Our curator feels that based on bone structure that these are really originally Caucasian, but he is not certain.

Upon hearing this information, Muttie bee-lined an abrupt exit from the museum. Indeed, they were not authentic Indian bones, but they were authentic human bones! Unquestionably, Muttie is concerned about human bones even when they are probably of a gentile. I was also fairly certain that Muttie would not want to rely on the fact that the remains are inside a glass display.

Alas, Poor Yorick!

At this point, I remembered a cute little theater that performs actual Shakespeare plays. What could be wrong with Shakespeare? Until I inquired, and discovered that one of the props for Hamlet is a real skull! I had just about given up on this idea, when I mentioned it to Rabbi Katz. He commented: "Check it out. I remember once discovering that these skulls are not complete, and that there is a *halachah* that a damaged skull does not convey *tumah* throughout a building."[2]

Off I went, to check Hamlet's skull. Much to my surprise, they were willing to show me the actual skull that they used, although they told me that they have no crossbones. Sure enough, I discovered that the top of the skull had been replaced with a metal plate. I am no Torah scholar, and had no idea whether this would be acceptable.

I called Rav Gross myself and described to him the Shakespearian skull, explaining the family situation so that he would realize that I was not hunting for a lenient opinion. He told me that there was no *kohein* issue.

> If one removes enough of an area of the skull such that a live person would not be able to survive, the remaining partial skull no longer spreads *tumah* unless it is touched or carried.[3] The subsequent repair with a metal plate does not cause the skull to spread *tumas ohel*, although it would spread *tumas ohel* if the removed skullcap was in the same room.[4]

Since I did not envision Muttie or his sons joining the cast of Hamlet, it seemed that we would be able to take them to the Shakespeare Theater as a special activity for Chol HaMoed. I thanked Rav Gross for sharing his scholarship with me, at which point he made the following observation:

> Are you sure that this is the type of entertainment that your brother-in-law and his children would appreciate?

Admittedly, this question had not even occurred to me. What could be risqué about Shakespeare? But then again, Muttie's priorities in education are very different from mine. I am not sure if this is the type of Chol HaMoed outing that he would consider memorable.

Look but Don't Touch

So I resigned myself to try to verify if any of our museums are kosher for *kohanim*. I asked the local *vaad ha'ir* if they have ever researched the museums. They told me that although it is a good idea, they have never done so, but would be very eager to follow up on whatever I discover.

I called the information desk at the Children's Science Museum, and explained that I have company from out of town who are unable to visit the museum if it contains any human remains. I realized that they must have thought I was absolutely bonkers! I can just imagine the conversation that transpired among the receptionists on their lunch break!

Although the information desk notified me that there were no human remains to be had anywhere in the museum, I did not get any sense that they took me seriously and decided that I would have to take a trip there to check it out myself.

I decided the best way to handle the situation was to call Muttie directly, and try to get direction from him as to what the parameters are.

I received quite an education from Muttie. If I can paraphrase what he told me:

> A close friend of mine, who is not a *kohein*, often visits museums to verify whether a *kohein* may enter. Among the most common remains he finds are mummies, human bones, skeletons, and preserved fetuses, and occasionally he has even discovered preserved human organs or entire cadavers. One museum had an empty stone casket that had been found in Eretz Yisrael with an obvious Jewish name on it. Since the supports of a grave are also sometimes *tamei*,[5] we had a *she'eilah* whether this contaminated the entire museum.
>
> Often displays of these items are not inside glass-enclosed areas, which increases the halachic concerns. For example, my friend discovered such artifacts as Aztec musical instruments carved from the femurs of captured prisoners, as well as bowls hollowed out from skulls displayed on museum shelves.

These bowls, Muttie noted, pose a problem only if the *kohein* touches them or picks them up – boy, was he impressed when I was able to explain to him why! (Actually, I found out later that my reasoning was wrong, but the explanation will have to wait for a different time.)[6]

On one visit, Muttie recounted, his friend noticed a display of a giant, which he assumed was a mannequin, but on closer inspection turned out to be a giant whose remains had been preserved in formaldehyde!

Muttie's friend feels that a *kohein* who would like to visit a particular museum should first have a knowledgeable non-*kohein* carefully research the entire museum. From firsthand experience, he can attest that one should not rely on the information desk personnel – they are often uninformed of what the museum owns. In one instance, the information desk insisted that a museum displaying ossuaries containing human bones had absolutely no human remains!

The curators also often make mistakes. In one museum, there was a skull on display. We asked the curator whether it was real. She told us that she knows that the museum purchased it from a supplier who sells only replicas and not real skulls or skeletons. I asked her if there was any way that one could look at a skull and tell if it was real. She responded that one can usually tell by making a very careful inspection of its teeth. To demonstrate the difference between the replica and a real skull, she opened the display to show him – and discovered, much to her surprise, that the skull was real! It turned out that the museum had purchased it at a time that the supplier sold real specimens!

Lesson to learn: be careful, and ask lots of probing questions.

Sorry I Opened That Drawer

Muttie then told me an interesting bit of information:

> When approaching a museum, one should ask if it contains any remains that fall under the NAGPRA act, the Native American Graves Protection and

Repatriation Act. This was a law passed by Congress requiring many institutions to return Native American cultural items and human remains to their respective peoples. Under one provision of this law, these institutions are required to catalog all Native American burial items and religious artifacts in their collections in order to identify the living heirs, or on behalf of culturally affiliated Native American tribes or Native Hawaiian organizations who are interested in the remains or artifacts.

Someone trying to find out whether a museum contains *tamei* remains can easily begin his conversation with the curator or collection manager by mentioning NAGPRA. Since they are familiar with the requirements of this law, the subject of human remains and their cataloging in the museum's collections are no longer so strange to them. One can use this as an entrée to discuss what a *kohein* is and what our halachic concerns are. I have found that the curators are usually very helpful; however, one must ask very specifically about each type of item, such as skeletons, skulls, bones, preserved organs, and mummies, since they are not thinking about *tumah* but about science. A museum curator categorizes these different items according to their branch of science: either as biology, anatomy, ancient history, or anthropology.

Furthermore, sometimes the curators themselves do not know what the museum has in storage. Here one often gets into very interesting halachic questions that one needs to discuss with a first-line *posek*. For example, while looking at one museum, someone discovered that a different floor of the building contained drawers filled with all sorts of human remains.

"By the way," Muttie noted, "there are other things to be concerned of in museums even if one is not a *kohein*. Many museums contain actual idols that constitute real *avodah zarah*. The question arises whether one may even look at them."

At this point, my brother-in-law pointed out that when the Torah states *al tifnu el ha'elilim* (do not turn to idols),[7] the prohibition includes looking at idols.[8] The *Magen Avraham*[9] explains that the Torah prohibits only gazing at an idol, but does not prohibit glancing at it. Therefore, seeing it is not prohibited, but intentionally looking at it is. Thus, one must be wary of this prohibition when visiting a museum that may include idols, statues, and images.[10]

Play Ball!

While I was contemplating the last fact, Muttie called me back to our original topic with the following comment:

> Jerry, do you know what kind of massive undertaking this is? The reason I rarely take the family to museums is that I am always uncertain about what they contain, and I know how difficult it is to really determine what they have. The curators themselves often don't know.
>
> I must tell you. I am so appreciative of your putting this effort into making sure we have a nice time. But for the next few weeks until Yom Tov I am sure that you have plenty of other responsibilities. Besides, my kids are not at all oriented towards museum visits – they spend most of their time in yeshivah, and they much prefer spending time playing ball and running around in the park. I am sure your wonderful boys have nice friends, and the cousins and the friends can play ball together. For my kids that will be seventh heaven – and a much more memorable outing.

I must admit that it had not even occurred to me that the cousins would enjoy just playing ball together. Indeed we had an absolutely wonderful Yom Tov that the cousins will all remember for years to come! And I left the job of researching whether the local museums are *kohein*-appropriate to someone else. Are *you* interested in working on this project on behalf of Klal Yisrael?

NOTES

1. See *Shu't Maharsham* #215.

2. *Ohalos* 2:3.

3. Ibid.

4. This conclusion is based on *Ohalos* 2:6 and 3:1.

5. It would seem that according to *Rashi* (based on his explanation in *Eruvin* 15a and *Kesubos* 4b and other places) and other authorities, this would qualify as a *dofek* that spreads *tumas ohel*, see *Ohalos* 2:4. However, for a variety of different reasons, most later authorities would be lenient in this instance.

6. The reason that there is no *tumas ohel* in this instance is because there is not enough bone to present a problem, see *Ohalos* 2:1, 3. However, even a very small amount of human bone will cause *tumah* if it is touched or carried, see *Ohalos* 2:5.

7. *Vayikra* 19:4.

8. *Yerushalmi, Avodah Zarah* 3:1; Rambam, *Hilchos Avodah Zarah* 2:2; *Sefer HaMitzvos, Lo Saaseh* #10; *Sefer HaChinuch* #213.

9. 307:23.

10. See chapter 10, where this topic is discussed in greater length.

25

Grave Issues about Graven Images

Real Problems Associated with Icons

A woman named Miriam recently asked me these two questions regarding *avodah zarah*:

1. I received some figurines from a museum shop which resemble various Egyptian gods. May I keep them to demonstrate at the Seder what silly gods the Egyptians worshipped?

2. My nonobservant but very respectful father has a rather eclectic collection of various art objects – including a four-foot-tall bronze statue of some Hindu figure. Do I have any obligation to say or do anything?

Zev, a chess enthusiast, asked me the following:

3. I just received a present of a very nicely carved chess set. Unfortunately, the king has a cross. May I keep the set as is, or must I break the cross off of the king?

Jack, an archeology student, sent me an e-mail:

4. As part of my studies, I will be joining a dig. What happens if we find an idol? Even though it is not worshiped today, would the *mitzvah* of destroying it still be applicable? Also, in examining the object, one has to gaze at and familiarize oneself with the piece. Does this violate the prohibition of gazing at *avodah zarah*?

Each of these actual *she'eilos* that I was asked revolves around the question of whether a Jew may own an item that has idolatrous overtones, even though he has no idolatrous intentions. Is this lack of intent sufficient to avoid any Torah violations?

As we will see, there are several potential *she'eilos* that we must analyze to determine the *halachah*:

1. May a Jew *look* at an icon?

2. Does it make a difference whether the icon is still worshipped?

3. May a Jew *own* an icon that represents an idol, even if it was never worshipped?

4. If owning this icon infringes on no other prohibitions, does it violate *maris ayin*, doing something that gives the impression that one is engaged in wrongdoing?

Graven Images in the Torah

In *Parshas Eikev*, the Torah commands:

> Burn their carved gods in fire. Do not desire and obtain the silver or gold that is upon them, lest you become ensnared by it, for it is repugnant to Hashem your G-d. Nor shall you bring this abomination into your house and become banned like it. Abhor it and revile it, for it is banned.[1]

This *pasuk* includes the following *mitzvos*:

1. "Burn their carved gods in fire" commands us to destroy *avodah zarah*.[2]

2. "Do not desire and obtain the silver or gold that is upon them" prohibits benefit even from the decorations on an idol.[3] One may not own or sell idols, even if one thinks that they are the silliest things on earth, since he gains financially or in other ways.

3. "Nor shall you bring this abomination into your house" bans bringing an idol into one's house and also forbids benefiting from idolatry.[4] Benefiting from idolatry, in effect, "brings" the idol into one's use and possession.

4. Furthermore, the Torah states, *al tifnu el ha'elilim* (do not turn to idols).[5] What is included in this proscription? Does it include looking at idols or images that represent idols?

The *Sifra*[6] quotes two interpretations of this verse. One prohibits studying idolatry, including its beliefs and how the idol is worshipped. A second approach understands the verse to forbid even looking at idols.[7] The *poskim* rule that both approaches are accepted *halachah*: the Torah thus prohibits studying idolatrous practices and beliefs, as well as looking at idols.[8] (The Rambam states that one receives *malkus* for violating this prohibition.[9] Therefore, someone who violates either interpretation of this *mitzvah* is halachically invalidated from providing testimony, even if he has no idolatrous intent.)

Glancing vs. Looking

Does this mean that even glancing at an idol violates the Torah? The *Magen Avraham*[10] explains that the Torah prohibits only gazing at an idol, but does not prohibit glancing at it: *seeing* it is not prohibited, but intentionally looking at it is.

Icon or Idol?

Is it prohibited to look at articles that merely represent the actual idol, even though they themselves are not worshipped (icons), or is the prohibition limited to idols that are actually the object of worship? The answer to this question depends on how one understands the following passage of Gemara in *Meseches Shabbos*:

> One may not look at the image itself...because one thereby violates "Do not turn to idols." How do we derive this law from this verse? Rav Chanin explained, "Do not face figures created by man."[11]

This unclear passage implies that one may not look at any image, even one not worshipped.

On the other hand, elsewhere, the Gemara praises the Talmudic scholar Rabbi Menachem ben Sima'ie as a holy man, because he never looked at the images that one finds on coins.[12] This implies that an especially holy person does not look at likenesses, but a person who observes *halachah* without stringencies may do so. Thus, we are faced with a seeming inconsistency: one Gemara statement prohibits looking at any image; the other implies that one may (although it is meritorious to avoid it).

The Rishonim suggest many different approaches to explain the Gemara in *Shabbos*. Here are two differing approaches that resolve the above quandary in very different ways:

1. Some contend that the prohibition of looking at an image applies only to one that was manufactured for worship, which is obviously not the case of the image on a coin. According to this opinion, although the Gemara seems to derive that one may not look at any portrait or image whatsoever, it really means to limit the prohibition to actual idols. Nevertheless, it is praiseworthy not to look at any portraits or images at all.[13]

2. Others understand that one may not look at any image whatsoever.[14] If this approach is correct, why does the Gemara in *Meseches Avodah Zarah* imply that Rabbi Menachem ben Sima'ie's acts are meritorious, but not required, when the Gemara in *Shabbos* prohibits looking at any image?

To answer this question, some authorities explain that although it is prohibited to look at any image, this applies only when one's attention is diverted to the image. Since coins are in common use all the time, glancing at them is not considered as constituting a diversion.[15]

Egyptian Figurines

Whether one may own a replica of an ancient Egyptian icon depends on the above-quoted dispute among the Rishonim. According to the first opinion quoted above, since these icons were meant for educational purposes, rather than for encouraging worship, it is technically permitted to look at them (although it is meritorious to refrain from doing so). On the other hand, according to the second opinion, even looking at these pieces violates the Torah's *mitzvah*, since only items as common as coins are excluded. Certainly, owning these items is problematic.

How does the *Shulchan Aruch* adjudicate this question?

Surprising as it may seem, the two statements of the *Shulchan Aruch* appear to contradict one another. In *Orach Chayim*,[16] he cites the above-mentioned Gemara in *Shabbos* in a way that implies that he prohibits looking at any image at all. On the other hand, in *Yoreh Deah*, in the laws on idolatry, he limits the prohibition to looking at bona fide, worshipped idols. We should also note that there he cites a different reason for prohibiting looking at idols: enjoying the artwork is considered benefiting from idolatry.[17]

However, the major commentators on the *Shulchan Aruch* in both places note that the accepted practice is to prohibit only icons manufactured for worship.[18]

Collecting Icon Stamps

A stamp dealer and collector asked Rav Moshe Feinstein whether he could own, buy, and sell stamps that contain pictures of crosses and other idolatrous images. Rav Moshe ruled that since stamps are a common item, like coins, one may own or sell their images, and may also look at them. Rav Moshe mentioned that it is meritorious not to, presumably for the same reason that Rabbi Menachem ben Sima'ie of the Gemara avoided looking at coins.[19]

Zev's Chess Set

According to the reasons we have applied so far, Zev may be able to keep his fancy carved chess set. No one worships the cross on the king, and one could, perhaps, argue that this is familiar enough that no one is led astray by these pieces. As mentioned above, it is meritorious not to have any images at all, and certainly not to have anything that is reminiscent of idolatry. Thus, there is good reason for the custom to break off the cross of such chess pieces.

Hindu Statue

Miriam's dad's Hindu statue involves a more serious halachic problem. First, if this image was manufactured for worship, all opinions prohibit looking at it and having any enjoyment from it. Furthermore, if it was once worshipped, then several other Torah violations are involved, including that of having an *avodah zarah* in one's house and benefiting from *avodah zarah* (because he enjoys looking at the artwork). In addition, there is a *mitzvah* to destroy it.

Is one required to assume that the Hindu statue was worshipped? After all, it looks as if it was created as a collector's item, not for worship.

The answer is that if this statue was manufactured in a place where images of this nature are worshipped, one must assume that it is a bona fide idol.[20]

Maris Ayin

In addition to the halachic problem of looking at these idols, the Gemara raises an additional factor to take into consideration: is there concern that someone might suspect that the owner worships them?[21]

Are we, today, still concerned that someone might worship idols?

The subject of *maris ayin* is extensively explained elsewhere in this book (see chapter 10, "What Will the Neighbors Think?"), and the bottom line is that if *circumstances* dictate that people will assume that nothing wrong was done, there is no violation of *maris ayin*. Indeed, even in cases where there was *maris ayin* at the time of the Gemara, the prohibition is rescinded in places and times when the concern no longer exists.

Concerning *maris ayin* and the prohibition of *avodah zarah*, the *poskim* conclude that if no one worships these icons anymore *anywhere in the world*, one need not be concerned about suspicion that they are being worshipped.[22] If these idols are still being worshipped *somewhere*, one must be concerned about *maris ayin*.

Thus, it makes a difference whether this particular idol is still worshipped somewhere in the world. Since, unfortunately, Hinduism is still being practiced in the world, one is not allowed to own an idol that they might worship, because of the prohibition of *maris ayin*, even if no other prohibition against owning it exists. On the other hand, since no one worships the ancient Egyptian idols any more, it is not *maris ayin* to own these figurines.

Teaching Ancient Religions

I mentioned above that the *Sifra* rules that studying idolatry, including the religious beliefs involved and how an idol is worshipped, is prohibited *min haTorah* as part of the *mitzvah* of *al tifnu el ha'elilim* (do not turn to idols).

Does this include studying ancient religions or archeology? Does this prohibit reading mythology as a form of literature?

In Nisan 5740 (1960), Rav Yehudah Parnes, a prominent *rosh yeshivah*, asked Rav Moshe Feinstein a *she'eilah* regarding an observant public school teacher, whose required ancient history curriculum included teaching the beliefs of ancient Greece and Rome. Rav Parnes inquired if the fact that these religions are not accorded respect in the modern world would permit studying and teaching their beliefs.

Rav Moshe rules that the prohibition of studying idolatry exists, regardless of the reason one studies the religion. This also prohibits reading mythology that includes idolatry, even as a study of ancient literature.

However, Rav Moshe contends that the Torah prohibits studying only that which is authored by a proponent of the religion. One may study something written by someone who scoffed at the religion, just as one sees that even the Torah sometimes describes the way idolaters worshipped in order to ridicule the practice. Rav Moshe rules that one may study these subjects only if the teacher derides their beliefs and does not have the students read texts written by those who believe in the idols.

Rav Moshe points out that the students may even benefit from this instruction, if they realize that, although most of the world's population once accepted these ridiculous beliefs, this does not demonstrate that they are true. Similarly, the fact that millions of people accept certain other false notions as true is not evidence of their veracity.[23] Truth is not determined by democratic means!

Conclusion

In conclusion, in reference to our original questions, Miriam may save the Egyptian figurines, although it is praiseworthy to dispose of them; however, her father may not hold onto his Hindu statue, even as art, or even in order to mock it. Zev may keep his chess set. Jack is prohibited from gazing at an idol that he unearths, and furthermore, he would be required to destroy such an idol. Since I presume this could get him into trouble with the authorities, he would have a different question – is he required to destroy the idol, knowing that he may get into legal trouble? This is a topic for a different time.

Our belief in Hashem is the most basic of *mitzvos*. Praiseworthy is he who stays far from idols and their modern substitutes and directs his heart to Hashem.

NOTES

1. *Devarim* 7:25–26.
2. Rambam, *Hilchos Avodah Zarah* 7:1. We should note that this *mitzvah* is also mentioned in *Devarim* 12:2.
3. *Sefer HaChinuch* #428.
4. Rambam, *Hilchos Avodah Zarah* 7:2.
5. *Vayikra* 19:4.
6. Ibid.
7. *Yerushalmi, Avodah Zarah* 3:1.
8. Rambam, *Hilchos Avodah Zarah* 2:2; *Sefer HaMitzvos, Lo Saaseh* #10; *Sefer HaChinuch* #213.
9. *Sefer HaMitzvos* ad loc.
10. 307:23.
11. *Shabbos* 149a.
12. *Avodah Zarah* 50a.
13. *Tosafos, Shabbos* 149a.
14. *Rashi; Tosafos Rid.*
15. *Tosafos, Avodah Zarah* 50a.
16. 307:16.
17. *Shulchan Aruch, Yoreh Deah* 142:15, quoting Rabbeinu Yerucham.
18. *Shach; Magen Avraham.*
19. *Shu't Igros Moshe, Yoreh Deah* 1:69.
20. *Rema, Yoreh Deah* 141:3 and *Shach, Yoreh Deah* 17.
21. *Avodah Zarah* 43b.
22. See *Rema, Shach,* and *Biur HaGra, Yoreh Deah* 141:3.
23. *Shu't Igros Moshe, Yoreh Deah* 2:53.

26

Do the Clothes Make the Kohein?

Identifying the Materials of the Bigdei Kehunah

I n the year 5017 (1257), several hundred Baalei Tosafos, led by
Rav Yechiel of Paris, left Northern France on a journey to Eretz
Yisrael. Rav Eshtori HaParchi, who lived two generations later,
records a fascinating story he heard when he went to Yerushalayim
to have his *sefer*, *Kaftor VaFarech*, reviewed by a *talmid chacham*
named Rav Baruch. Rav Baruch told him that Rav Yechiel had
planned to offer *korbanos* upon arriving in Yerushalayim! Rav
Eshtori writes that he was too preoccupied with his *sefer* at the
time to realize that there were several halachic problems with Rav
Yechiel's plan.[1] In *Kaftor VaFarech*, he mentions some of his own
concerns; in addition, later *poskim* discuss many other potential
difficulties. Among the concerns raised is identifying several of
the materials necessary for the *kohanim*'s vestments.

Vestments of the Kohein

The Torah describes the garments worn by the *kohanim* in the Beis HaMikdash as follows: "Aharon and his sons shall don their belt and their hat, and they (the garments) shall be for them as *kehunah*, as a statute forever."[2] The Gemara[3] deduces, "When they wear their special vestments, they have the status of *kehunah*. When they are not wearing these vestments, they do not have this status." This means that *korbanos* are valid only if the *kohein* offering them attires himself correctly.

The regular *kohein* (*kohein hedyot*) wears four garments when serving in the Beis HaMikdash. Three of them – his undergarment, his robe, and his turban – are woven exclusively from white linen. The Torah does not describe how one makes the fourth garment of the regular *kohein*, the *avneit*, or belt, but it does mention the material of the belts worn by the Kohein Gadol. On Yom Kippur he wears a pure linen belt, whereas his regular belt also contains *techeiles*, *argaman*, and *tolaas shani*, different colored materials that I will describe shortly. The Gemara cites a dispute concerning whether the *kohein hedyot*'s belt also includes these special threads, or whether he wears one of pure linen.[4] The Rambam concludes that the *kohein hedyot*'s *avneit* does include threads of *techeiles*, *argaman*, and *tolaas shani*.[5]

Assuming that Rav Yechiel concluded that the *kohein hedyot*'s *avneit* also includes *techeiles*, *argaman*, and *tolaas shani*, his proposal to offer *korbanos* required proper identification of these materials, a necessary prerequisite to offering *korbanos*. This essay will be devoted to the fascinating questions that we must resolve to accomplish this task.

What Is *Argaman?*

The *Midrash Rabbah* writes that *argaman* is the most valuable of these four threads and is the color of royal garments.[6] The Rishonim dispute its color, the Rambam ruling that it is red, whereas the Raavad understands that it is a multicolored cloth, woven either from different species or of different colored threads.[7] The Raavad explains that the word *argaman* is a composite of *arug min*, meaning "woven of different types." This approach appears to be supported by a *pasuk* in *Divrei HaYamim*[8] that lists *argavan*, rather than *argaman*, as the material used in building the Beis HaMikdash.[9] The word *argavan* seems to be a composite of two words, *arug gavna;* meaning *woven from several colors*, an approach that fits the Raavad's description much better than it fits the Rambam's.[10]

The Raavad's approach that *argaman* is multicolored is further supported by a comment in the *Zohar*[11] that describes *argaman* as multicolored. However, the Radak[12] understands the word *argavan* according to Rambam's approach, and the *Kesef Mishneh* similarly states that the primary commentaries follow Rambam's interpretation. The Rekanti[13] quotes both approaches, but implies that he prefers the Raavad's approach.

By the way, the Ibn Ezra[14] implies that *argaman* might have been dyed silk rather than wool, whereas most opinions assume that it is wool.[15] Rabbeinu Bachyei[16] contends that silk could not have been used for the Mishkan or the Beis HaMikdash, since it is manufactured from a nonkosher species. This is based on the Gemara's[17] statement that nonkosher items may not be used for *mitzvos*. I will discuss this point further below.

Argaman: Color or Dye?

It is unclear if the requirement to use *argaman* thread means that the thread used for the *kohein*'s belt must be a certain shade of color, or whether it must be dyed with a specific dye. Rambam implies that the source for the *argaman* color is irrelevant. These are his words: "*Argaman* is wool dyed red, and *tolaas shani* is wool dyed with a worm."[18] (It should be noted that the Hebrew word *tolaas*, which is usually translated as *worm*, may include insects and other small invertebrates.) The Rambam's wording implies that the source of the *argaman* dye is immaterial, as long as the thread is red. Thus, there may be no halachically required source for the dye, provided that one knows the correct appearance of its shade.

Tolaas Shani

One of the dye colors mentioned above is *tolaas shani*. In addition to its use for dyeing the *kohein's* belt and some of the Kohein Gadol's vestments, *tolaas shani* was also used for some of the curtains in the Mishkan and the Beis HaMikdash, in the manufacture of the purifying ashes of the *parah adumah*,[19] and for the purifying procedure both of a *metzora* and of a house that became *tamei* because of *tzaraas*.[20]

Tolaas shani is a red color.[21] This presents us with a question: according to the Rambam who maintains that *argaman* is red, the source of which is irrelevant, what is the difference between the shade of *argaman* and that of *tolaas shani*? The Radak explains that they are different shades of red, although he provides us with no details of this difference.[22]

Must *tolaas shani* be derived from a specific source, or is it sufficient for it to be a distinctive shade of red, just as I suggested above that *argaman* is a color and not necessarily of a specific dye source?

The words of the Rambam that I quoted above answer this question: "*Argaman* is wool dyed red, and *tolaas shani* is wool dyed with a worm." These words imply that although *argaman* can be used from any source that produces this particular color, *tolaas shani* must be from a very specific source.

A Worm-Based Dye

Can the *pesukim* help us identify what *tolaas shani* is? The description of *tolaas*, which means *worm*, implies that the source of this dye is an invertebrate of some type. For this reason, some authorities seem to identify *tolaas shani* as *kermes*, a shade of scarlet derived from scale insects or some similar animal-derived red color.[23] Support for this approach could be rallied from a *pasuk* in *Divrei HaYamim*,[24] which describes the *paroches* (curtain) that served as the entrance to the Kodesh HaKodoshim, the Holy of Holies of the Beis HaMikdash, as woven from the following four types of thread: *techeiles*, *argaman*, *karmil*, and *butz*, which is linen. The Torah, in describing the same *paroches*, refers to it as made of *techeiles*, *argaman*, *tolaas shani*, and linen. Obviously, *karmil* is another way of describing *tolaas shani*.[25] Similarly, in *Divrei HaYamim* II,[26] when describing the artisans sent by the Tyrian King, Hiram, to help his friend King Shlomo, the *pasuk* mentions *karmil* as one of the materials in place of *tolaas shani*. Thus, *karmil*, a word cognate to *kermes*, is a synonym for *tolaas shani*.[27]

Kosher Source

However, as I mentioned above, Rabbeinu Bachyei takes issue with this approach, insisting that only kosher species may be used for building the Mishkan and the garments of the *kohanim*. He bases his opinion on the Gemara[28] that states that "only items that one may eat may be used for the work of heaven," which teaches that only kosher items may be used in the manufacture of *tefillin*. How does this fit with the description of *tolaas shani* as a worm derivative?

The Rambam states that the dye called *tolaas shani* does not originate from the worm itself, but from a berry that the worm consumes.[29] Thus, according to the opinion of Rambam and Rabbeinu Bachyei, although *tolaas shani* and *karmil* are the same, they are not from nonkosher sources, but from kosher vegetable sources.

Nonkosher Source

Although this is probably the primary approach we would follow in a halachic decision, we cannot summarily dismiss those who identify *tolaas shani* as *kermes* or a different invertebrate-based dye. Although Rabbeinu Bachyei objects to a nonkosher source for *tolaas shani*, those who accept that its source is *kermes* have several ways to resolve this issue. One possibility is that this *halachah* applies only to a substance used as the primary item to fulfill the *mitzvah*, but not if it serves only as a dye.[30]

Others resolve the objection raised by Rabbeinu Bachyei by contending that the color derived from these nonkosher creatures may indeed be kosher. Several different reasons have been advanced to explain this approach. Some contend that this coloring is kosher, since the creatures are first dried until they are inedible, or, because a dead insect dried for twelve months is considered an innocuous powder and no longer nonkosher.[31] (The halachic debate on this issue actually concerns a colorant called carmine red that is derived from a South American insect called cochineal. This color, which is derived from the powdered bodies of this insect, is used extensively as a "natural red coloring" in food production. To the best of my knowledge, all major *kashrus* organizations and *hechsherim* treat carmine as nonkosher, although I have read *teshuvos* contending that it is kosher.)

A similar approach asserts that *kermes* dye is kosher, since it is no longer recognizable as coming from its original source.[32] This approach is based on a dispute among early *poskim*, as to whether a prohibited substance remains nonkosher after its appearance has been completely transformed. The Rosh[33] cites Rabbeinu Yonah, who permitted using musk, a fragrance derived from the glands of several different animals, as a flavor, because it has been transformed into a new substance that is permitted. The Rosh disputes Rabbeinu Yonah's conclusion, although in a responsum[34] he quotes Rabbeinu Yonah's approach approvingly.

A Similar Dispute

It is noteworthy that this dispute between the *Rosh* and Rabbeinu Yonah appears to be identical to a disagreement between the Rambam and the Raavad[35] in determining the source of the *mor*, one of the ingredients burnt as part of the fragrant *ketores* offering in the Beis HaMikdash.[36] The Rambam rules that *mor* is musk, which he describes as the blood of an undomesticated Indian species. (Although the Rambam calls it blood, he probably means any body fluid.) The Raavad disagrees, objecting that blood would not be used in the construction of the Beis HaMikdash, even if it were to be derived from a kosher species, and certainly from a nonkosher one. In explaining the Rambam's position, *Kesef Mishneh* contends that once musk is reduced to a powder that bears no resemblance to its origin, it is kosher. Thus, the disagreement between the Rambam and the Raavad as to whether a major change of physical appearance changes the *halachos* of a substance may be identical to the dispute between Rabbeinu Yonah and the Rosh. It turns out that the Radak, who implies that *tolaas shani* derives from nonkosher invertebrates, may also accept the approach of Rabbeinu Yonah.

Only for Holy Writings

Some authorities have a different approach that would explain how *tolaas shani* may be acceptable for Beis HaMikdash use, even if it derives from a nonkosher source. They contend that the rule prohibiting the use of nonkosher items applies only to *tefillin* and other *mitzvos* that utilize *kisvei hakodesh*, holy writings, but does not apply to most *mitzvos* or to items used in the Beis HaMikdash.[37] This approach requires some explanation.

The Gemara states that *tefillin* may be manufactured only from kosher substances, deriving this *halachah* from the following verse: *Lemaan tihyeh toras Hashem b'ficha* (In order that the law of Hashem should always be in your mouth);[38] i.e., whatever is used for the Torah of Hashem must be from kosher items that one may place into one's mouth. In order to resolve a certain question that results from the Gemara's discussion, some authorities explain that this *halachah* refers only to items that have words of the Torah or Hashem's name in them, such as *tefillin*, *mezuzos* or a *Sefer Torah*, but does not include the garments worn by the *kohein hedyot* in the Beis HaMikdash, which do not contain Hashem's name.[39] (The *halachah* requiring kosher substances would still apply to the *tzitz* and the *choshen*, garments of the Kohein Gadol, both of which carry Hashem's name.)

Techeiles

The next material or shade we need to identify, the *techeiles*, is also a factor in the daily wearing of *tzitzis*. Indeed, the Torah requires us to wear *techeiles* threads as part of this *mitzvah*. Nevertheless, Jews stopped wearing *techeiles* about thirteen hundred to fifteen hundred years ago, and with time, its source has been forgotten. Although the Gemara[40] mentions a creature called the *chilazon*, whose blood is the source of *techeiles*, and even discusses how to manufacture the dye, the use of *techeiles* ended sometime after the period of the Gemara. The Midrash states "now we have only white *tzitzis*, since the *techeiles* was concealed,"[41] which implies that Hashem hid the source for the *techeiles*. Indeed, some *poskim* interpret the writings of the Arizal as saying that *techeiles* should not be worn until Moshiach comes.[42]

Attempts to Identify the *Techeiles*

In 5647 (1887), the Radziner Rebbe, Rav Gershon Henoch Leiner, *ztz"l*, published a small *sefer, Sefunei Temunei Chol,* which concluded that the *mitzvah* of wearing *techeiles* applies even today. In his opinion, the Midrash quoted above means that *techeiles* will become unavailable, but one is both permitted and required to wear it. Based on his analysis of every place the Gemara mentions the word *chilazon*, the Radziner drew up a list of eleven requirements whereby one could identify the *chilazon*, and concluded that if one locates a marine animal that meets all these requirements, one may assume that it is the *chilazon*.

He then traveled to Naples, Italy, to study marine animals that might fit all the descriptions of *techeiles*, and concluded that a squid-like creature called the cuttlefish, which in many languages is called the *inkfish*, is indeed the *chilazon* from which one produces *techeiles*. The Radziner then published his second volume on the subject, *Pesil Techeiles*, in which he announced his discovery of the *chilazon* and his proofs as to how the cuttlefish can be identified as the *chilazon*. Subsequently, the Radziner published a third volume, *Ayn HaTecheiles*, to refute those who disagreed with him.

The Radziner attempted to convince the great *poskim* of his generation to accept his thesis, particularly Rav Yitzchok Elchonon Spector (the Rav of Kovno and the *posek hador* at the time), the Beis HaLevi (then the Rav of Brisk), Rav Yehoshua Kutno (author of *Yeshuos Malko*, the Rav of Kutno), the Maharil Diskin (who had been Rav of Brisk and was living in Yerushalayim), and Rav Shmuel Salant (the Rav of Yerushalayim). None of these *rabbonim* accepted the Radziner's proposal, although the Maharsham, the *posek hador* of the time in Galicia, felt that the Radziner's approach had merit and wore a *tallis* with the Radziner's *techeiles*, although apparently only in private. Nowadays, only Radziner Chassidim and some Breslover Chassidim wear the *techeiles* that the Radziner introduced.

Some later authorities have attempted to identify the *techeiles* as being one of several varieties of sea snail, although the objections raised by the generation of *poskim* of the Radziner's own time apply to these species as well.

Among the many objections to both of these identifications of the *chilazon* is the contention that neither the cuttlefish nor a snail could possibly be the source of the *techeiles*, since they are not kosher. In addition to the reasons I mentioned above, the Radziner presents a novel approach to explain why *techeiles* may derive from a nonkosher source. He contends that although the flesh of a nonkosher fish is forbidden *min haTorah*, the blood of a nonkosher fish is forbidden only *mid'Rabbanan*. Since *min haTorah* one may eat this blood, it is permitted as a source for a kosher dye.

Techeiles: Color or Dye?

It is noteworthy that a prominent nineteenth-century *posek*, Rav Tzvi Hirsch Kalisher, contended that the garments of the *kohein* do not require *chilazon* as the dye source, only the color of *techeiles*. In his opinion, *chilazon* dye is only necessary for *tzitzis*.[43] In Rav Kalisher's opinion, it is sufficient to dye the threads of the *avneit* the correct *techeiles* color in order to perform the service in the Beis HaMikdash. However, not all *poskim* accept this interpretation, but require the specific dye source of *chilazon* to dye the vestments.[44]

Review

In review, what we know for certain is that the regular *kohein* (*kohein hedyot*) wears four garments when performing the service in the Beis HaMikdash, including the *avneit*, or belt, which the Rambam rules includes threads of *techeiles, argaman,* and *tolaas shani.* In identifying these materials, however, we have several disputes:

1. Whether the *techeiles* must be derived from a *chilazon* in order to offer *korbanos,* or if merely dyeing clothes the appropriate color is sufficient.

2. Whether the *chilazon* has been and will remain hidden until Moshiach comes.

3. Whether the *chilazon* must be kosher or not.

4. In identifying the *argaman,* we are faced with a dispute between *rishonim* whether its color is red or a mix of different colors.

5. In identifying the *tolaas shani,* we face a dispute as to whether its source is a berry that worms eat or a worm of some type.

All of these questions will need to be resolved before we can again manufacture kosher *bigdei kehunah,* either by having Eliyahu HaNavi teach us how the *bigdei kehunah* were made, or by having the *poskim* of Klal Yisrael determine the *halachah.*

Several earlier *poskim* devoted much time and energy to clarifying the correct procedures for offering *korbanos,* because of their intense desire to bring sacrificial offerings. Let us cultivate a similar desire within ourselves, and in that merit, may we soon see the *kohanim* offering the *korbanos* in the Beis HaMikdash in purity and sanctity, *amein.*

NOTES

1. Vol. 1, p. 101 in the 5757 edition.
2. *Shemos* 29:9.
3. *Zevachim* 17b.

4. *Yoma* 6a, 12a, 69a.

5. *Hilchos Klei HaMikdash* 8:2; cf. Rashi, *Pesachim* 26a s.v. *Kesheirim.*

6. *Bamidbar Rabbah* 12:4.

7. *Hilchos Klei HaMikdash* 8:13.

8. II, 2:6.

9. See also *Daniel* 5:7; Rashi on *Divrei HaYamim* II, 2:6.

10. See Ibn Ezra on *Shemos* 25:4.

11. *Parshas Naso.*

12. *Divrei HaYamim* II, 2:6.

13. *Shemos* 25:3.

14. *Shemos* 25:4.

15. Rambam, *Hilchos Klei HaMikdash* 8:13; *Rashi, Shemos* 25:4; 26:1; *Rashbam, Shemos* 25:4.

16. *Shemos* 25:3.

17. *Shabbos* 28a.

18. *Hilchos Klei HaMikdash* 8:13.

19. *Bamidbar* 19:6.

20. *Vayikra* 14:4, 49.

21. See *Yeshaya* 1:18.

22. *Divrei HaYamim* II 2:6.

23. See Radak on *Divrei HaYamim* II 2:6.

24. II 3:14.

25. Rashi, ibid.

26. 2:13.

27. See *Radak* on *Divrei HaYamim* II 2:6.

28. *Shabbos* 28a.

29. *Hilchos Parah Adumah* 3:2; see *Rashi* on *Yeshayah* 1:18 who explains it in a similar way.

30. *Shu't Noda Be'Yehudah* II, *Orach Chayim* #3.

31. See *Shu't Minchas Yitzchak* 3:96:2.

32. *Psil Techeiles,* p. 48 in the 1990 edition.

33. *Berachos* 6:35.

34. *Shu't HaRosh* 24:6.

35. *Hilchos Klei HaMikdash* 1:3.

36. See *Shemos* 30:23.

37. *Shu't Noda Bi'Yehudah* 2, *Orach Chayim* #3; cf. *Magen Avraham* 586:13.

38. *Shemos* 13:9.

39. *Shu't Noda Bi'Yehudah* 2, *Orach Chayim* #3.

40. See *Menachos* 42b.

41. *Midrash Tanchuma, Shelach* 15; *Bamidbar Rabbah* 17:5.

42. *Shu't Yeshuos Malko* #1–3.

43. He based this approach on the wording of the Rambam in *Hilchos Tzitzis* 2:1–2.

44. *Likutei Halachos, Zevachim* chapter 13, p. 67a in the original edition.

27

Should a Kohein Be Afraid of Confederate Ghosts?

Permissibility of a Kohein to Enter Lincoln Park

From early 1843, until August 1859, the only authorized burial location within the city of Chicago was a place then known as City Cemetery. This plot also included the first Jewish cemetery in the city of Chicago. During the Civil War, this graveyard served as the final resting place for thousands of Confederate prisoners of war who died in nearby Camp Douglas, which was used as a prison camp. About 153 years ago, this cemetery was closed to new burials, and later many of its graves were dug up. Subsequently, the city constructed residential sections, commercial areas, and city streets atop the seventy-two acres of the cemetery. The remainder of the cemetery was annexed to adjacent parklands and is now called Lincoln Park, which includes a zoo.

Lincoln Park and its zoo are very popular, particularly as locations for family Chol HaMoed outings. Our halachic question is: may a *kohein* visit the park and its zoo, or must he be concerned about the *tumas meis* to which he may be exposing himself?

Historical Background

In 1843, the city designated a sixty-acre zone as a cemetery. Three years later, a Jewish organization paid $45 to purchase a small part of this land for a cemetery of its own. Four years later, in 1850, the city purchased an adjacent area of twelve more acres to expand the cemetery, so that it now encompassed seventy-two acres.[1] Eventually, the cemetery included a large "potters' field" for burying the destitute and unclaimed bodies.

During the late 1850s, a prominent physician, Dr. John Rauch, requested that the cemetery be closed. Dr. Rauch was concerned that the cemetery was too close in proximity to Lake Michigan, which at the time served as the city's water supply, and that the cemetery might become a source of disease. Up until that point, this cemetery was the only authorized one in the city; it included a large "potters' field," or expanse for burying the destitute and the unidentified.

Two years later, an area located directly north of the cemetery was designated for a park. During this time, the city gradually ceased using the cemetery. However, an estimated four thousand Confederates who died in custody were interred in the "potters' field."

In 1866, the cemetery was officially closed, due in part to Dr. Rauch's health concerns. By now, the Civil War was over, and the surviving Confederate prisoners had been repatriated. The city officially decided to move the remains buried in this cemetery to other locations. Over the next thirty years, there were numerous scattered reports of moving some of the graves to new locations. Despite attempts to relocate graves, a conservative speculation is that the majority of the remains were never removed. At one time, the cemetery held an estimated thirty-five thousand graves – including the resting place for those who made the ultimate sacrifice for the Confederacy – and the subsequent records imply that most of these graves were never removed.

Fast-forward to the contemporary era. In 1962, workers digging a foundation for the zoo's new barn discovered a skeleton and a casket. They reburied the casket *in situ* and poured the foundation right on top. During 1998, workers constructing a parking lot in the area discovered eighty-one skeletons and an iron casket containing a cadaver. At least nineteen more reports of human bones found in the disused cemetery's location were recorded.

Thus, the *she'eilah* is whether a *kohein* may walk through the streets and enter businesses located on this former burial ground.

Steve Katz lives and works in this city and is well aware of the history of the park and its environs. His boss assigns him to attend a business meeting at a hotel that is located in the area that was originally part of the cemetery. Since Steve is a *kohein*, may he attend the meeting? If he cannot, how will he explain his refusal to his gentile employer?

Steve made an appointment to discuss the problem with his *rav*, Rav Goldberg, whom he can count on to explain all aspects of the *she'eilah*.

Will the Tumah Rise from the Ground?

Rav Goldberg begins by explaining some of the pertinent halachic background. When human remains are buried, under most circumstances the *tumah* rises directly overhead and contaminates the area above the remains. If a building is constructed directly above a grave, *tumah* may spread throughout that building, although sometimes it may only travel through the bottom floor, and possibly only into the room constructed directly above the grave. On the other hand, if there is no building, tree or overhang over the gravesite, one becomes *tamei* only if one walks or stands directly above the gravesite.

The details of which factors affect how far *tumah* will spread through the structure are beyond the scope of this essay.

Safek Tumah Birshus Harabim

"However, the specific situation that you are asking about may be judged more leniently," explains the *rav*, "because of a concept called *safek tumah birshus harabim, sefeiko tahor*, which basically means that if there is doubt about whether an entity in a public area became *tamei*, the *halachah* is that it remains *tahor*.[2] Notwithstanding our usual assumption that *safek d'Oraysa lechumra* (we rule strictly on doubts concerning Torah prohibitions), we rule leniently concerning a doubt in matters of *tumah* when the object in question is located in a 'public' area, a term that we will define shortly."

There also exists an inverse principle that *safek tumah birshus hayachid, sefeiko tamei*, which means that in cases when one is doubtful whether someone or something contracted *tumah* when it was in a private area, the entity is considered *tamei*.[3] (All of these laws are derived from *pesukim*.)

Which Areas Are Considered "Public"?

For the purposes of these two principles, "public" is defined as an area to which at least three people have ready access,[4] and "private" denotes a location that is accessible to less than three people. Thus, someone who discovers that he may have become *tamei* while walking down the street remains *tahor*. However, if he discovers that he may have become *tamei* while he was in a private area, he is considered *tamei*.

"I know that there is more to explain," interjected Steve, "but it would appear that one could have a situation in which one may enter a building, but one may not use the bathrooms or have a private interview."

"This may indeed be true, sometimes," responded the sage. "However, there are other factors to consider before we reach a definitive ruling."

May the Kohein Intentionally Enter?

At this point, Steve raised a sophisticated point: "I understand that a person who entered this area would subsequently be considered *tahor*. But, may I enter the area knowing that I *may* be contaminating my *kehunah*?"

The *rav* explained: "You are asking whether a *kohein* may, *lechatchilah*, rely on the principle of *safek tumah birshus harabim*, or whether this principle is applied only after the fact. In general, one must be stringent when there is concern that one may be violating a Torah prohibition, and it is prohibited *min haTorah* for a *kohein* to contract *tumah* from a *meis*. Thus, one might assume that a *kohein* should not enter an area where there is a possibility of *tumah*. However, many authorities rule leniently in the case of a *safek tumah birshus harabim*.

They contend that the Torah prohibited a *kohein* only from becoming *tamei*, but not from entering a situation where he will be ruled as *tahor*.[5] Thus, a *kohein* could enter any publicly available area, including an office or residential building, constructed over the city's defunct cemetery. However, he could not enter an area restricted to less than three people.

"Others contend that since the Torah prohibits a *kohein* from being in contact with a *meis*, he is similarly prohibited, because of *safek d'Oraysa lechumra*, to enter a place where he might be exposed to a *meis*."[6]

Chazakah

Steve raised another point: "In fact, we know that this area was once a cemetery and we are fairly certain that not all the graves were exhumed. Does this make matters worse?"

"You are raising a very insightful question. Even assuming that a *kohein* can rely on the principle of *safek tumah birshus harabim*, this principle might not apply here, since we know that this area was once a cemetery, and we are fairly certain that some graves remain. Thus we have a *chazakah* that the area was once *tamei meis*, and we are uncertain whether the *tumah* was removed. In such a situation, perhaps the principle of *safek tumah birshus harabim* does not apply, since this rule may apply only where there is no *chazakah*.[7]

"Nevertheless, in our particular case, we have some basis to be lenient. Although this entire area was once set aside as a cemetery, it is very unlikely that it became filled wall-to-wall with graves, and also, only the places directly above the graves were *tamei*. Furthermore, we do know that some, and even perhaps most, of the graves were removed. Thus, any place within the cemetery would have been *tamei* because of doubt, not because of certainty."

Jewish vs. Non-Jewish Graves

"There is another reason to permit entering the hotel for your meeting," the *rav* continued. Researchers have ascertained the exact location of the original Jewish cemetery, which is now the location of one of the ball fields. Thus, although I would advise you and your sons not to play ball on that particular diamond, we can certainly be more lenient regarding entering the hotel constructed in the area, as I will explain."

Steve replied: "But how can we be certain that no Jews were ever buried in the non-Jewish cemetery? There definitely were some Jewish soldiers in the Confederate army, and it is likely that some Jews were buried in the non-Jewish cemetery or in the potters' field."

His *rav* replied: "You are correct that some Jews were probably buried in the non-Jewish parts of the cemetery. Nevertheless, since we do not know this for certain, we may work with the assumption that there are no Jews there."

"But even a non-Jewish body conveys *tumah*, so I still have a problem."

"This depends on whether remains of a gentile convey *tumas ohel*, that is by being under the same roof, cover, or overhang that is at least three inches (a *tefach*) wide."

Do Non-Jewish Remains Transfer *Tumah*?

"Although all authorities agree that the remains of a non-Jew convey *tumah* via touching and carrying," the *rav* said, "the Gemara cites the opinion of Rabi Shimon that remains of a non-Jew do not convey *tumas ohel*.[8] The Rishonim dispute whether this position is held universally, and in addition, whether this is the way that we rule. It appears that most Rishonim conclude that a *kohein* may enter a room containing the remains of a gentile, because they follow Rabi Shimon's position. Others contend that we do not follow Rabi Shimon's position, and that the *tumah* of a gentile does spread through the *ohel*. The *Shulchan Aruch* considers the question as unresolved and advises a *kohein* not to walk over the graves of non-Jews."[9]

At this point, Steve commented. "It seems from what you are saying that it is not a good idea for a *kohein* to enter buildings in this area, but one may enter if there is a pressing reason."[10]

The *rav* responded: "This is the conclusion of many authorities. Some are even more lenient. One famous responsum by the *Avnei Nezer* permits a *kohein* to enter a field that he purchased without realizing that it contained an unmarked gentile cemetery. The author permits this by combining two different leniencies, each of which is somewhat questionable. One leniency is that perhaps a gentile does not spread *tumah* through *ohel*, and the other leniency is that some early authorities contend that once a *kohein* becomes *tamei*, he is not forbidden from making himself *tamei* again.[11] Although we do not rule according to this last opinion, the *Avnei Nezer* contends that one can combine both of these ideas to permit the *kohein* who purchased this field unwittingly to utilize his purchase."[12]

"If the *Avnei Nezer* ruled leniently in the situation that he had, then my case should certainly be permitted," noted Steve. "After all, in his case, there was no attempt to clear out the cemetery."

"You are correct. For this reason, I would certainly not find fault with someone who chooses to be lenient and indiscriminately enters the area that was only a gentile cemetery, relying on the ruling that gentile remains do not contaminate through *ohel*, and on the principle of *safek tumah birshus harabim*."

"It still seems that one should avoid the ball fields that are located right over the old Jewish cemetery."

"I would certainly advise this," closed the *rav*.

So Steve does not need to explain to his boss that he cannot attend business meetings at the hotel because of lost Confederate ghosts.

Although there may be little reason to panic over such issues, as we have discussed, one should be aware that the discovery of old cemeteries beneath modern cities is a fairly common occurrence.

Cemeteries, particularly Jewish ones, were always consecrated on sites outside the city limits, in order to avoid the obvious problems of *tumah* affecting *kohanim*. Unfortunately, when Jews were exiled, the whereabouts of many cemeteries became forgotten, and in addition, as cities expand they incorporate areas originally outside the city limits that often include former cemeteries. Therefore, similar predicaments are likely to continue cropping up. In each case, a *posek* must be consulted to find out whether, and to what extent, a *kohein* need be concerned.

NOTES

1. The historical information included in this article is based on the following website: http://hiddentruths.northwestern.edu/home.html. Also note that an article on this topic was written by Rabbi Mordechai Millunchek in his book *Midarchei Hakohanim*.

2. See *Nazir* 57a.

3. Ibid.

4. Ibid.

5. *Tosafos, Kesubos* 28b s.v. *Beis*; *Shu't HaRashba* #83; *Binas Adam* 157; *Pischei Teshuvah* 369:4, quoting *Shu't Chasam Sofer*; *Minchas Chinuch* 263:13 s.v. *Vehinei*.

6. *Tzelach, Berachos* 19b; *Achiezer* 3:1:1, 3:65:7; *Kovetz Shiurim*; *Teshuvos VeHanhagos*.

7. In *Mikvaos* 2:2, this seems to be the subject of a dispute between Tannaim. See also *Tosafos, Niddah* 2a s.v. *Vehillel*.

8. *Yevamos* 61a.

9. *Yoreh Deah* 372:2.

10. See *Shu't Avnei Nezer, Yoreh Deah* #470.

11. *Raavad, Hilchos Nezirus* 5:15, as explained by *Mishneh LaMelech, Hilchos Aveil* 3:1.

12. *Shu't Avnei Nezer, Yoreh Deah* #466.

28

Sifting the *Makom HaMikdash*

Handling Artifacts Discovered on *Har HaBayis*

S omeone recently asked me a *she'eilah* that involves what is probably one of the most heartbreaking issues I was ever asked. The question was: "Are there any halachic issues involved in sifting through the earth removed by the Waqf from the *makom haMikdash*?"

During the past number of years, the Waqf, the Muslim "trust" that controls the holiest place on earth, Har HaBayis, has been "renovating" the area. The renovations included the construction of yet another mosque – this one located near Shaarei Chuldah, which is the southern entrance to Har HaBayis. These gates are called Shaarei Chuldah, because Chuldah the Prophetess stood between these two gates and admonished the Jews to do *teshuvah*.

Har HaBayis

The Kosel HaMaaravi where we *daven* is part of the Western

Wall of the Har HaBayis, known in English as "the Temple Mount," which is the top of the mountain called Har HaMoriah. The Beis HaMikdash included open courtyards, as well as the structure that stood on the Har HaBayis, but occupied only a small area of the mountain. Although the Har HaBayis has much more *kedushah* than that of Yerushalayim, the Beis HaMikdash has much greater *kedushah* than that of the Har HaBayis. Someone entering the area where the Beis HaMikdash once stood is *chayav kareis*, an extremely severe punishment.[1] Although the Har HaBayis has far less sanctity than the Beis HaMikdash, nevertheless, most contemporary *poskim* prohibit ascending the Har HaBayis nowadays. Some *poskim* permit entering areas of the Har HaBayis that are not part of the Beis HaMikdash to *daven* or perform a *mitzvah*, after one has performed certain *taharah* procedures. However, most *poskim* prohibit entering the Har HaBayis under all circumstances.

Muslim Construction

The Muslim construction is without any permits and is illegal. However, the Israeli authorities refuse to interfere, citing concerns about violence! One of the Waqf's goals is to obliterate any remnants of the Batei HaMikdash from the Har HaBayis so that they can persist with their lies that Jews never lived in Israel, and that the Batei HaMikdash never existed. The Waqf has removed hundreds of truckloads of "debris" from the Har HaBayis, which they dumped in the Kidron Valley and other sites around Yerushalayim.

With the help of volunteers, Israeli archeologists are painstakingly sifting through the rubble removed from the Har HaBayis, to look for artifacts. (Thus, there is no halachic concern of ascending Har HaBayis.) One of these volunteers asked me whether he may participate in this work, citing the following potential *she'eilos*:

1. Is there a halachic concern that someone may be using property of the Beis HaMikdash for one's own benefit, which violates a Torah prohibition called *me'ilah*?

2. Since we are all *tamei*, is there concern that one might

be rendering impure (i.e., making *tamei*) property or the stones of the Beis HaMikdash?

3. What is one required to do with stones or earth that were originally part of the Beis HaMikdash or Har HaBayis?

4. The remnants being unearthed include bone fragments, some of them human. This leads to two specific questions:

A. May a *kohein* work in this project?

B. Is there a halachic concern of mistreating the dead, since these human remains will not be buried afterwards, but will be stored and used for scientific research and study?

5. Some artifacts that surface are clearly from what were once idols. Is there a halachic requirement to destroy them? Is it the finder's responsibility to destroy them, something which the archeologists do not permit?

Archeological Finds

Before answering the above questions, let's examine what the search is uncovering, so that we can explain the halachic issues raised.

Everything found on Har HaBayis has a dark-gray ash color, rather than the typical white limestone color of Yerushalayim earth. This is because the various fires of destruction that raged on Har HaBayis discolored its earth.

Every bucketful of sifted earth contains numerous historical items, including coins, pottery and glass fragments, arrowheads and other primitive weapons, and pieces of human or animal bone. Coins unearthed date from as early as the second Beis HaMikdash to as late as the period of Napoleon III (mid-nineteenth century). The pieces of animal bone are presumably from what people ate there – possibly, leftovers from *korbanos*, but also leftovers of non-Jewish meals of the last centuries.

Other remnants unearthed are connected with the *churban*, such as Babylonian and Roman arrowheads, and Roman catapult projectiles – all sad reminders of the Jews who died there during the two *churbanos*.

(Probably a greater reminder of the *churban* is the general attitude of the Muslims, who, in effect, rule over Har HaBayis today. One would think that the Muslims would treat Har HaBayis with some level of sanctity, since they claim that it is one of their holy sites. Unfortunately, this is not true. The workers loiter and smoke there, and children play soccer. Their chief concern seems to be to ensure that Jews do not pray there.)

We can now begin to answer the questions raised above.

Beis HaMikdash Property

Question 1: Is there a halachic concern that in the unearthing of these items someone is receiving personal benefit from property of the Beis HaMikdash, thus violating the severe Torah prohibition called *me'ilah*?

Much broken pottery has been found among the artifacts. These items are of great archeological curiosity, because they establish who used Har HaBayis and ate their meals there over the millennia. Halachically, we know that *kohanim* ate meat of the holier *korbanos* only in the Beis HaMikdash area. After cooking these *korbanos*, the *halachah* required that the earthenware pots used be broken in a holy area of the Beis HaMikdash.[2] The shards discovered may indeed be remnants of these vessels. However, these earthenware pieces have no sanctity, since all holy vessels were manufactured from metal only.

Remnants of Holy Vessels

Many types of holy vessels, such as bowls, baking dishes, forks, and numerous other items were used in the service in the Beis HaMikdash. What is the *halachah* if someone finds a usable metal item that might be one of the holy vessels of the Beis HaMikdash, or something that might be a remnant from the *mizbei'ach* (altar)? Is there a prohibition of *me'ilah* in using these items?

Because of complicated halachic issues, the *poskim* disagree as to whether one would violate *me'ilah* in such a case. Allow me to explain. Based on a *pasuk* in *Yechezkel*,[3] the Gemara presents us with a halachic concept referred to as *ba'u peritzim vichilaluhu* (when the lawless entered, they removed its sanctity), meaning that under certain circumstances, misuse of Beis HaMikdash vessels defiles them and removes their *kedushah*.[4]

The Rishonim dispute concerning when this concept applies. The Baal HaMaor explains that when the Hellenized Jews used the *mizbei'ach* of the Beis HaMikdash inappropriately (during the events prior to the Chanukah story), this defiled usage removed the sanctity from the stones of the *mizbei'ach*. In his opinion, the other vessels of the Beis HaMikdash still maintain their sanctity, and furthermore, only Jews cause the *kedushah* to be removed, not gentiles. Thus, according to the Baal HaMaor, someone who uses a vessel of the Beis HaMikdash today violates the severe prohibition of *me'ilah*.

The Ramban disagrees with the Baal HaMaor, explaining that when the gentiles entered the Beis HaMikdash to destroy it, they profaned the sanctity of the building and its vessels. In his opinion, someone who subsequently made use of these vessels for his own personal purposes would not violate any prohibition of *me'ilah*. As a result of this dispute, one should not use a metal utensil found in the Har HaBayis ruins, because of the possibility of committing *me'ilah*, based on the Baal HaMaor's stricter opinion.

Profaning Beis HaMikdash Property

Question 2: Since we are all *tamei*, is there concern that one might be profaning (i.e., making *tamei*) the property or stones of the Beis HaMikdash?

I could find no halachic literature directly discussing this *she'eilah*. One is prohibited from making something *tamei* in the Beis HaMikdash.[5] However, I am unaware of any halachic source that prohibits making these items *tamei* once they have been removed from the Beis HaMikdash grounds. Furthermore, stones themselves do not become *tamei*.[6]

Stones and Earth

Question 3: What is one required to do with stones or earth that were originally part of the Beis HaMikdash or Har HaBayis? Is there a responsibility to bury the broken stones?

The *halachah* is that damaged stone from the Beis HaMikdash or its vessels must be buried, just as we bury worn-out *sifrei Torah*.[7] Thus, the *halachah* requires that stone or other remains from the Beis HaMikdash be respectfully buried. Unfortunately, today, the stone and other remains that have no archeological value are simply abandoned at the worksite.

Does the earth from Har HaBayis have sanctity?

The *Mizbach Adamah*,[8] whose author, Rav Shmuel Meyuchas, was the *rav* of Yerushalayim during the eighteenth century, discusses a *she'eilah* about whether grapes grown on Har HaBayis are prohibited because of *me'ilah*. From his discussion, it is clear that he considers all earth of Har HaBayis to have *kedusha* that might create a prohibition of *me'ilah*. Thus, the same concerns I raised above about the stone exist concerning the earth itself, and it must be buried in a respectful way.

Human Bones

Question 4: The remnants unearthed include bone fragments, some of them human. This leads to two specific questions:

A. May a *kohein* participate in this project?

B. Is there a halachic concern of mistreating the dead, since these human remains will not be buried afterwards, but will be stored and used for scientific research and study?

The discovery of human bone fragments on the Har HaBayis is puzzling, since Jews would never have buried anyone there. In all likelihood, these are bones of non-Jews that were interred there, or perhaps of Jews who were killed on Har HaBayis and, unfortunately, not buried according to *halachah*. Even if one assumes that these are bones of non-Jews, even a fragment the size of a barleycorn will convey *tumah,* if moved or touched. Therefore, since there is a reasonable chance that a *kohein* might touch or lift a human bone fragment, he should refrain from participating in this project.

Burial

Does a non-*kohein* need to be concerned about the possibility that he will locate bones, and that he now has a *mitzvah* to bury them?

If one can assume that the bones discovered were from non-Jews, there is no *mitzvah* to bury them, but only to be certain that they do not render a *kohein* impure. Even if the bones are from a Jew, it is unclear whether the *mitzvah* of burying a Jewish *meis* applies to such a small amount. The *Mishneh LaMelech*[9] rules that the *mitzvah* of *kevurah* does not apply to *part* of a corpse, whereas the Tosafos Yom Tov[10] rules that one is required to bury a piece of a Jewish *meis* as small as a *kezayis.* However, it is unclear how small a piece of bone requires *kevurah.*

Avodah Zarah

Question 5: Some artifacts that surface are clearly from what were once idols. Is there a halachic requirement to destroy them? Is it the finder's responsibility to destroy them, something which the archeologists do not permit?

Some background to this *she'eilah*: It is prohibited to benefit from an idol; furthermore, there is a Torah *mitzvah* to destroy idols in a way that no one can ever benefit from them.[11] The suggested method is to grind up the idol and scatter the filings to the wind or the sea. One may also not benefit from a broken idol, and the same halachic requirement exists to destroy it.[12] Obviously, the archeologists overseeing the work will not allow this *halachah* to be fulfilled.

Conclusion

Thus, in conclusion, it appears that one does not need to be concerned about rendering property of the Beis HaMikdash impure or using Beis HaMikdash property while sifting earth removed from Har HaBayis. It also seems that a non-*kohein* may participate in these activities *if* he can have control over the items that he finds and can destroy the idols and bury the human bones and any remains from the Beis HaMikdash that he may find. However, he may not participate as a member of a "dig team," where he is forced to follow the instructions of an archeologist who is not following halachic guidelines.

Postscript

From photographs I have seen of the new mosque, it appears that the Waqf did very little actual construction, but simply hollowed out one of the underground archways as it was originally constructed when the Beis HaMikdash was built. Explaining this underground construction is, in itself, a fascinating halachic subject.

Archways on Top of Archways

Someone who stands above a buried corpse or part of a corpse becomes *tamei* (with the exception of the case I will describe below). When the Beis HaMikdash was built, the building was constructed in a way that it was impossible to become *tamei*, even if someone was once buried in the earth beneath the Beis HaMikdash, itself an almost impossible scenario. In order to eliminate the possibility of someone becoming *tamei* from such a corpse, they constructed the Har HaBayis complex with "archways on top of archways."[13]

To explain this construction, I will elucidate how *tumas ohel* works. If there is *tumas meis* under a building, *tumah* spreads throughout the building, but does not spread *above* the building. Therefore, someone walking along the roof of the building remains *tahor*, even though he is walking directly above the *meis*.

Similarly, if one constructs an archway, and there is *tumah* under the roof of the archway, the *tumah* spreads underneath this entire archway, but not above it. This is because an archway is a building – *tumah* spreads underneath it, but the archway prevents *tumah* from rising above it.

However, if the *meis* was buried beneath the *pillar* of an archway, the *tumah* is not inside the *ohel*, but under the pillar – and the *tumah* rises vertically and contaminates the area directly above it.

The way to prevent this *tumah* from proceeding upward and rendering people above it impure is to construct another archway directly above the pillar. This way, although the *tumah* will rise through the pillar of the lower archway, it will then remain within the *ohel* of the upper archway and not spread above it.

This is the concept of "archways on top of archways" – where both of the upper archway's pillars rest on the arch of the lower archway, which effectively blocks any *tumas ohel* from spreading from the ground below to any area above the double archway. If the *meis* is beneath the *arch* of the lower archway, the lower archway blocks *tumah* from rising above it, and if the *tumas meis* is beneath the pillar of the lower archway and its *tumah* rises above the lower archway, it will be blocked by the upper archway.

Thus, to avoid any possible *tumas meis* in the Beis HaMikdash, the entire Har HaBayis was constructed with underground double sets of archways, thereby guaranteeing that no *tumas meis* could spread upward from a *meis* below. The Waqf apparently cleared out the debris accumulated under one of these archways, and used it as the roof of their mosque!

Incidentally, this method of making "archways on top of archways" is used to correct the problem of roads discovered to pass over graves or cemeteries. In this instance, very small "archways" are constructed, but this is sufficient, because to accommodate this halachic problem, each section of archway-*ohel* needs to be only a *tefach* high.

We all hope and pray that the day will soon come when the Beis HaMikdash returns as the Bayis Shlishi, and we will ascend Har HaBayis in purity, sanctity, joy, and awe to serve Hashem with complete devotion.

NOTES

1. *Kaftor VaFerech*, chapter 6; *Kesef Mishneh*, *Hilchos Beis HaBechirah* 6:14; *Magen Avraham* 561:2; *Shu't Binyan Tziyon* #2.
2. *Zevachim* 93b.
3. 7:22.
4. *Avodah Zarah* 52b.
5. *Eruvin* 104b; Rambam, *Hilchos Bi'as HaMikdash*, chapter 3.
6. Rambam, *Hilchos Keilim* 1:6.
7. *Tosefta*, *Megillah* 2:10; Rambam, *Hilchos Beis HaBechirah* 1:15.
8. Cited by *Machazik Bracha*, addendum to *Orach Chayim* 151.
9. End of *Hilchos Aveil*.
10. *Shabbos* 10:5.
11. Rambam, *Hilchos Avodah Zarah* 7:1; *Shulchan Aruch, Yoreh Deah* 146:14.
12. *Shulchan Aruch, Yoreh Deah* 146:11.
13. *Parah* 3:3; Rambam, *Hilchos Beis HaBechirah* 5:1.

29

Here Comes the King

What *Berachos* Will We Recite When Moshiach Comes?

An acquaintance of mine named Shimon asked me what *berachos* we will recite when Moshiach comes, and when we will recite those *berachos*. I must admit that, surprisingly, no one had ever asked me this *she'eilah* before. I did discover two short responsa on the topic, both discussing only certain aspects of the subject.

Subsequently, my son showed me a pamphlet that included a list of *berachos* that one will recite upon the auspicious occasion. However, the list included errors and was very incomplete. Hopefully this essay will prepare us better for the occasion we *daven* for three times a day, and will itself hasten the redemption.

Before discussing the *she'eilah*, we must first clarify an important fact, one that a surprising number of Jewish people do not know.

Moshiach and His Endeavors

Moshiach will be a Torah scholar descended from Dovid HaMelech, who will reestablish the halachic Jewish monarchy in

Eretz Yisrael and influence the entire Jewish People to observe *halachah* meticulously.[1] He will be wiser than his ancestor, Shlomo HaMelech, and he will be a prophet almost as great as Moshe Rabbeinu. Moshiach will teach the entire people how to serve Hashem, and his advice will be sought by all the nations of the world. He will gather the Jews who are presently scattered to all ends of the world, expand Jewish territory more than ever before, and rebuild the Beis HaMikdash. (This follows the approach of the Rambam, *Hilchos Melachim*, chapter 11. There is a dispute as to whether the third Beis HaMikdash will be built under Moshiach's supervision, or whether it will descend from heaven.[2] There is also a dispute regarding whether the ingathering of the exile will be performed by Moshiach or will occur immediately prior to his arrival. We will find out for certain when the events unfold.)

After Moshiach establishes his dominion, there will be no more wars, famine, jealousy, or competition, since the entire world will be filled with only one desire: to know Hashem and draw close to Him.[3]

Combined *Berachah*?

The fact that Moshiach is both the political leader of Klal Yisrael and also a leading *talmid chacham* caused Rav Shmuel Hominer, a great *tzaddik* and *talmid chacham* of the previous generation, to ask Rav Shlomo Zalman Auerbach the following *she'eilah*, which I paraphrase:

When we merit meeting Moshiach, one will be required to recite four *berachos* to praise Hashem upon the occasion:

1. *Chacham harazim*, the wise One Who knows all secrets

2. *Shechalak meichachmaso lirei'av*, Who bestowed of His wisdom upon those who fear Him

3. *Shechalak mikevodo lirei'av*, Who bestowed of His honor upon those who fear Him

4. *Shehecheyanu*

Rav Hominer then proceeded to ask whether the second and third *berachos*, both of which begin with the word *shechalak* should be recited as two separate *berachos*, or if they are combined into one *berachah*, *shechalak meichachmaso u'mikevodo lirei'av* (Who bestowed of His wisdom and honor upon those who fear Him). Let me explain his question:

Chazal instituted the following blessing, to be made when one sees a Jewish king: *Baruch Atah Hashem Elokeinu Melech ha'olam shechalak mikevodo lirei'av* (Who bestowed of His honor upon those who fear Him). A different albeit similar *berachah* was instituted to be recited upon seeing a tremendous *talmid chacham*: *Baruch Atah Hashem Elokeinu Melech ha'olam shechalak meichachmaso lirei'av* (Who bestowed of His wisdom upon those who fear Him).[4]

(Chazal also instituted the recital of similar *berachos* when one sees a non-Jewish king, *shenasan mikevodo lebasar vadam* (Who gave of His honor to human beings); and when one sees a gentile scholar, *shenasan meichachmaso lebasar vadam* (Who gave of His wisdom to human beings).[5]

Note that the *berachos* recited over a Jewish king or scholar use the word *shechalak* whereas the *berachos* recited over gentiles use the word *shenasan*. The word *shechalak* implies that the recipient of this power or wisdom recognizes that these are gifts received from Hashem, and that Hashem retains total control over them.[6] However, the gentile king or scholar views these Divine gifts as his own accomplishments and does not recognize Hashem's ongoing involvement in his success.)

Since Moshiach will be both a king and a Torah scholar, Rav Hominer assumed that someone meeting him should recite both *berachos*. However, Rav Hominer queried about whether these two similar *berachos* are combined into one *berachah*, *shechalak meichachmaso umikevodo lirei'av* (Who bestowed of His wisdom and honor upon those who fear Him).

Rav Shlomo Zalman replied that one does not combine these two *berachos*, even when seeing a Jewish king who is also a *talmid chacham.*[7] He pointed out that *berachos* are generally kept separate, even when their themes are similar. As Rav Shlomo Zalman pointed out, an earlier author, the *Teshuvah Mei'Ahavah,*[8] discussed this same *she'eilah* in the eighteenth century and reached the same conclusion.

Several *poskim* contend that we no longer recite the *berachah shechalak meichachmaso lirei'av* upon seeing a noteworthy *talmid chacham,* maintaining that our generations no longer possess Torah scholars of the stature required to recite this *berachah.*[9] Nevertheless, both Rav Hominer and Rav Shlomo Zalman assumed that one will recite this *berachah* upon witnessing Moshiach, either because they held that one does recite this *berachah* today, or that Moshiach will clearly be a scholar of this league.

Baruch Chacham Harazim – Knower of Secrets

In the above-quoted correspondence with Rav Shlomo Zalman, Rav Hominer mentioned that one will recite two other *berachos* when greeting Moshiach: *Baruch chacham harazim* and *shehecheyanu.* What is the *berachah* of *Baruch chacham harazim*?

The Gemara[10] records that someone who witnesses six hundred thousand Jews gathered together recites: *Baruch Atah Hashem Elokeinu Melech ha'olam chacham harazim* (the wise One Who knows all secrets).[11] This *berachah* praises Hashem for creating such a huge multitude of people, each with his own unique personality and physical appearance. (The Gemara records a different *berachah* to recite when observing a similarly large-sized throng of gentiles.) The wording of the *berachah* notes that only Hashem knows the secrets that each of these people thinks.[12]

Rav Hominer pointed out that since the entire Jewish People will surround Moshiach, there will be no doubt at least six hundred thousand Jews together, enabling us to say this *berachah.* Note, however, that one will recite this *berachah* upon seeing the huge crowd, and will not recite the other two *berachos* until one actually sees Moshiach.

Shehecheyanu

The fourth *berachah* mentioned by Rav Hominer is *shehecheyanu*, based on the *halachah* that if one sees a close friend whom one has not seen for thirty days, one recites *shehecheyanu* because of one's excitement.[13] Certainly, seeing Moshiach for the first time will generate more excitement than seeing a close friend whom one has not seen for thirty days![14]

Shehecheyanu or Hatov Vehameitiv?

However, I would raise the following query: should one recite *shehecheyanu* or *hatov vehameitiv* (He who is good and brings benefit) upon seeing Moshiach?

The Mishnah teaches: "Upon hearing good tidings, one recites *baruch hatov vehameitiv*."

One who builds a new house or purchases new items recites *baruch shehecheyanu vekiyemanu vehigiyanu lazman hazeh*.[15] When one hears good tidings that are beneficial only for him, he recites *shehecheyanu*; if others benefit as well, he recites *hatov vehameitiv*.[16] Similarly, when acquiring new appliances, one recites *hatov vehameitiv* if other people benefit; if only one person benefits, as is usually the case when purchasing new clothes, then he or she recites *shehecheyanu*.[17]

So, which *berachah* will one recite upon the coming of Moshiach, *shehecheyanu* or *hatov vehameitiv*? After all, it's not just the excitement of seeing Moshiach, but the realization that he will change the entire world for the better that generates the excitement and *berachah*.

In my opinion, one will recite both *shehecheyanu* and *hatov vehameitiv*, but not at the same time. One will certainly recite *hatov vehameitiv* when one *hears* the wonderful tidings of Moshiach's arrival. After all, if one recites the *berachah* when hearing that one receives any kind of bounty, how much more so for the gift of Moshiach's long awaited arrival!

In addition, according to Rav Shmuel Hominer and Rav Shlomo Zalman, one will recite *shehecheyanu* upon *seeing* Moshiach the first time, due to the personal pleasure of witnessing him.

Although this now completes the list of *berachos* mentioned by Rav Hominer, I believe at least one more *berachah* should be added to the list:

Returning the Widow to Her Property

The Gemara[18] teaches us that someone who sees Jewish houses in Eretz Yisrael that have been restored after the *churban* recites the *berachah matziv gevul almanah*, "Who reestablishes a widow in her borders," referring to the restoration of the Jewish People to the Holy Land. Rashi explains that this Gemara applies to a period such as that of Bayis Sheini, when the Jews returned to Eretz Yisrael after the exile, and the *Rif* states that it refers specifically to the restoration of *shuls* and *batei medrash*. Obviously, one will recite this *berachah* the first time one sees either the restored Beis HaMikdash or the *batei medrash* and *shuls* of a rebuilt Yerushalayim.

Why Don't We Recite This *Berachah* Now?

We do not recite this *berachah* until Moshiach arrives and we no longer need worry about our enemies.[19] However, as soon as Moshiach has accomplished his purpose, one will recite this *berachah* on every rebuilt *shul* and *beis medrash* one sees in Eretz Yisrael. Thus, one might recite this *berachah* even before actually seeing Moshiach himself!

An Earlier *Teshuvah*

There was actually an earlier responsum, discussing what *berachos* one will recite when *Moshiach* arrives. Someone asked Rav Chaim Falaggi, *ztz"l*, a great nineteenth century *posek* who was the *rav* of Izmir, Turkey, the following *she'eilah*: "When Moshiach redeems us, what *berachah* will one recite upon the redemption and in appreciation of Hashem's benefiting us?"

Here is his response:

> It appears that one should recite a *berachah* of *"gaal Yisrael"* (Who redeemed us from exile), similar to when one completes retelling the story of our

Exodus on Pesach and recites "and we thank You and recite a new song on our redemption," and one concludes with the berachah "Who redeemed Israel." After the future redemption, one will recite a similar berachah. One will also recite shehecheyanu for experiencing this wondrous time, since, without question, this day will be established as a Yom Tov.[20]

Recently, I saw someone rule that we will recite a berachah Baruch Atah Hashem Elokeinu Melech ha'olam go'el Yisrael as soon as Moshiach arrives. However, I believe this to be an incorrect understanding of Rav Falaggi's teshuvah. Nowhere do Chazal record a berachah with the text Baruch Atah Hashem Elokeinu Melech ha'olam go'el Yisrael, nor do they cite a berachah to be made when one is redeemed. Rather, what Rav Chaim Falaggi contended is that the Sanhedrin of the Moshiach era will institute a celebration to commemorate the wondrous events that transpire, and will presumably institute the recitation of a berachah similar in structure to the berachah that one makes immediately prior to drinking the second cup of wine at the Seder, which closes with the words gaal Yisrael. In addition, the Sanhedrin will, presumably, make the day of Moshiach's arrival into a Yom Tov that will be celebrated with the berachah of shehecheyanu, just as one recites this berachah to commemorate every Yom Tov.

Six Berachos

Thus, we now have a total of six berachos to recite when Moshiach arrives:

1. *Hatov vehameitiv* when one hears of his arrival

2. *Matziv gevul almanah,* each time one sees a newly reconstructed *shul* or *beis medrash,* and when one sees the Beis HaMikdash

3. *Chacham harazim,* upon seeing six hundred thousand or more Jews assembled

When one actually sees Moshiach, one will recite three *berachos:*

4. *Shechalak meichachmaso lirei'av*

5. *Shechalak mikevodo lirei'av*

6. *Shehecheyanu*

In what order should one recite these last three *berachos?*
I believe that the following Gemara[21] demonstrates that *shehecheyanu* should be the last of this triad:

> Rav Pappa and Rav Huna, the son of Rabi Yehoshua, were traveling when they met Rav Chanina, the son of Rabi Ikka. They told him, "when we see you, we recite two *berachos: asher chalak mei'chachmaso lirei'av* and *shehecheyanu.*"

Thus we see that *shehecheyanu* is recited after the other *berachos.*

Which *Berachah* Is Recited First?

Having resolved earlier that one will recite two different *berachos, shechalak meichachmaso lirei'av* and *shechalak mikevodo lirei'av,* which of these *berachos* is recited first?

I found no reference made by any *posek* concerning this question. On one hand, perhaps one can demonstrate that the *berachah* on a *talmid chacham* is first, since we have a general rule that *mamzer talmid chacham kodem leKohein Gadol am haaretz* (a *mamzer* who is a Torah scholar is given more honor than a Kohein Gadol who is boorish).[22] On the other hand, the Gemara[23] cites a dispute between the prophet Yeshayah and King Chizkiyahu as to whether a king commands more respect than a prophet or vice versa. The Gemara implies that the king commands more respect. Thus, one could infer that the *berachah* relating to Moshiach being king should be recited before the *berachah* on his being a *talmid chacham.*

What if One Can't See Moshiach?

Now a practical question:
What if you cannot actually see Moshiach because of the large

throngs that are there, but you know that he is present? Do you recite these *berachos* anyway?

It would seem that whether one recites these *berachos* under these circumstances depends on a dispute among authorities, which is, in turn, dependent on two versions of a passage of Gemara:[24]

1. "Rav Sheishes, who was blind, joined others who went to see the king. When the king arrived, Rav Sheishes began *reciting the blessing.*"

According to this version, Rav Sheishes recited the *berachah* for seeing the king, although he could not and did not see him. Thus, someone may recite this *berachah* to Hashem for "seeing" (i.e., perceiving) the honor that the king receives, even though he does not actually see the king himself[25]

However, there is another version to this text.

2. "Rav Sheishes, who was blind, joined others who went to see the king. When the king arrived, Rav Sheishes began *blessing the king.*"

What is the difference between the two versions? According to the second version, Rav Sheishes blessed the king, meaning he gave him an appropriate greeting, but there is no evidence that he recited the *berachah* on *seeing* a king, since he could not see him. It is very likely that one may *not* recite these two *berachos* unless one actually sees a king or a *talmid chacham*; it is insufficient just to be aware of his presence.[26]

Conclusion

In conclusion, one may recite a total of eight special *berachos* when Moshiach arrives, in the following order.

1. When we first hear from a reliable source the good news of Moshiach's arrival, we will recite: *Baruch Atah Hashem Elokeinu Melech ha'olam hatov vehameitiv.*

2. When we see the huge throngs of Jews assembled to greet him, which will no doubt number at least six hundred

thousand people, we will recite: *Baruch Atah Hashem Elokeinu Melech ha'olam chacham harazim.*

3. When we see the rebuilt Beis HaMikdash or rebuilt *shullen* or *batei medrash*, one will recite: *Baruch Atah Hashem Elokeinu Melech ha'olam matziv gevul almanah.* Theoretically, one might recite this *berachah* before the *berachah chacham harazim*, if one sees the rebuilt Beis HaMikdash before one sees the huge throngs.

4. When we actually see Moshiach, we will recite *Baruch Atah Hashem Elokeinu Melech ha'olam shechalak mikevodo lirei'av.*

5. Immediately after reciting this *berachah*, we will recite the *berachah Baruch Atah Hashem Elokeinu Melech ha'olam shechalak meichachmaso lirei'av.* According to some *poskim*, one may recite these last two *berachos* when one is aware that Moshiach is nearby, even if one cannot see him.

6. When one actually sees Moshiach, one should recite *shehecheyanu.*

7–8. According to the *Lev Chayim*, on the anniversary of Moshiach's arrival, we will again recite *shehecheyanu* to commemorate the date, and we will recite a long *berachah* mentioning some of the details of the miraculous events of his arrival. This *berachah* will close with the words *Baruch Atah Hashem gaal Yisrael.*

Now that we have completed our discussion and review of these *halachos*, let us *daven* hard that we soon have the opportunity to recite these *berachos, bimheirah veyameinu, amein!*

NOTES

1. Rambam, *Hilchos Melachim*, chapter 11.

2. *Rashi, Sukkah* 41a; *Yerushalmi, Maaser Sheni* 5:2 and *Meleches Shlomo*, ibid.

3. Rambam, *Hilchos Melachim*, chapter 12.

4. *Berachos* 58a.

5. *Berachos* 58a; *Tur* and *Shulchan Aruch* 224; cf. Rambam, *Hilchos Berachos* 10:11, who records a different text to these *berachos*.

6. *Avudraham*, quoted by *Beis Yosef, Orach Chayim 224.*

7. *Minchas Shlomo* 1:91:27.

8. *Teshuvah Mei'Ahavah* 2:237.

9. This approach is quoted by *Shu't Teshuvah Mei'Ahavah*, 2:237; *Ben Ish Chai, Parshas Eikev* 1:13; and *Aruch Hashulchan* 224:6, whereas *Chayei Adam* 63:8; *Kaf HaChayim* 224:18; and *Shu't Shevet HaLevi*, 10:13 rule that one does recite this *berachah* today. Several anecdotes are recorded about great *talmidei chachamim* who recited the *berachah* upon seeing *gedolim*, such as the Ragetchaver Gaon, the Chazon Ish, the Brisker Rav, and Rav Gustman. See, for example, *Piskei Teshuvos*, chapter 224, footnote 17.

10. *Berachos* 58a.

11. *Tur* and *Shulchan Aruch, Orach Chayim* 224:5.

12. *Rashi, Berachos* 58a.

13. *Berachos* 58b and *Tosafos*, ibid.

14. Compare this to *Shulchan Aruch, Orach Chayim* 225:2.

15. *Berachos* 54a.

16. *Berachos* 59b; *Shulchan Aruch, Orach Chayim* 222:1.

17. *Shulchan Aruch, Orach Chayim* 223:3, 5.

18. *Berachos* 58b.

19. *Beis Yosef, Orach Chayim* 224; *Maharsha, Berachos* 58b; *Shu't Har Tzvi* #84; cf. *Magen Avraham* 224:8.

20. *Shu't Lev Chayim* 2:42.

21. *Berachos* 58b.

22. *Horiyos* 13a.

23. *Berachos* 10a.

24. *Berachos* 58a.

25. *Magen Avraham* 224:6.

26. *Elyah Rabbah* 224:6.